One Bright Spot

One Bright Spot

Victoria K. Haskins

palgrave
macmillan

First published 2005 by
PALGRAVE MACMILLAN
Houndmills, Basingstoke, Hampshire RG21 6XS and
175 Fifth Avenue, New York, N. Y. 10010
Companies and representatives throughout the world

PALGRAVE MACMILLAN is the global academic imprint of the Palgrave Macmillan division of St. Martin's Press, LLC and of Palgrave Macmillan Ltd. Macmillan® is a registered trademark in the United States, United Kingdom and other countries. Palgrave is a registered trademark in the European Union and other countries.

ISBN-13: 978–1–4039–4743–7   hardback
ISBN-10: 1–4039–4743–0   hardback
ISBN-13: 978–1–4039–4744–4   paperback
ISBN-10: 1–4039–4744–9   paperback

This book is printed on paper suitable for recycling and made from fully managed and sustained forest sources.

A catalogue record for this book is available from the British Library.

Library of Congress Cataloging-in-Publication Data
Haskins, Victoria K. (Victoria Katharine), 1967–
    One bright spot / Victoria K. Haskins.
        p. cm.
    Includes bibliographical references and index.
    ISBN 1–4039–4743–0 – ISBN 1–4039–4744–9 (pbk.)
        1. Women, Yuin–Australia–Wallaga Lake Region (N.S.W.)–Social conditions.
2. Women, Yuin–Relocation–Australia–Wallaga Lake Region (N.S.W.) 3. Women, Yuin–Pulic welfare–Australia–Wallaga Lake Region (N.S.W.) 4. Yuin (Australian people)–Australia–Wallaga Lake Region (N.S.W.)–Social conditions. 5. Wallaga Lake (N.S.W.)–Race relations. 6. Wallaga Lake (N.S.W.)–Politics and government. 7. Strack, Joan Kingsley. I. Title.

DU125.Y85H37 2005
305.48′899150944–dc22   2005047297

10   9   8   7   6   5   4   3   2   1
14 13 12 11 10 09 08 07 06 05

Printed and bound in Great Britain by
Antony Rowe Ltd, Chippenham and Eastbourne

Dedicated to

Victor John Townsend
(1943–2004)

who saw the importance of this story

For none of us liveth to himself, and no man dieth to himself ...

Romans, 14:7

Contents

Acknowledgements

I am indebted to many people for their practical assistance, time and moral support in the process of researching and writing this book. To Jan Kociumbas, who supervised my research in its first incarnation, as a history thesis. To Craig Cormick, an inspirational writer of unwritten histories, for his excellent guidance on how to turn it into a book. To Briar Towers, Jill Lake, Ruth Willats and the staff at Palgrave Macmillan; and to Flinders University's research support committee, for making it a reality.

I am also grateful to Millie Ingram for her wholehearted support and help negotiating the archives of the Protection Board. Thanks also to Melissa Jackson at Mitchell Library and John Sharman of the department of Family and Community Services.

Many other people have been very helpful to me in providing me with access to obscure or private historical records, especially Tess de Araugo, Richard and Lesley Bate, Sean Burke, Beverley and Don Elphick, Merri Gill, Jack Horner, Norm Hoyer, Lorraine Kelly and Eric Naylor, Rona Mackay, Madeline McGrady, Laurelle Pacey and Inara Walden. A special thanks to Lorraine and Eric of the Umbarra Cultural Centre for their generous hospitality at Wallaga Lake, and for giving me an insight into the spirituality of their people and place.

For valuable advice and encouragement at crucial moments I thank Anna Cole, Angela Woolacott, Simone Penketheman, Tina Baum, Djon Mundine, Jackie Huggins, Sylvia Scott, Alison Holland, Tikka Wilson, Yuin Kelly, Gordon Briscoe, Heather Goodall, Wendy Brady, the staff at Link-Up NSW, Peter Read, Fiona Paisley, Julia Smith, Anna Haebich and the late Herb Simms. The community of scholars I've met in South Australia, especially Karen Vered, Sue Sheridan and Sharyn Roach-Anleu, have offered a supportive friendly environment to work in. The many kind and helpful individuals who helped me to locate the descendants of the people I was writing about are too numerous to mention, but I would like to thank Gloria Ardler, Agnes Coe, B. J. Cruse and Emily Walker especially for their personal introductions.

Thank you to the families of the Aboriginal women, and especially to John, Kevin, Herb, Alice, Irvine, Donna, Bev, Val and May, whose interest, encouragement and involvement were crucial to my work. I am overwhelmingly grateful for their trust and support, and appreciate the extent of the emotional as well as practical demands on them in giving this. Thank you also to my own family for their support, especially my grandmother, Jan Haskins, and my aunt, Melody Haskins. Yes, it is true that our histories are kept in the houses of our aunties!

This book has taken three babies to write, so my special thanks for their patience goes to Ganur, Kaiyu and Kirrin-Yurra, and of course John Maynard, my sweetheart and my soul-mate, who made the whole process a joy. Your creativity and love combined inspires me.

List of Figures

1
Introduction: More than my own mother to me

In a quiet Sydney suburb in May 1934, Joan Kingsley-Strack, fashionably dressed North Shore mother of three and organizing genius of the British Empire pageant the year before, was writing a eulogy to her grandmother, Maggie Hobbes, in her diary. Sitting by the old lady's deathbed, she reflected on her romantic past – an orphan of the British Raj, she had fled cold guardians in Scotland to the remote British colony of New South Wales, to end up, almost single-handedly, running a vast dairying property overlooking Wallaga Lake on the far south coast. In particular, Joan dwelt on Maggie Hobbes' legendary kindness to her Aboriginal neighbours, the Yuin, who lived adjacent to her on the local Aboriginal reserve. 'Mrs Hobbes mothered nursed & cared for the Aboriginal women and babes at the Wallaga Lake settlement which adjoined Merriwinga adding to the meagre rations of these ill treated people whenever possible,' she wrote:

> The love care and understanding which she expended upon these simple & lovable people has never been forgotten. She patched up their quarrels she fed & clothed them until they came to look upon her as their own 'little Missus' ... . She always said [they] had been infamously treated ... . On several occasions she came to Sydney simply to demand justice for these defenceless people, once having a manager of the Station removed because of his dishonesty ...

It was the 1930s and an era was drawing to a close. The obituaries in the papers were full of similar sentimental panegyrics to 'the last of our pioneer women', those who had gone before into a world now forgotten. But for Joan Strack, in the midst of her own struggle against the Aboriginal authorities, there was a special significance in the way she imagined her grandmother's relationships with Aboriginal people.

Figure 1   Narrelle and Mary, East Kew, Victoria, 1923 Author's collection.

Many decades later, I had no idea that Joan Strack – my great-grand-mother – had had any relationships with Aboriginal people whatsoever. Seventy-five when I was born, she had been a little old lady from the earliest time I can remember. Even now, I recall only her thin, fluffy hair, her watery eyes, the soft, papery skin of her trembling hands. I remember asking, when I was quite young, why our family called her 'Ming' and being told that the odd nickname had been given to her, as far as anyone knew, by my father whom she looked after as a baby. Apart from this singular aspect of curiosity, I knew nothing about her life. Genteel and faded, like the pastel-painted china gathering dust in the gloom of the rooms of her flat, she was from another world, another time.

I certainly did not know that at the time she was penning her tribute to her dying grandmother, Ming was herself 'demanding justice' for Aboriginal girls and women forcibly removed from their families and indentured under a now infamous policy of state governments. And I could certainly not have imagined that Ming would go on to become an activist in the Aboriginal citizenship rights movement of the 1930s. Her story was not passed down to me via my family oral tradition of memory; rather, it had, literally, been shut up and forgotten for nearly half a century. Like other women who did not follow the conventional scripts allotted to them, Ming's life was painful, the price was high, the anxiety intense.[1] By the mid-1940s, Ming had put all that behind her and barely spoke of it again. In 1993, I stumbled on her remarkable papers, and within them, a story of a white woman's relationship with her Aboriginal servants, a white experience of the Stolen Generations that is embedded in my own family history.

My journey to recover Ming's story began one mild, blue, jacaranda-spring day, in the small fishing village where my Gran lived on the north coast of New South Wales. From her balcony I could gaze out over the township to the sparkling sea; a cool breeze swayed the tall bangalow palm and shook its down-turned skirt of ripening nuts. Gran had brought out some treasured old photographs to show me as we whiled away the morning over coffee, talking about her memories. A hand-tinted sepia snapshot of an Aboriginal woman, dressed in a white apron and cap and embracing Gran, then a fair-haired toddler, imme-diately captured my attention:

'Who's *this*?'

Gran took the photograph from me, and smiled. 'Oh yes,' she said. 'That was Mary. Dear old Mary. She was *such* a beautiful person. Do you know – she was more than my own mother to me.'

I looked again. Mary was smiling shyly, but proudly, the two of them beaming in the bright sunlight. A plump, comfortable-looking young woman with a round, open face and smoothed back hair, she looked gentle, guileless, sweet-natured. Bemused, I turned the photograph over and read, 'Narrelle and Mary, East Kew'. I was intrigued, but my Gran was at a loss to explain how Mary had come to be with her. Perhaps I might find the clue in the papers that Ming had left.

Although the photograph was tantalizing, I was somewhat less enthusiastic about Gran's idea of getting me to 'do' our family history. Looking back, I realize now that she was simply trying to give me something to do. In my mid-twenties, I was dissatisfied, disenchanted, bored and, like a good many of my generation, without a clue what to do.

For the past year or so I had been attempting to put together a relevant and interesting history of race relations between Aboriginal and white Australian women, and was in despair. When I set out to research a history of Aboriginal–white relationships, my impulse arose from personal experience. When I was twelve, my geologist father was transferred from his work with a mining company in northwestern Australia, in the remote east Kimberley, to the bustling city of Sydney. I'd gone abruptly from one side of the continent, with its glowing red earth and blue sky where I was the sole white girl in a sea of laughing black kids playing basketball and riding bikes, to the other side and the cool green suburbs of Sydney's leafy North Shore, a bastion of Anglo-Australia, where my fair hair and blue eyes confirmed my place in a huge majority. Ever since, I had been hungry to hear the Aboriginal side of Australian stories, which were so glaringly absent from everything around me. Why were Aboriginal people seemingly gone from the southeastern swathe of the continent and in particular from where we now lived? What had happened here in our past? What bound our shared existence? And, as I became more politically aware and began meeting Kooris in Sydney while I was at university, were we to be locked into racial injustice and conflict forever?

When a university scholarship allowed me to embark on such a project in the early 1990s, I was plunged into the argument that white academics were only perpetuating colonialism by writing Aboriginal people's history. Any historian who has ventured to write an Australian history in which Aboriginal people play a key role will be familiar with the ideological problems I confronted – issues I had never been forced to acknowledge in my undergraduate studies of Russian, American and Asian histories. Repeatedly, at conferences, in seminars, in journals, I was told that white Australians should not, *could* not, try to speak for Aboriginal people, nor try to represent the Aboriginal experience. So I took the escape route chosen by many in my position at a time when the concept that our perception of reality – historical and otherwise – as a social construction was a fresh and radical idea. Instead of studying the nuts and bolts of history, I would study *images* (cartoons, book characters, newspaper accounts) of Aboriginal and white women and of their relationship with each other, in white Australian popular culture. But a year of sophisticated discussion of representations of relationships had only compounded my sense of futility.

Looking for inspiration – or legitimation – I returned to my home town Kununurra, in the company of my old best friend Sophie, then living at Borroloola. But here I felt a profound sense of alienation. Not only had Sophie's life turned out so dramatically, so harshly, different from my own. Her unexpected impatience when some Aboriginal people visiting from Wave Hill told me a creation story of the country round Top Dam – *her* country, which they had no right to tell – brought home to me my uncomfortable position. As a *kartiya* (white person; literally, I later learned, one who cannot hear) and an outsider, in a place I had long treasured as my own, my problem was clarified rather than resolved. Without the right (or was it the ability?) to hear, let alone to tell, my research was a mere mirage, reflecting a meaningless world. Back in Sydney, my sense of unreality about the whole project intensified. It was at this point that my father's sister, my Auntie Mel, asked me if I would mind her house and her market stall bookshop while she went overseas. And so I decided to put my project on hold and set off for the far north coast of New South Wales.

Not really a local, not really a tourist, I had roots here of sorts. My Gran lived nearby. In her yard stood a sprawling, shady poinciana which she had planted on the day of my birth. My grandfather's ashes were scattered beneath it. On the other side of the yard, a solitary and dark-leafed avocado tree that fruited bountifully every year stood as testimony to his life. A farmer, who gave up farming in his later life for the less rigorous life of a sea fisherman, he had brought my Gran to live here some years before I, their first grandchild, was born. It was a regular destination for Christmases throughout my life and the one unchanging place in my nomadic childhood existence. And so there I was, half-heartedly agreeing to trace the family history on my grandmother's behalf while I suspended my candidature. I could not help feeling that this despised pursuit was appropriate to my uselessness as a 'real' historian.

But that photograph, with its evocative, faded depiction of a memory I did not know our family had – *that* was interesting. I knew that the image of an Aboriginal servant to a white mistress dominated the few popular historical depictions of black and white women's relation-ships. I had not thought of family photographs – perhaps I might find more images buried in Ming's boxes; perhaps I might yet find a spark to rekindle an interest in my work.

When Ming died in 1983, the formidable boxes of papers and belong-ings she left behind had been passed from one family member to anoth-er. Nobody had had the heart to throw them out, but equally nobody knew what to do with them, until they reached my father's sister, Melody. Gran had retrieved the photograph of Mary when the boxes had first been opened, and then hurriedly closed again. Then, for almost a decade, they had lain undisturbed on the floor of my aunt's garage.

Not hoping to find much more than perhaps few more photographs, I was stunned to find, on the top of the very first box, a folder on which was written, 'Abo. Citizen Committee'. It was the minutes of a group for Aboriginal citizenship rights in Sydney from the late 1930s. Initiated by the prominent Aboriginal activists of the 1930s, Bill Ferguson and Pearl Gibbs, the inter-racial Citizenship Committee pro-vided political and financial support to their Aboriginal-only organiza-tion, the Aborigines Progressive Association. Little was known or had been written about it, largely due to the fact that only fragmentary doc-umentary evidence of its existence survived. Now I found that Ming, this apparently conventional and ultra-conservative old lady, had been its enthusiastic secretary between 1938 and 1940.

Delving further, I came across official correspondences, and pages and pages of barely legible, pencil-scrawled diaries, documenting Ming's experiences between 1920 and 1942 as an employer of not one, but four Aboriginal women channelled out from their communities to the Sydney suburbs by the state. Mary was but the first of a number of 'apprentice' servants she (or Ming's mother, Isobel, in the case of the last) hired through the New South Wales Aborigines Protection Board. As she recorded her experiences with her workers and the revelations she learned from them with a growing sense of outrage, it became increasingly apparent to Ming that the real menace to Aboriginal girls and women was the very body set up to protect them. She even-tually became vociferously opposed to the so-called 'apprenticeship policy', her opposition hardening to such an extent in the late 1930s that she joined with Aboriginal activists in calling for the abolition of the Aborigines Protection Board and the full equality of Aboriginal people.

I was shocked, and not only by the realization of my direct and inti-mate connection to a history of colonial domination. You might think, given that I had been researching relationships between white and Aboriginal women, that I should have known about the policy of removing Indigenous girls and placing them in indentured domestic service. It was a policy pursued aggressively by state governments across Australia in the first half of the twentieth century, but I was not alone in my ignorance. In 1993, the history of forcibly removing Aboriginal children had yet to explode into the national consciousness. And despite this history having had a *direct* impact on my own family, Ming's struggle, both personal and political, in effect against her own privilege, had been forgotten by her descendants. Yet the fact that my great-grandfather, Ming's husband, Norman Kingsley-Strack, was connected with the ultra-right organization the New Guard *was* remembered, even with pride. Why this forgetting? Partly it is to do with the general lack of interest in women's lives; partly it is due to a general lack of interest in Aboriginal lives. But this silencing is more significant and more complex than neglect.

Ming's story defies categorization: an upper-middle-class, conservative woman, in many ways typical of those to whom the Board allocated apprentices, she found herself in the enemy camp, so to speak, as a direct result of her intimate contacts with her Aboriginal workers. I had done enough background reading in the two years leading up to my discovery of her papers to realize just how extraordinary her story was – and how difficult it was going to be to tell this long-silenced history, to tease out the complexities of her relationships with Aboriginal women.

Such histories are not only plagued by a paucity of sources; but our contemporary understandings of the ambiguities of cross-cultural relationships between women, where scripts of race and gender interweave and entangle, are profoundly limited by the urge to simplify and moralize. In opposition to the ubiquitous colonial mythology of kindly white mistresses – the so-called 'good fella missus legend' – we are left with the hard realities of the gross disparities of power between women, militating against mutual affection, let alone friendship.[2] Enhanced opportunities for brutal exploitation and abuse have bred a history of resentment and bitterness that is not easily forgotten or forgiven. As a collective of Aboriginal women historians admonished white feminists in the early 1990s:

just because you are women doesn't mean you are necessarily innocent. You were, and still are, part of that colonising force. ... In many cases our women considered white women to be worse than men in their treatment of Aboriginal women, particularly in the domestic service field.[3]

For Ming, the intrusion of the state into her private relationships would be the catalyst for her activism. But histories of Aboriginal child removal highlight only that such state intervention meant that Aboriginal servants were rendered even more vulnerable to abusive employers and exploitation. In fact, the great majority of white mistresses did *not* speak out against a system that, in most cases, operated in their interests; and the whole apprenticeship system on which the removal of Aboriginal children was based hinged on the acquiescence of these women. The absence of mistresses' narratives in this history is striking: such uneasy stories sit outside of accepted and understood categories of white women's behaviour. But Ming's story shows that the potential for some kind of alliance between women existed even in such a rigidly divided hierarchy of race and class; it shows also what a woman of the dominant race and class could – and would – do when confronted by the realities of the system. Ming's story is highly unusual, but it is an important one to tell, testimony to what could have been, and what could never be.

* * *

Having floundered for some time with the difficult politics of writing Aboriginal history as a white Australian scholar, it was with no small sense of relief that I set about recovering this hidden history, one that was so clearly my own. Yet writing about my great-grandmother, a woman so directly implicated in the policy of taking Aboriginal girls away from their families, induced a deep sense of self-consciousness in the way I approached her story.

When she wrote of *her* grandmother's life, Ming constructed Maggie to serve as a reflection for her own opposition to the Board. In many ways Ming was very much a product of her time. I am the product of a different time and as concerned as Ming was to eulogize her grandmother's life, so am I concerned not to romanticize Ming's life and actions, not to pursue a redemptive narrative of the beloved 'little missus', not to reinscribe white dominance over Aboriginal women.

Whenever Ming recalled the influences that had shaped her later attitudes and interests, she invariably referred not simply to her great-grandmother at Wallaga Lake but to her childhood memories of the Aboriginal people there. The Yuin made their camp opposite the land selected by Ming's grandfather in the 1870s, in the bushland overlooking the vast and tranquil lake, coastline to the east and the mountain Gulaga, the first landmark on the Australian coast sighted by James Cook in 1770, looming westwards. Throughout her childhood Ming regularly stayed with her widowed grandmother at Wallaga Lake for months at a time, and by her own account she was drawn to the company of the Yuin. 'Their generosity always amazed me & their goodness to each other & their gentle care of me, as a very small child,' she wrote. One venerable elder, Merriman, in particular had a powerful impact on her. Apparently taking pity on her, he fulfilled a surrogate fatherly role, taking her round the area and teaching her the legends, language and traditional food of the Yuin. In her memory the place became a sweet-smelling 'little paradise' and a 'sanctuary': 'Had not my old and dear friend Merriman last King of a dying tribe brought me here & told me so.' Indeed, Ming explained her political interest in the Aboriginal movement as being derived from a childhood vow to Merriman, made silently as her 'heart stood still' to hear the old man weeping.[4]

To my modern ear, these reminiscences were saturated with a cloying colonialist nostalgia for a world that never was, an invented landscape of grateful natives and kindly pioneers. In her later years, Ming even went so far as to tell people she had been born at Wallaga Lake, when in fact she had been born at her parents' house in Pymble, a suburb of Sydney – it was her mother who had been born on the far south coast. Blind to the enormity of her condescension, Ming also ignored the fact that her grandmother's land had formerly belonged to the very people now eking out a living on its margins, and that her privilege – and Ming's – derived directly from their dispossession.

But her stories did solve that longstanding puzzle over her name – in one, she described Merriman calling her 'Mingi', or 'little woman', as a child. It seemed that Ming had reinstated this name for herself some-time soon after the birth of my father in 1941.

'King Merriman', or Umbarra (his Aboriginal name), was indeed a recognized leader of his community during Ming's early childhood; his memory as a spiritual leader is honoured by the Yuin community at Wallaga Lake today. I gathered up a bundle of Ming's 'legends' and memories and went to Wallaga Lake myself. Both the Yuin people of Wallaga Lake Community Village and the local townspeople of Tilba Tilba greeted me with a warmth and an interest that made me feel that I had somehow returned, even though nobody remembered the Hobbes, who had left the area in the 1920s. Despite the obvious good relationships between the present-day Yuin and the white townspeople, there were clear differences in their understandings of the past in the histories I was told, especially about Umbarra, a figure both mystical and historical, who seems to have been many things to many people. Stories merged, converged, conflicted, dovetailed, slid between each other. There were the occasional outright denials and contradictions, but more often, simply many different angles and facets of the same thing, a shimmering interweaving of past lives and memories that was connected only by what seemed, essentially, to be a relationship to the place. The stories I had brought down with me, Ming's memories of Merriman that I had so awkwardly proffered to the Yuin, contained a core reality, which was a historically embedded connection between different people and the same place. Taken to see the site of the old house – nothing remained save an ancient, gnarled stump of a rose bush and a brick chimney, the sparse ruins looking out across the same breathtaking vista of sea, land and mountain Ming would have known – I felt my anxieties over the fancifulness of Ming's legends ebbing. By the time I left Wallaga I felt that I understood Ming better; or rather, that sense of unknowable but certain meaning she tried so awkwardly to convey in her own self-explanation.

* * *

For the first time, too, I could genuinely appreciate the bemusement with which many Aboriginal people view those who study histories that are not their 'own'. Returning to study Ming's papers afresh I saw graphic evidence of the harrowing experiences of the succession of young Aboriginal women coercively brought into her household: Mary, gentle and forsaken; affable Alma; high-spirited, quick-witted Del with her indefatigable hopes to improve the hand that life had dealt her; dignified, defiant, tragic Jane. Supporting acts in Ming's story, they were, of course, the lead characters in their own; but their stories are not mine to tell.

'Women will starve in silence until new stories are created which confer on them the power of naming themselves,' it has been said.[5] But to protect the privacy of their descendants and the peace of their families, I have, with the advice of senior members of each family, conferred on each of them a pseudonym. My great-grandmother alone has the honour of bearing the name she chose herself. There are important reasons for this.

Tracing and then meeting the descendants and relatives of the four women employed by Ming gave me a profound sense of the person I was writing about and of the ongoing effects of this history on lives today. But in my meetings with them, it was apparent that the Aboriginal women too had not spoken of their experiences under apprenticeship, or of their resistance. Like Ming, these Aboriginal women were not immune to the pressure to be silent.

I have sat and drunk tea and talked to people who were complete strangers to me, and I to them, about the most painful and private experiences of their mothers, grandmothers and aunts. For no other reason than being the descendant of a white woman who was given control and custody of four Aboriginal women under a genocidal and oppressive government policy, I not only found I was the 'keeper' of their stories, but that I had a significant degree of control over their re-telling. There are many reasons why each woman may have kept her silence, and in order to proceed with my work I had to reflect on what these may have been and the ethics of 'making them speak' posthumously.

Along the journey, I have come to realize how important relationships of trust and respect are to understanding the contingencies of silence. And so, in their individual stories which I have reconstructed in consultation with their senior descendants, I have given them names that will not identify them to the wider community. By this I mean to show respect for their decision – whatever the reasons – to keep their silence in their own lifetime. The truth is that my access to these stories was a direct consequence of this policy – and also, that I hear these stories of the Aboriginal women only through the way that Ming heard and told them. And so the story I tell here is of my great-grandmother and of those women whom we might expect to have had some knowledge and some responsibility to bear for the history that was carried out in their families, in their homes.

Yet the very keeping of these papers is a statement in itself. Ming was unable to expose the actions of the Aborigines Protection Board, which both outraged and motivated her to act. My belief is that she entertained the hope that the exploitation, struggle and suffering of Aboriginal women under the Board's policies would one day be exposed, even if not in her lifetime. Out of respect to her memory, and the memories of Mary, Alma, Del and Jane, I hope that throughout this discussion of their relationships with Ming, the reader can truly get a sense of the underlying and fundamental message contained in these documents – the brutality of the regime under which Aboriginal women in service, situated at the crossroads of race, class and gender oppressions, lived out their lives.

Part I
Mary

2
My One Bright Spot

Outside the glass-panelled door standing open to a fine new house on Highlands Avene, Pymble, set proudly on the hillside of a bushland of turpentines, elms, giant gums and great oaks, their leaves turning gold, a trim, pleasant-faced woman in her early fifties stood knocking. No answer. She gave a puzzled look at the young, neatly dressed Aboriginal girl standing beside her, and called into the long, high-ceilinged hallway.

'Joan – Jo –? Where are you, dear? ... I've got someone here for you.'

My great-grandmother lifted her face from the ceramic basin she was holding in her hands. 'I'm out the back, Aunt ... come on through.'

'Oh there you are, darling ... Oh dear, not sick again? You poor old thing.' Aunt Jean put her arms around Ming's shoulders and gave her a warm squeeze, then pulled back and looked at her, her brown eyes gazing directly into the younger woman's, their blue accentuated by her red rims. 'Oh, you don't look at all well, Joan. She doesn't look at all well, does she, dear?'

This last remark was addressed to the dark girl who had followed her down the hall and out onto the broad wooden verandah, and now stood there quietly, gazing down at the flagstone steps that led into the garden. Her eyes widened and she hesitated for a moment. 'No, missis,' she answered softly.

'Well, my dear, now Mary's here to help you, I expect you to really take care and make sure you *rest* now,' she said, patting the curve of Ming's belly under her tunic. 'I don't want anything more happening to my precious one, hmm? And you, you scamp' – this to the snub-nosed, ginger-haired boy at Ming's skirt – 'this is Mary and she's here to look after you and Mummy now, so you be a good boy for her.'

'Mary, take this, dear,' Jean handed her Ming's basin, 'and bring us back a nice fresh bowl of water and a cloth. You'll find the jug in the kitchen in the ice chest just there, and cloths in the pantry.'

'She's a lovely girl, Joan. Mrs Phillips told me she's been ever so pleased with her, wouldn't be letting her go at all, only I told her how desperately you needed help, and quickly, and did need a *good* type of girl, one you'll be happy leaving little Pete with.'

Ming smiled weakly. 'Oh, Aunt Jean, you're so good to me. I'm sure she'll be perfectly wonderful. Just seeing her makes me feel better – she does remind me of being at Granny's.'

'Well, everything's fixed up, my darling, I've paid for her up to the next quarter so there's nothing to worry yourself about, or Norman ... Oh, thank you, Mary. Now, you sit back, Joan, and put this over your eyes – there – and Mary, how about fixing us a nice pot of tea, then?'

* * *

I'm only guessing that it was Jean who arranged Mary's transfer to Ming in 1920, directly from a situation at Wahroonga. Mary was 19 years old; she had already been in service for three years and began working for Ming under the terms and conditions laid down by the New South Wales Aborigines Protection Board, on the third year Aboriginal 'apprenticeship' rate of 3s 6d a week. Mary's previous mistress was quite likely a friend or acquaintance of Ming's mother or aunt: a network of female employers which existed among the cliques of Sydney's upper-middle-class society was in the habit of transferring Aboriginal servants between metropolitan households. Jean, who lived on a property in far western New South Wales, had been visiting her sister's family in Sydney when Ming first fell ill, and had organized the services of a private nurse for her.

Ming had been married for three years. Now 27 years old, married life had fallen far short of her expectations. A war bride who had conceived virtually on her wedding night in 1916, she had been a mother for most of her marriage. Obliged to take in piecework to bring in extra money, a situation she found shameful, she was distressed at being unable to enjoy her new baby and cynical about the acclaim she received for doing 'her duty' as a woman in producing 'a son – a son', simply 'to replenish the ranks of manhood again!' The strain of reconciling her romantic ideals of motherhood with her situation was evident in her recollection of these early years, written soon after Mary's arrival. '[A]n Aboriginal nurse girl came to me, a dear soft eyed little soul, full of affection for us both,' she concluded, with evident relief. [1]

Figure 2   Mary with Narrelle, Sydney. Author's collection.

By that time the large house Norman Kingsley-Strack had been building on a substantial plot of land next door to Ming's parents home at Pymble was ready to move into. Ming was pregnant again and suffering from severe morning sickness. She was also recuperating from recent surgery and needed somebody to help her with the care of three-year-old Peter during her convalescence.

Ming's invalidism at the outset of Mary's employment set the tone for their relationship. Ming had been traumatized by the operation, which involved the removal of one ovary, her appendix and 'some other part of the anatomy!' unknown to her. Told by the doctor that her unborn child 'must be removed' also, Ming's distress was intensified by Norman's absence, who was 'holidaying' and could not be located. The private nurse Jean hired, a 'wonderful woman' who 'never left me for a moment', had provided her with a much-needed sense of solidarity, supporting her (unsuccessfully) in her objection to the operation and insisting that a specialist be called in when complications arose. Ming's description of this episode in her life reflects her sense of physical vulnerability as a woman, 'frantic with fear' and at the mercy of her own body as well as of an errant husband and overbearing male doctors.[2]

Mary's support was vital in practical terms, as she took over the nurse's role as well as the housework. Ming's unborn baby – my grandmother – did survive, but when she arrived five months later (premature and weighing just 3 lb) Ming would have depended even more on Mary, emotionally as well as physically.

The theme of illness and convalescence dominates Ming's narrative of the years during which Mary worked for her. The Stracks gave up their fine house in Pymble and, in the midst of constant moves between Sydney, Melbourne and Brisbane, plagued by 'accursed sickness' and bouts of hospitalization, Ming gave birth to her third and last child, Helen. It was a period of instability and insecurity for Ming, who became more and more disenchanted with her marriage. Not only were the couple temperamentally ill-suited, but Norman, an ex-Army officer who had suffered head injuries during the war, found it very difficult to settle down to supporting a wife and family. His inability to hold down a variety of jobs resulted in regular upheavals. In addition, he borrowed heavily, and Ming felt that they were constantly under a burden of debt. For her, these were 'those dreadful years' through which Mary was 'faithful, gentle, always at hand to help or cheer me'. Indeed, 'if it had not been for the affection & the faithfulness & understanding of an Aboriginal girl who lived with us,'

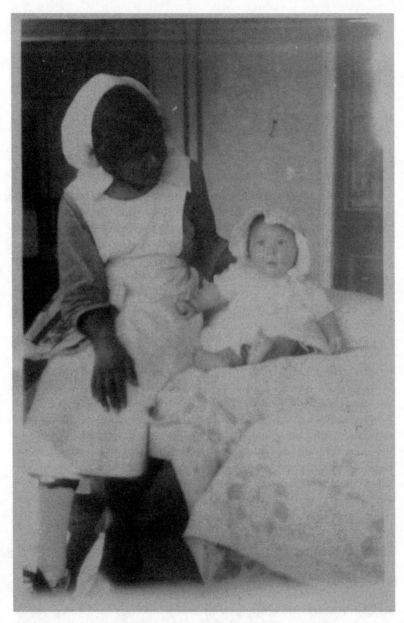

Figure 3 'Mary and Baby (Helen)', Brisbane, 1925. Author's collection.

Ming would write years later of her early years of marriage, 'I never could nor would have attempted to live with Norman.'[3]

* * *

'Mum and Nean [Ming's sister Helen] thinking they had best depart! I might have the plague! Oh dear I wish they would *go*. They are terrified. They rang Dr Bidge and he said it was the Dengue,'[4] Ming wrote in her diary in February 1926. '*Oh* the pain is *unbearable*,' she continued fretfully, '– why don't they go home, there is nothing to do for me – and if there is, Mary my old faithful will do it without fear or crossness. She is my one bright spot.'

Ming was staying with the children and Mary at her father's paint-ing cottage (he was a minor artist of the Sydney 'bush school') at Davistown, on the central coast just north of Sydney, having taken a 'holiday' away from Norman. This, her earliest reference to Mary, shows the extent to which she felt Mary was her only female family support, and this was also reflected in her rather paranoid claim on their return to the city in May that her mother and sister had 'told poor old Mary most wild things *about me*'.

Narrelle, my grandmother, who was five at the time, remembers this disastrous holiday clearly. The two-roomed cottage was set in the bush down a long track from the Davistown jetty, surrounded by swamp-land, with no neighbours in view. They took their baths in a large bowl in front of the kitchen fire, the other room being a bedroom, with beds made of flour sacks slung between four 'forky' sticks. There was no mesh on the windows, and fever-bearing mosquitoes were rampant. Gran remembers Mary spreading some kind of paste of leaves, a home-made remedy, on her mother to ease her illness. With her brother Peter, playing in a flat-bottomed boat on the beach, she saw a man hauled from the water onto the jetty and doused with kerosene after being attacked by a shark. Later, she spent what seemed to be hours lost in the mangrove swamp. Gran's memories of the holiday, dominated by these episodes, are overwhelmingly fearful. Ming, for her part, made no further diary entries at Davistown, record-ing wearily on her return home in May, 'Arrived Brisbane. All safe and sound but *very* tired – the most truely awful 3 months I have ever spent ever – under the name of "holiday".' It must have been truly awful for Mary too, coping with a sick mistress and three young children on her own.

But constructing how Mary felt is more difficult: unlike Ming, she left few traces of her feelings. Mary sent Ming a letter in the early

1920s when they were living in Melbourne, Ming evidently being away. Mary's tone was tender. 'My Dear Mistress', she wrote,

> Just a few line to say that little Narrelle [and] Peter are quite well and allso Mrs Commons [Ming's mother, visiting at the time] and Mr Strack all [so] myself. I do miss you very much. I am telling Mrs Commons all the nice thing about you, you are just like a mother to me when you are at home.

'No need to worry you self about the children ther quite all right,' she reassured Ming, before filling her in on what they had been doing in the past week. 'Well dear Mistres,' she concluded,

> I think I have told you all the news for this time have a good rest and dont worry so much about you little childrens the are quite all right Narrelle is getting a dear little pet, and so is dear old Petes good by lot of love from us all
> Mary.[5]

Mary had not seen her own mother since the Aborigines Protection Board took her away in 1915. Perhaps she had indeed transferred her filial affection to Ming, but the graceful way in which she let Ming know she had told Ming's mother, Isobel, that Ming was 'like a mother' to her suggests that Mary also recognized her role as bolster to Ming's image in her family's eyes. Ming delighted in the compliment, keeping Mary's letter with the notation on the envelope, 'Letter from my little Aboriginal girl "Mary"'. Such symbolic acts and signs of deference and maternalism as these were indeed rituals that have traditionally underpinned the domestic service relationship.[6]

With her crisp white apron and cap contrasting against her dark skin, marking her as Ming's human possession, Mary not only alleviated the private disappointments of Ming's life, she also enabled Ming to present a public face of marital and financial success, enhancing Ming's prestige in the eyes of her friends and family. One of Ming's cousins came to dinner with the family soon after they had moved to Brisbane at the end of 1924 and was impressed by the sight of Mary bringing dishes out to the table from the kitchen at the summons of a bell, as well as tending lovingly to the children. The couple 'seem happy', Ming's cousin wrote approvingly afterwards. They had a 'very nice' house, beautiful children, 'a car to use whenever they want it', and Ming 'still has the black girl & she adores the children'.[7]

Another year on and Ming clearly assumed she would always have Mary. When she returned to Brisbane from her trip to Davistown to find that the Aborigines Protection Board had sent an 'offer' of a holiday for Mary, Ming was no doubt nonplussed: she had given no thought to the possibility of Mary ever leaving.

But in the eyes of the Board, Mary – and the wages of her labour – remained state property. At the end of the previous year, around Christmas 1925, Mary's wages had been raised to the fourth-year apprentice rate of 5 shillings a week. Mary was now 25 years old, and had been working for Ming for five years, and as an apprentice for close on a decade. Perhaps the Stracks did not want to pay the wage rise, low as it was, and Mary might herself have offered to apply for her trust monies, when they all realized that her term of apprenticeship theoretically should have expired five years earlier. According to Ming, the Board, however,

> promptly refused but insisted that she *'must have a holiday!'* She would not go away and after persuasion and threats on our part they condecended [*sic*] to send her £5.0.0 but on condition that she left me and went for this 'holiday'.[8]

Although Mary's application for her wages was not recorded, the minutes of the Board show that her case received the special and unusual attention of a Board meeting in May (remarkably, being the only entry to be indexed at the front of the minute book). In connection with her case, the Board stated its commitment to the principle of allowing apprentices who completed five years' service to return to their reserves to afford them the opportunity for marriage.[9] Such a principle had been Board policy since 1916, but had evidently not been regular practice, or Mary's case would not have drawn such special notice.

In hindsight Ming would interpret this, quite rightly, as a reaction to Mary's claim on her trust monies, but at the time she could not understand what was happening. The conflict between Ming and the Board over who 'owned' Mary illustrates the contradictions inherent in the apprenticeship system, where the bureaucratic state intervened in what was often imagined as being a private and personal arrangement. For its part, the Board's response was no doubt conditioned by their sensitivity to recent press criticism (galvanized by a newly emergent Aboriginal political movement) that its policy of removing Aboriginal girls and placing them in indentured domestic service was 'exterminating the race'. In their defence, the Board had been claiming their intention was only to train Aboriginal girls to be good wives in preparation for their eventual return to their communities.[10] Ironically, Mary may have been one of the first of the apprentices to be returned to the reserves in the face of public pressure.

I expect Ming was very relieved when Mary returned from Brungle. And having got her back, from the beginning of July 1926, Ming began paying Mary her wages directly.

How much Mary was paid was possibly quite little; the Stracks were already in debt and Norman had lost his job. Ming wrote of Norman's depression as he tramped the streets looking for work. At home he 'sits and gazes at me till I am almost crazy, won't talk, just sits and looks aimlessly around, plays with the revolver laconically. Through it all I have to sit and appear not to notice, an *awful* strain,' she agonized in her diary. Her frightening experience was not isolated, and the threat of deadly violence was real: there was in fact an 'enhanced tendency to use firearms upon the marital front' in Australia in the aftermath of the First World War.[11] Ming hid the gun, and within a few months Norman had found work again, but their unhappiness continued. 'N. not quite so blue, wonders what is the matter with me – I wish I knew – sometimes I *hate* him when I think of the chances he misses of being a success and of all the misery and hatefulness that follows us just through his want of balance.' By October 1926, Norman had lost that job too, as well as the company house that went with it. Ming sat down and wrote a letter to an imaginary confidante (Jean perhaps?), confessing that they were in serious trouble:

> I have been seriously thinking that the best thing we could do, the children & I, would be to live somewhere else right away from Norman, & I'll earn my own living I cannot & *will* not live like this any longer ...
> ... I pretend not to notice it [*the gun*] at all & that seems the best way, but it is frightening. Life is really not worth living when there is no pleasure or happiness for either of us, & there are children to be thought of as well which makes it a million times worse.
> This is quite a nice house & we were just beginning to feel that things were on a safe footing for once in our lives, when this bomb-shell came & we are right back to the beginning again ...[12]

One can only imagine how Ming would have reacted to the news she received that night – not only had Norman decided to try his luck in

Sydney again, with or without her, but Mary was pregnant. Mary's child, to an unnamed white man, had apparently been conceived during the three-month trip she had taken with Ming to Davistown. Mary would have been about six months pregnant at this stage. Presumably Ming had been unaware of her predicament before that. Years later, Ming recorded, 'I was almost distracted – put the matter in the hands of the police but they could do nothing,'[13] and at the time she wrote that she had called on a 'Mrs D' at Mary's request, but there are no further clues to the circumstances in which Mary became pregnant. In her diary entry that night, Ming was curiously complacent about Mary's 'trouble', merely adding it to the litany of catastrophes that afflicted her.

Ming's aunt Jean wrote to Ming commiserating: 'I am terribly sorry for you dear, & Norman, as well as Mary, *what* a thing to have happened just now – too dreadful when you are all needing her most ...'[14] Their attitude highlights Mary's position – the significance of her pregnancy was not how it affected *her* life, but how it impinged on the life of Ming and her family. But with the birth of her own child, a child whose unexpected appearance demonstrated indisputably that Mary was a grown woman with the potential to be a mother in her own right, the relationship she had with Ming would change forever.

* * *

The steamer SS *Canberra* arrived in Sydney's Circular Quay from Brisbane in November 1926, unloading its cargo of tropical Queensland fruit, together with Ming, the three children and Mary. As they stretched their limbs after the long, cramped voyage, shaking off the sickly-sweet smell of the rotting mangos and paw-paws, the acrid powder-blue air of the city harbour seemed bright and refreshing. Norman met them on the wharf, with a gigantic teddy bear for six-year-old Narrelle, and took them by train to Ming's parents' house at Pymble.

There they were then, bedraggled, poverty-stricken, on the run from their debts, with a pregnant Aboriginal maid, on the doorstep. Ming was humiliated beyond anything she had previously experienced. Ming's mother arranged for them the use of a family friend's house at nearby Wahroonga over the Christmas period, but in early January they would have to leave. The following day Ming took Mary, now eight months pregnant, into town to be admitted to Crown Street Women's Hospital. The two women would never again share a roof.

3
All girls shall leave the Reserves

My grandmother was six when she last saw Mary. Mary's unexplained disappearance marked the end of Narrelle's early childhood, with its vaguely remembered smells and sounds, snatches of old, yet startling sensations, and uncanny moments. What Gran remembers most intensely of Mary is a soft hand caressing the nape of her neck to wake her, gently, in the still grey hours of the morning on the day they left Brisbane. She does not remember why Mary was there or why she left. Nobody thought it necessary to tell her. It was not until I embarked on my own search for Ming's and Mary's story, beginning with Ming's old boxes, that Gran learnt of Mary's child.

As it turned out, I *did* find more photographs of Mary in Ming's boxes. She alone of Ming's servants, it seems, was photographed by Ming during the years she worked for her. I find her image scattered throughout Ming's papers: Mary on the beach, in the backyard, on the verandah; sometimes serious, sometimes smiling; always with one or more of the Strack children, reflecting that her relationship with Ming revolved around the care of the other woman's children. These glimpses through a Brownie lens literally represent Ming's view of Mary, and of their relationship. There is a captivating pair of snapshots taken on the beach, depicting Mary, and then Ming, playing with Narrelle and Peter. Two women, one sunny day, taking turns at photographing each other at play with the babies. An idyll of feminine harmony. But it strikes me that there are no photographs of the two women together – and the contrast between the trim, fashionably dressed white woman and the plump and softly bundled black woman is disturbingly redolent of the Old Slave South.

These images speak of colonialist nostalgia and, further, a memory triggered that today marks Ming as unambiguously complicit in the

Figure 4   Mary on the beach with Peter and Narrelle, Melbourne, 1922. Author's collection.

Figure 5   Ming on the beach with Narrelle and Peter, Melbourne, 1922. Author's collection.

Aboriginal child removal policy. There is one other surviving photograph of Mary, a formal, Victorian-style portrait of her standing alone in a hallway, solemn, wide-eyed, her slender dark hand resting on a stand. This was not among Ming's papers. It remains in the archives of the New South Wales government. Having been taken from her own family and community, Mary was sent to work for Ming by and under the terms of the New South Wales Aborigines Protection Board. The two women would not have laid eyes on each other, let alone photographed one another, were it not for the existence of this unseen third party.

* * *

The policy of forcibly removing Aboriginal children from their communities and placing them in white households, was followed by colonial and state governments around Australia. In New South Wales from the late nineteenth century until the 1940s the policy was directed overwhelmingly at female Aboriginal children. Established in 1883, when Social Darwinism, positing the inevitable extinction of the Aborigines, was hegemonic, the New South Wales Aborigines Protection Board (APB) secured legislative powers in 1909 and 1915 to hasten this process by placing Aboriginal girls as servants in the households of privileged white women.[1]

The Board was set up at a time when moves were underway to establish the New South Wales (NSW) colony as part of a federated 'White Australia'. In 1876 the NSW Parliament had heard the pastoralist W. H. Suttor demand an inquiry into the 'problem' of the perpetuation of Aboriginal communities around the state, who were now increasingly calling for 'land in our own country' to support themselves.[2] The missionaries' endeavour had been to transform the Aborigines into a settled, Christian yeomanry, and there was evidence that where Aboriginal people were able to manage their own affairs from a secure farming base, their communities were thriving. Indeed, some observers went so far as to condemn the missionaries for mistakenly maintaining a race destined for extinction.[3] Following a petition for land to the Governor from 42 Maloga mission men, an official 'Protector of Aborigines' was appointed in 1881 and immediately initiated a census of Aborigines in the colony. It indicated that there were 8,919 Aboriginals in the colony, 2,379 of whom were classified as 'half-castes', a figure that shook the notion that the Aboriginal people had practically disappeared.[4] Appointed chair of the new APB set up after the critical King and Fosbery report in 1883 into the missionaries' administration, he was replaced a month later by the Police Inspector-General and co-author of the report, Edmund Fosbery. Thereafter, until 1938, the chief executive of police was automatically the chairman of the Board.

The political response to the vitality of Aboriginal communities was to claim, as Suttor had, that growing numbers of 'nearly white' people were swelling the supposedly doomed Aboriginal minority. (Suttor in

Figure 6   Portrait of Mary, NSW Aborigines Protection Board. Reproduced with permission of the Australian Institute for Aboriginal and Torres Strait Islander Studies, Canberra, State Records, NSW, and the Department of Aboriginal Affairs, NSW.

1876 asserted that there were only 1,000 'full-blood' Aboriginals left in the colony even though the census taken that year enumerated 6,510.) Thus the survival of these communities was attributed to 'white blood', so providing a neat ideological solution. By 'absorbing' their younger generations into the white working class, the new Board could effect the disappearance of the original occupiers. This was crucial not just in terms of the immediate contest for land, but in the long-term issues centring on indigenous people's ill-defined status under the doctrine of *Terra Nullius*. Six years after the Board's formation, the Privy Council in England announced that Australia's east coast had been 'practically uninhabited' in 1788.[5] The obsession with the 'whiteness' of the Aboriginal survivors also reflected the racial anxieties of the colonists as the colonies headed towards independent nation status and Federation. As potential mothers reproducing the next generation of the obdurate indigenous communities, girls and young women in the founding Australian colony were to be the key targets of what was, to all intents and purposes, a planned programme of eradication.

The Board was quite open in its aim of using apprenticeships as a way of removing girls from their communities and 'absorbing' them into the white working class. From the outset, following the recommendations of the King and Fosbery report, fairer-skinned mission girls were indentured to this end. They were sent out from a Girls Home established on the Warangesda mission and also from a dormitory on the new, government-controlled reserve, Brewarrina. The Board secured legislative powers to arrange formal apprenticeships in 1909, subject to the provisions of the Apprentices Act of 1901, which required parental consent or a court finding of neglect. In 1915 the Board secured additional powers to indenture Aboriginal children where parental consent was withheld ('the almost invariable experience', according to the Board), without recourse to the courts. This had been an irksome requirement, given that 'the difficulty of proving neglect where children are fairly clothed and fed is insurmountable'.[6]

In its argument for such extraordinary powers, the Board made its intentions explicit, the object of the original and now unsatisfactory 1909 legislation having been, quite simply and as stated by Board member and politician Robert Donaldson at the time, to take the children from their communities.[7] The Board's campaign was accompanied by annual reports threatening that, in the absence of such intervention, the number of lighter-skinned people on the reserves was 'increasing with alarming rapidity' and would eventually become a 'positive menace to the State'.[8] The Colonial Secretary J. H. Cann, however, put a more euphemistic spin before the Legislative Assembly:

> It is not a question of stealing the children, but of saving them ... . The moral status of these aboriginals is very different from that of white people. A young girl 13 years of age may be an asset to an aboriginal woman ... . If we give the board the powers I am seeking to bestow under this amending bill these half-caste children will be given a chance to better themselves, and instead of the Government being called upon to maintain stations all over the state for the protection of the aboriginals, the aboriginals will soon become a negligible quantity and the young people will merge into the present civilisation and become worthy citizens. I am asking that power be given to the board to enable these children to have a chance ...

'If ever in the cause of humanity there was reason for children to be protected it is now,' he concluded piously, 'and the House ought readily to accede to the proposal, and give these poor little ones a chance.'[9]

Despite intense debate in the Assembly, the proposed amendment was passed with an overwhelming majority and enshrined in law under a Labor government as clause 13(a) of the Aborigines Protection (Amendment) Act 1915. Dissenting Labor members were compelled to vote on the party line, there being bipartisan support for the Board's aim of putting 'things into train on the lines that would eventually lead to the camps being depleted of their population, and finally the closing of the reserves and camps altogether'.[10]

The Cootamundra Home, housed in an old hospital acquired by the Board in 1911 to replace the Warangesda dormitory, had begun functioning in a small way in 1912. That year the Board made two female appointments, a matron for Cootamundra, Emmaline Rutter, and a 'Homefinder', Alice Lowe, whose responsibility was 'to make inquiry as to suitable homes for female apprentices, and to visit such apprentices in their situation'.[11] As a holding station for Aboriginal girls prior to their indentures, the Home derived from the nineteenth-century method of dealing with girls and young women from the 'dangerous classes'. It was the brainchild and primary responsibility of a Board member, George Ardill, an old-fashioned religious philanthropist who believed in 'saving' unmarried mothers by putting them to work as servants whilst placing their children in Christian institutional care. As secretary of the missionaries' lobbying body, the Aborigines Protection Association, Ardill had formerly managed the indentures of young women from Warangesda. In October 1897 he was appointed to the Board, and by 1909 was Vice-President and the Board's 'effective policy-maker', taking a prominent role in the campaign for increased removal and apprenticing powers between 1912 and 1915.[12]

His triumph in 1915 was short-lived. Only a month after being appointed to take control of all matters regarding the Cootamundra Home, Ardill resigned. In April 1916, two months later, the Chief Secretary reconstituted the Board. It was now dominated by high-level public servants. Of the seven Board members, only two, the politicians R. Scobie and W. Millard, were not bureaucrats; the other five represented the departments of the Police, Chief Secretary, Public Health, Education and Agriculture. In the words of the Board's Secretary, Alfred C. Pettitt, himself a public servant appointed in 1909, 'the idea was to team up, they were liaison with the Departments that really have something to do with Welfare, Health, Education'.[13]

The reconstituted Board directed that 'All girls on reaching the age of 14 years ... shall leave the Reserves'. This marked a change in the original emphasis of the Board, which stated in 1915 that fairer children were the target of the legislation; darker children to be apprenticed far from their communities only in 'exceptional circumstances'.[14] Nevertheless, throughout 1914, the Board's Secretary A. C. Pettitt, had been directing reserve managers to supply lists of 'all' Aboriginal girls and youths aged between 14 and 18, particularly those 'suitable for apprenticeship'. The Secretary had expressed his frustration at the inability of the managers 'to understand what is required'.[15] Certainly there was confusion over the Board's intention regarding darker children. Reiterating the earlier caution against placing 'the full blooded and dark coloured' children in situations far from their communities,[16] the Board now directed that Aboriginal mothers were to find their daughters domestic positions living off the reserves within a month of notification, or the Board would remove them itself. Girls were to return to their communities only temporarily, if at all, for 'a holiday', during which time they had to reside with the Board staff, were to be encouraged to marry and then to move off the reserve with their husbands. Having stated clearly in the 1914 debates that their policy was not to allow children who had 'been removed from camp life to return thereto',[17] this grudging concession was due to the authorities' fear of lone Aboriginal women 'at loose' in society, or indeed on their own reserves. A fear reflected also in the further direction that girls considered 'unsuitable' for apprenticeship were not to be expelled from the reserves, but rather should be sent to disciplinary institutions. The following year the Board abruptly turned down Ardill's request for financial assistance for his private homes; at the same meeting they welcomed the head of the State Children's Relief Board, Alfred Green, as a new Board member. Green's appointment was to facilitate the transfer of fair-skinned Aboriginal children removed under Board legislation to his department.[18] Although the Board Secretary later asserted that existing policy was only intensified, rather than redirected, the restructuring of the Board reflected a definitive move away from a missionary-style preoccupation with the 'moral' reclamation of fair-skinned Aboriginal girls towards a rigorous secular policy aimed at the most effective dismantling of the reserve populations.

The rationalization of the Board in 1916 was a major development, and one that would have fundamental and long-reaching effects. The policy of removal was pursued aggressively throughout the inter-war period, Aboriginal communities around the state being depleted of all their adolescent girls, who were sent to institutions or directly into domestic service. It is unlikely that *any* Aboriginal family in NSW was unaffected by this policy, if not through the taking of their own daughters, then through the removal of girls from the extended family and kinship networks. It was the years between the end of the First World War and the beginning of the Second World War, under the regime of bureaucrats, that witnessed the most intense creation of a Stolen Generation of Aboriginal girls – perhaps anywhere in Australia.

* * *

In the eyes of Ming's family having an Aboriginal servant was not exploitation, let alone a strategy by which Aboriginal communities might be 'broken up entirely', but a mark of benevolence and an indicator of enhanced social status. Ming had a particularly feudal attitude towards Aboriginal people, especially towards Mary, which can be traced to the influence of her mother's family. While Mary was her first servant, Ming was the third generation of her family to use Aboriginal labour, and she accepted it as her right.

The scraps of family history Ming recorded follow the contours of the 'Australian legend', with its story of the free British immigrants, drawn by promises of wealth for toil to a boundless new land where old class distinctions would melt away and democracy triumph. This was despite the fact that Ming herself, and no doubt the rest of the women of her family, felt compelled to maintain the myth that they were descended from the gentry. In fact, Ming's maternal grandfather, John T. Hobbs, had worked as a valet to that champion of working-class education,

John Ruskin, in his former life in London, while his mother and sisters worked in the Ruskin household as domestic servants. But his fortunes improved dramatically in the colonies, where he passed himself off as the great man's secretary and landed a plum position as Secretary of the Sydney School of Arts. After his re-marriage in 1862 to Maggie Goldie, who by then, having escaped her guardians in Scotland and in Australia, had found a job as a governess to his children by his late wife, 'J. T.' added an 'e' to his name and selected land on the far south coast under the Free Selection Acts of NSW.

The Hobbes gradually amassed substantial holdings in the district through the simple expedient of selecting land in the name of their sons, and are now numbered among the pioneers of the district. In 1874 they had chosen their property at Wallaga Lake on which they built their homestead and raised their numerous children. After J. T.'s death in 1892, Maggie took over the dairy farm herself, quickly establishing herself as a wealthy woman in her own right and purchasing more land in the area. 'Granny Hobbes', as she became known, straight-backed and fichu-collared, in the classic mould of the Victorian

Figure 7   Granny Hobbes with her daughters, *c.*1910. Ming's favourite aunts, Narrelle and Jean, stand behind Maggie, Narrelle in the middle and Jean to the right. Author's collection.

matriarch, continued to run the property until she was well into her seventies. The site of one of the earliest government-managed Aboriginal stations, the Wallaga Lake camp, located opposite Maggie's property, had been formally gazetted as an Aboriginal reserve with a Protection Board manager appointed in 1891, the year before both Ming's birth and the death of her grandfather, John Hobbes. Maggie relied on the labour of her Yuin neighbours, including two married women, to work in the house in return for credit at the local store. Her daughters, Ming's assorted aunts, marrying in the rural districts, followed her example. This use of Aboriginal labour was apparently undertaken with an air of *noblesse oblige*, masking Ming's family's dependence on the Yuin and their role in their dispossession. Ming undoubtedly modelled herself on her aunts, especially Jean. In 1913 Jean's husband wrote approvingly of his wife (known in the district as 'the Little Missus') that she had thrown a generous Christmas dinner for the local Aboriginal people at Weilmoringle.[19] This public persona of kindly benevolence must, however, be balanced against a private letter written to Ming written several years later, which gives a different insight into the complacent way such women regarded their role as mistress. Jean and Mina (her white 'lady's companion') had just done a 'big wash' and the 'hard work' of cooking, due to her cook having cut her finger. 'These women I have are frauds,' she complained to her niece:

> I detest them lazy hounds, it will serve them right to have you and the children, for when I go away they only loaf, Mina detests them too, we do most of the work as you will see. I am getting rid of them as soon as Easter is over & I can get others – they don't know & are quite pleased with themselves. My arm is tired, so this will only be a note. Aunt Kit helped rinse & hang out … . You will like seeing Mina again, & can have music together, she loves it. I am so glad to have her with me – we swear together at large! over these women.[20]

Ming's family were made aware early on in 1900 of the Board's plans to intervene in such employment arrangements, when another of Ming's aunts unwittingly incurred the displeasure of the Board when she took a local Yuin girl to Moree to work for her without first seeking Board sanction, at a time when the Board was first setting up the scheme and had no legislative powers.[21] In the Board records I found that Maggie had also made personal representations to the Board over ration stoppages and corrupt ration-tendering practices. (It is worth noting that milk rations were supplied to the reserve from Ming's grandmother's dairy at the end of the following year.) Her clashes with a manager over two Yuin men she employed and over the erection of a boundary fence between her property and the reserve may well lie behind that story Ming recorded in her draft obituary for Maggie, of her having a 'dishonest' manager removed[22] (although ·it is hard to be sure, as during the time that Maggie was at Wallaga Lake, four of the five managers were removed in disgrace). But whatever the intricacies of Maggie's engagement with Yuin affairs, Ming's grandmother's activities seemed to have been motivated by economic self-interest and supported rather than challenged the underlying causes of the Yuin's dependence. Almost certainly, Maggie recognized no connection between their unhappy position and the denial of their access to land. Her own selection was of course taken from the Yuin, and she herself had earlier pushed for the resumption of a portion of the reserve land so she could graze her stock there.[23]

Ming was, however, powerfully influenced by her childhood memories of apparently harmonious relations between grateful, child-like 'Natives' and the bountiful white settlers who had usurped their land. Ming not only romanticized such colonialist relationships, but attempted to put them into practice in her own life. Her maternalistic outlook towards Aboriginal people had a significant bearing on her decision to become a mistress of an Aboriginal servant in 1920. But she would find problems and contradictions with which Maggie Hobbes never had to contend, and her attempt to recreate her grandmother's imagined relationships with Aboriginal women would bring her, eventually, into direct conflict with the bureaucratic administration of the Aborigines Protection Board.

* * *

I first met Keith, the son of Mary's firstborn child, walking a horse in the light scrub skirting the central New South Wales town where he lived. I had written to him some weeks earlier and, receiving no reply, drove down to meet him. When I pulled up outside the modest house, a little girl, about four or five years old, fled inside. 'Nan, Nan! *Waijin* comin' to see you!' Keith's wife, Mavis, met me on the doorstep, somewhat concerned. There was that familiar jolt of awkwardness for me. But recognizing my name, Mavis told me how excited they'd been when they received my letter, which she had, folded in her purse. She told me I would find her husband with the horses down the road. I went to the edge of the town where the bush started and called, somewhat sheepishly, into the air. A rustle, a bay-brown horse emerged, and then a man in his fifties or thereabouts, with faded blue eyes crinkling in a weatherbeaten face, greeted me. A softly spoken man, there was an air of calm about Keith which seemed to melt imperceptibly into the quiet of the bush around him and the tranquil, rippling currents of the river nearby.

I had been looking for Mary's descendants for a while by the time I found him. I had located the families of all the other women who'd worked for Ming before I had found Mary's family, and was beginning to worry that she had entirely disappeared. So many Aboriginal women have disappeared without trace in this history of dislocation.

For Aboriginal people, 'doing family history' has an explicitly political significance. The fact that their families have been consistently attacked and torn apart by the state makes it a wholly different enterprise from the way I saw 'doing family history'. For me, tracing one's genealogy was a trivial, bourgeois pursuit, driven by middle-class anxieties and a denial, in the face of impending death, of one's own insignificance – the province of mildly ridiculous ageing relatives, searching for the dates of their ancestors' arrival in the colonies. One the other hand, 'real' history for me meant the big stuff, the affairs of political leaders, the clanking of the vast machineries of social and economic forces. Aboriginal writers have overwhelmingly preferred the personal approach when reflecting on their history. It is seen as an approach not just more accessible than traditional Western historiography, but one that counterbalances the inadequacies of the official records and allows an emphasis on important personal ties to family and community. Life narratives by Aboriginal women in particular have been described as 'the catalyst for the reconstruction of our identities'.[24] I understood these differences, but in an academic way. It was not until I came face to face with people who actually have been denied not only the stories of their ancestors but the most basic knowledge of where they come from that the real impact of this difference hit me.

I had hoped that Keith would be able to tell me something of who Mary was, what she was like, where she came from. Ming's papers certainly gave no hint of that or how she had been taken. As it turned out though, Keith had never met his grandmother, had never even seen a photograph of her – she, whose face smiled up at me from Gran's treasured collection of memories! Mary had died before he was born, when his mother (the child she was carrying when the Stracks returned to Sydney) was only a child herself. Not only had Keith not known his grandmother, but he had never known the original land of his maternal line. Such a bereavement of kin and country is of no small significance to Indigenous people today.

For the first time I realized how family history and genealogy, such a tiresome embroidery exercise to me, was alive and shot through with politics and conflict for Aboriginal people. The dislocation of families and individuals over successive generations of enforced removal from their land and of their children left people bereft of a personal identity that most of us take for granted. The irony is that many of these lost and stolen family histories are recorded in the dusty, intimidating archives of government.

With Keith's permission I was able to search these records in Victoria as well as New South Wales to trace his maternal line as far back as Mary's grandparents, Charley and Hannah. The pattern of destruction and resistance that emerged not only gave me the fullest explanation for Mary's presence in my great-grandmother's home, but illuminated for me a disturbing parallelism between white and Aboriginal family histories in this country. As I pieced together my own family history at the same time, a surreal symmetry emerged.

* * *

Mary's name appears as one of the earliest entries in the Protection Board's register of wards, that heavy, dusty book listing the children taken from their families between 1916 and 1928. In 1916, aged 15, Mary had been among the first major haul of girls seized after the passage of the 1915 Aborigines Protection Amendment Act. Like Ming, Mary also had a family tradition spanning three generations, a continuity of experience that stretched from the time of the migrant selectors to that of the post-war urban bourgeoisie. But if Ming's family's experience represented the white Australian dream, Mary's family's represented the nightmare that is hidden beneath it.

Mary's mother, Cecily, had been through the mill of domestic service indentureship in Victoria and had seen her younger sisters go through it also. Mary's maternal grandparents, Charley and Hannah, were Kurnai people from the Gippsland region of Victoria. Of Hannah I could find no detail other than her name; Charley's origins were uncertain when the missionary John Bulmer, noting the names of those he had persuaded to come onto his newly established mission at Lake Tyers, recorded him as having had little contact with Aboriginal people since being taken to work for squatters as a child.[25]

Charley's background is recorded not in the annals of proud pioneer history, but in the whispered stories, both black and white, that haunt that same history. He had been a child survivor of the Milly Creek massacre, one of the more notorious of the many killing fields of the Gippsland frontier in the mid-nineteenth century. Brought up by his captor, who bestowed on the small boy his own name, Charley grew up to be 'an excellent stockman'.[26] An industrious and intelligent man by Bulmer's account, it seems that Charley was determined to forge a new identity for himself. He resisted Bulmer's entreaties to remain on the mission and, like Ming's grandfather, applied for a grant of land soon after his marriage in the 1860s, under the new Victorian Crown Lands Alienation Act. But unlike Ming's grandfather, his application was rejected. Charles was thwarted by the Victorian Aborigines Board's refusal to support his application to the Lands Department and was forced to continue to earn his living precariously as a landless labourer. Living on the old run of Tongiomungie, he worked for two white men, selectors who had been able to acquire land under the same Act. By the 1880s he was destitute. Hannah fell ill in 1883. The local doctor, fearing he wouldn't be paid for his services, refused to treat her and she died, leaving seven children ranging in age from six months to 20-year-old Cecily, who was sick herself with a badly injured arm. Charley had no choice but to bring his family to Lake Tyers mission.[27]

Cecily formed a relationship there and had two daughters before her partner died and she, now single and being deemed a 'half-caste' as her mother Hannah had been so classified, was compelled by the recent Victorian Aborigines Protection Act to leave the mission. This draconian legislation of 1886 forced 'half-caste' Aboriginals – those who, it was claimed, had some white descent – under the age of 34 to leave the government reserves and stations.[28] Aimed at 'absorbing' Aborigines into white society, and underpinned by the assumption that 'full-bloods' would die out on the reserves, it must have been bitter news for Charley. He was the only one of the family who did not have to leave. He took his family back to his wife's people, and Cecily got a position as a domestic servant to a local white woman. The following year the Lake Tyers manager found the family in a 'bad way'. Charley and his youngest son were returned to the mission; his two younger daughters were placed in domestic service indentures. Cecily was more of a cause of consternation, being pregnant again, yet as 'according to the law she is a white woman', she was not allowed to remain on the mission. It was decided to send her to a refuge in Melbourne, and her two daughters were placed in a reformatory school in Melbourne. Mary's grandfather died on the mission shortly afterwards, bereft of the family he had strived to hold together. The people there were pained by the pathos of his death, and blamed the 'Half Caste Laws' for it, as well they might.[29]

A year later, arrangements were made for Cecily to be indentured to a pastor and his wife, but the prospective employers demanded that she come without her baby. Eventually, Cecily was compelled to go to them and her baby was taken from her. She wrote to the Victorian Board's Secretary Hagenauer asking if she could visit her children, but was advised against it, the Secretary writing that it was better not to press things: 'You must not get out of your mind because that will only do you harm.' Perhaps as a concession, Hagenauer placed her sister in a service position near her. Then, with three months of her indenture left to go, at the end of 1895, it seems her former employer offered to employ her. Hagenauer refused Cecily permission to go back there, as it was where 'she came to such shameful grief before'. He proposed that she get married at Coranderrk Aboriginal Station. But Cecily was not amenable to this plan, expressing her desire to 'look after herself and find a place to live'.

Two months after her indenture expired, however, in January 1896, she reluctantly submitted to a Board-arranged marriage at Coranderrk Aboriginal Station with the man who would become Mary's father. In the wedding photo that survives, Cecily stares directly at the camera, her expression hollow with pain and resentment. Her hopes for the return of her children may explain why she married, but her newly respectable status was not enough to grant her the return of one or more of her children, although she was told she might inquire how they were. Three years later she was again refused permission to have them with her, nor would she be told where they were 'at present'. That year the first child of this marriage, a boy, was born. Mary followed in 1900, Sarah in 1902 and Amelia two years later.

Cecily successfully applied to have one of her older daughters, Hilda, visit her at Coranderrk in 1901 for a couple of weeks, and she was there when the little boy died that year. After the death of her husband in 1908, Cecily again asked if Hilda, now 17, could come to live with her. (Cecily's other daughter and her third child disappear from the records.) The Board refused, but Cecily did not give up. She found Hilda at the Salvation Army Home at Bendigo and asked them to send Hilda to her. By the end of the following year they were reunited.

During this time, a NSW man by the name of Hollis, visiting his mother at Coranderrk station, had informed the Victorian Board, as he was obliged to by law, that he intended to marry Cecily. The Victorian Board gave their permission to the marriage, but demanded as a condition that Cecily and her children leave the state. The couple were married at Coranderrk about two months later, but they did not go to NSW for some years.

However, in the space of a few months Cecily had lost her daughter Hilda forever. As part of their strategy of absorption, and as a way of pushing people off the reserves, the Victoria authorities prevented 'half-castes' – both men and women – from marrying those designated 'full-blood'. Thus having been refused permission, as a 'half-caste', to marry a 'full-blood' resident soon after her mother's remarriage,[30] Hilda was reportedly 'going out of her mind'. She was sent to a mental asylum, where she died within a fortnight of her committal.

By October 1914, Cecily had left Victoria with Alf Hollis, and they and her three daughters were living one and a half miles out of Brungle Aboriginal Station. At this point they came to the attention of the NSW Protection Board. Noting the presence of Cecily's family near the Brungle reserve, the Board concurred with the station manager's suggestion that the girls be sent to the Cootamundra Home. Cecily's refusal to relinquish her daughters, however, confounded this plan. The Board had yet to receive the legal authority to seize children, but having just submitted the draft amendments to the 1909 Act, were prepared to bide their time.[31]

Cecily was allowed only a brief respite before her other daughters were taken from her by the NSW government. Perhaps Cecily had hoped that these girls might escape the fate of her older children. But when the 1915 amendment Act came in, giving the Board powers to remove Aboriginal children without parental consent or a court finding of neglect, Mary's mother could do nothing to resist.

Six months after Mary and Sarah were taken, Cecily's death from heart failure was formally registered by the Cootamundra police sergeant, who witnessed her burial in a paddock just south of Cootamundra. This unusual formality was due to the Board securing control of the youngest daughter, who was committed that same day to Cootamundra Home by court order. She joined her sister Sarah there, but Mary had already left, two weeks before her mother's heart had apparently broken, to take up her first situation at Wahroonga.

Mistress and servant, Ming and Mary's relative positions in life at the opposite extremes of the social spectrum were the outcome of their backgrounds. A mere two generations earlier, Ming's family had been servants; as for Mary, her great-grandparents knew nothing of servitude at all. As the one family rose, the other fell, and the pivot of that shifting balance was land, and the weight of their measure was race.

4
If I am coming back to you all again

'The public should be taught that it is just as necessary to go to hospital for childbirth as for a surgical operation,' a prominent practitioner told his audience of doctors in 1920.[1] Nevertheless, most women, like Ming, preferred to have their babies at home with a midwife, or in a private 'Lying-in' establishment run by one. The public hospitals and their male doctors continued to cater to poor and working-class mothers, many of them single, many of them, like Mary, with nowhere else to go. A photograph of one of Crown Street's wards from the time shows a long, cavernous room, with a dark polished wood floor and iron-framed beds lining the walls.

Mary wrote a lengthy, chatty letter to Ming two days after her admission. She told of her difficulty sleeping – 'I could hear the babies crying all night long, makes me think of dear little Helen. I do hope she will be good for you all. I am always thinking of you all.' She asked Ming how they had got on going up to Davistown. She told Ming she had put Peter's missing shilling on the kitchen shelf at 'Nan's' (Ming's mother); told Ming not to 'work too hard, have a good old rest till I get back'; and asked her to send her some 'fancywork' to do. 'The nurse is so good to me,' she continued:

> We all call one another 'Mrs' here. Nurse called out to me this morning. 'Where is Mrs Hollis? I have something for you to do.' She told me to do out the bathroom and two other rooms and I did. She said I was a good Mrs Hollis.

Further down the page, as an aside: 'I don't like that name called Hollis,' she commented, 'make me think of that mad old Hollis in Gundagai.' Her wry observation on the pretence that she was a respectable married woman and not a pregnant black servant, and this allusion to her removal, could only have reminded Ming that she had nobody else to turn to. She signed off, 'Your fond girl'.[2]

Mary wrote again a couple of days later, asking Ming if she had received her first letter. She was 'quite well and getting on splendid', but 'feeling very homesick. I better not think so much about home till I am quite well again.'[3]

Reading Mary's next letter to Ming written a week later I imagine her sitting up in one of those austere, iron-framed beds, smoothing the thin notepaper carefully on the tray table. 'My Dear Mistress'. Pen sliding smoothly across the clean sheet, 'I had your very well come letter and was please to hear from you all'.

Pauses, stares at the ticking pendulum clock on the wall at the end of the room, the potted palm in the corner, the posy of flowers on the nurses' desk in the centre of the room, the curliques of the light fittings. 'I do hope you all are having a good time.' Feels the baby shift inside her. 'We had a big storm her[e] on Monday night and I could not sleep you could hear the nurse walking all night looking after the baby[s] I am feeling very home sick getting quite sick of it,' all in a rush, 'I do hope I will be home for –'

Mary stops, stares again at the clock, the palm, the posy, looks out the sash windows to the blue sky, and crosses out the 'for'. 'I do hope I will be home *soon*', she corrects herself. More carefully,

> One of the nurse was saying that there is a Home down at [illegible] where you can go for three week or a fortnight with them and stay with them. Lot of white girl are doing that and going out to work again if you tell Miss Low[e] [the Protection Board 'Homefinder'] about it that mean that I will not …

She turned over the page.

> return Back to you anymore.

Reading her words years later, I can virtually feel Mary stop and take a deep breath. 'I am feeling worry about that I think I had better tell Sarah [her sister, living at Brungle Station] about it and get it over.'

> I know that you told all your people about me. So I suggest that I or to [ought to] write to Sarah and tell her about it. I do hope I will not part from you and the children. I am feeling a bit up set about it. If you are down in town some time run out and see me I would love

to see you if you could fit it in I do miss you and the children thinking of you all ever[y] night. I give my love to Helen Narrelle Peter and Peggy [Ming's niece] and I hope I will see them soon – if I am coming back to you all again.

Resolutely, 'Oh I must tell you that I got the two feeder [bibs] that you send me to work for dear little Helen. I must stop now love from Mary.' Then a postscript, in small writing, 'we have tea at five lunch at 12. And breakfast at 7 every morning'. Maybe then it occurred to Mary that Ming might not even be in Sydney, perhaps she was still at Davistown. She writes, finally, painfully, 'Do you think you could send me some more fancy work to do if you are down at Woy Woy. I feel I must have some thing to do in the afternoon. We all sit down and look at one another till tea time.'[4] And she seals the letter, leaving me with the haunting image of full-bellied, blank-faced women, sitting in a silence broken only by the slow ticking of the wall clock.

Evidently, there had been some discussion between Ming and Mary over what would become of her. Mary's warning about Miss Lowe, the woman employed as an official 'Homefinder' by the Aborigines Protection Board, the woman who was responsible for arranging the placements of the Aboriginal apprentices, suggests that Ming had contemplated asking her to assist in providing a place for Mary to stay after the birth of her baby. The problem was that Ming did not yet have a home herself, and Norman did not even have a job. None of Ming's 'people' were able – or willing – to provide a place for Mary to stay in the interim.

Mary's baby girl was born on 26 January, Australia Day, 1927. Mary wrote a short note to Ming a few days later asking her to visit – 'I would like to have a talk to you'.[5] Her note reached Ming the day before the Stracks moved to a boarding house on the far western outskirts of Sydney. Two weeks later Mary wrote again, care of Ming's mother's address:

Do try and come and get me. I am longing to get back to you if I could get someone to take baby, nurses are so nice to baby and I think one of the nurses said that I would be able to dop [adopt] baby if all goes well ... Tell dear little Helen that I am coming home soon, if I am well. Love to you all, come in soon and take me to the home.[6]

Ming would later write that Mary had 'implored' her to take her baby as well as herself, and this Ming 'had intended to do and said so', despite the Board telling her that they would take charge of Mary's

Figure 8 Mary in the backyard in Brisbane, Queensland, with Helen and Narrelle. Author's collection. This is the last surviving photograph of Mary in Ming's papers.

baby.[7] But she was evidently not making her intentions clear to Mary, and Mary's alternatives, which were limited even for a *white* unmarried mother, were harshly constrained. An adoption arranged by herself might well have been Mary's best option. It appears that Ming had not replied to the news of the baby's birth, and Mary's next letter, with her tentative suggestion that she give up her baby, took a full month to reach Ming. But five days after writing, Mary and her three-week-old baby were transferred from the hospital to the Ashfield Infants Home, an institution for single mothers and their children utilized by the Board for pregnant apprentices.

From the Ashfield Home Mary again wrote to Ming, care of Ming's mother, and again the following month, care of the Stracks' old address at Pymble. These letters have not survived (only their envelopes), and there is no way of knowing if Ming replied. In July 1927, Mary and her baby were discharged from the Infants Home to the authority of Protection Board, transferred to Wallaga Lake Aboriginal Station (which was now a transit station between the NSW and Victorian reserves), and thence interstate to Lake Tyers Station in Victoria.

In later years, Ming insisted that she had been 'most anxious to have Mary again in my home' at the time, but the Aborigines Protection Board 'refused ... to allow her to return to me'.[8] The records of both the Board and the Infants Home suggest that the authorities might have been trying to locate Mary's stepfather, and might not have approached Ming at all.

Yet Ming herself had been in no great haste to have Mary back. There were several reasons, apart from the evident confusion in the correspondence, why Ming may not have responded immediately to Mary's pleas. The Stracks were in fairly straitened circumstances – Ming supplemented their rent at the boarding house by serving in the kitchen – and so were not in a position to accommodate Mary and her newborn baby. Although Norman found work in May 1927, they may not have been in their own home until September, when they were renting at Lindfield.

Ming was also preoccupied with the serious illness of three-year-old Helen, who contracted laryngeal diphtheria in June 1927. Ming contacted the Aborigines Protection Board then to tell them that, due to Helen's illness, she 'would take Mary a little later'.[9] This was presumably in response to Mary's last letter and strongly suggests that the Board had not 'refused' to allow Mary to go back to Ming at this stage. But when a drunken doctor attempted an emergency tracheotomy on the little girl at Ming's parents' home, Helen nearly died. She was rushed to hospital and hastily baptized, though thankfully she survived. But the timing was terrible. The day before she was sent to Victoria, Mary made one last attempt to see Ming, coming out to Pymble alone, but Ming was not there – she was at the hospital with Helen.

* * *

Ming's failure to find any kind of emergency, stop-gap solution until she did have a place for Mary implies that she assumed that Mary could be collected at her convenience – after years of toting her with her back and forth, Mary somehow 'belonged' to her. Since Mary had returned to her from the Board's 'holiday' and from then on was paid by Ming directly, Ming presumably considered Mary by this measure to be independent of the Board's control. But Mary was under no such misconception, as her letters from the hospital show. Ming however chose to disregard her warning.

As Mary was 25 years old and had completed her apprenticeship, the Board's usual strategy of removing the baby and placing the girl straight into another apprenticeship was not available. Their decision to send her interstate to Victoria no doubt had a great deal to do with her previous claim for the reimbursement of her trust fund monies. No reason for this location was given, in preference to Brungle Station where Mary's sister Sarah lived and where the Board had wanted to send her for a 'holiday' the previous year. As I would find out, she did have family connections in that state, but the Victorian Board that had so ungraciously rejected her mother years earlier was evidently not prepared to accept Mary. The manager of Lake Tyers wrote to the Victorian Board upon her arrival 'Mary Hollis from NSW arrived on Station and desires instruction', to which the Victorian Board responded by telling him she was allowed to stay there for yet another 'holiday'.[10]

Mary wrote again to Ming from the Victorian reserve and they kept up a correspondence throughout 1927 and 1928, Mary enlisting the aid of a solicitor at nearby Bairnsdale on Ming's recommendation. This solicitor wrote to the NSW Board on Mary's behalf within a few months of her arrival at Lake Tyers, but it was another year before she finally received the full balance of her trust account. This happened in October 1928, after her marriage at Lake Tyers in early August and an inquiry from the NSW Board to the Victorian authorities in September as to her 'bona fides'[11] (although they had apparently been happy to pay her out small amounts without such assurances). She was sent a cheque for £65, which represented more than ten years of her labour. Ming considered this to be far below the full amount, although the records held by the Board, at least, appear to be in order.

If Mary felt at all abandoned by Ming we do not know. Their correspondence appears to have been driven by Mary at least as much as Ming. Although her tone remained friendly, if somewhat reserved, tellingly Mary now addressed Ming as 'My Dear Mrs Strack' and made no emotional appeals to her – at least not in the one letter which survives. (Again, only empty envelopes attest to other correspondences.) Instead, she wrote confidently and happily of having found relatives in Victoria and of her 'dear little Baby', thanking Ming politely for her present of a bottle and blanket – 'thank you so much for thinking of baby like that'. Mary not only sought her former mistress's advice regarding the solicitor, but also a 'loan' of £2 to buy clothes for herself and her child. Mary pointed out quite firmly that her need was due to Ming's failure to send her own clothes down to her – clothes that constituted part of her wages to which she was rightfully entitled – even as she promised to pay Ming back 'next week'.[12]

After finally receiving her trust funds from the NSW Board, Mary left the reserve with her daughter and her new husband. Mary's husband, William, like Mary herself, had been an unwelcome presence on the Victorian station, the manager having unsuccessfully attempted to take action against him for trespass in 1927. As they simply disappear from the official records it is not clear whether they were expelled from Lake Tyers or left voluntarily. The Stracks also moved around the same time. Mary again wrote to Ming at this time, of which again only an envelope survives, which was forwarded to Ming's new address. It was the last Ming would hear of her for some years.

* * *

'My Dearest Old Mary,' Ming wrote, the hasty scrawl of her writing betraying her excitement. 'At last I have found your address.' It was February 1930, nearly two and half years since she had last seen Mary:

> I have written to you & sent parcels but have not had any letter from you since you left Lake Tyers. You poor old Mary! I was very sad to hear that you had lost your dear baby Mary. I *am* so sorry. How is the new little baby? Do write me a long letter, & Mary if you would like to come to me again, you can come whenever you like, just say, & I will send the money for your fare. You know that I will always love my old Mary & take care of you both.

Am sending 10/- in this letter & a parcel of clothes. I heard from one of your people at Lake Illawarra (where we stayed for 3 weeks) that you had been very ill & got so thin. I do hope you are well. Just fancy your coming back to Wallaga Lake! What a long way, Mary. Were you trying to come to Sydney? If I had only known I could have helped you. I wrote letters to every place I could think of & at last wrote to Mr Bell at Lake Tyers, but he did not answer it, & then Mrs Mason at Lake Illawarra told me all about you & that your step-father had taken you to Brewarrina. Are you happy Mary? Do write soon.

With love from Joan Strack

Ming addressed the envelope to Mary in both her married and maiden names and sent it off. But her information – including the news of Mary's baby's death – was wrong. Within a few days the letter came back. It had been opened, was stamped with an official stamp from 'Brewarrina Aboriginal Station,' and a note attached to it with a pin. It was from the manager of the Brewarrina Station. 'Dear Madam,' he wrote, '... no one here knows these names ...'[13]

* * *

Ming's relationship with Mary, however genuinely affectionate, was created within the framework of colonial dominance and subordination, in which symmetry of dependence and attachment was an impossibility. Ming's dependence, emotional and practical, on Mary was very real – her second child, even she herself, may well not have survived without Mary – but for Ming, Mary was essentially replaceable. After all, there was always another of Mary's kind, another Aboriginal apprentice supplied by the state. While this disparity in their relationship had become stark with the birth of Mary's child, Ming's opposition to the system did not develop overnight. Her application to the Board in 1931 for another apprentice, having unsuccessfully searched for Mary, shows that her perceptions of what had occurred had not yet widened into a general opposition to the Board's apprenticeship scheme and the recognition of her complicity in it as an employer. That the Board was more than happy to supply her with another servant also indicates that Ming herself was not seen by them to be 'subversive' or a threat in any way.

Indeed, it was in the Board's interests to keep Ming as a contented client. Most of the 850 or so employers registered with them by the early 1930s were women, and given that the apprenticeship policy was aimed at Aboriginal girls, the participation of white women in particular as employers was crucial to the success of the scheme. As the Board argued, it was the Aboriginal girls' experience of being in these 'first-class private homes' that was 'paving the way for the general absorption of these people into the general population'.[14] But unlike the Aboriginal workers, the participation of white women was entirely voluntary.

The Board had originally found, when it first began considering introducing a systematic indenturing system in 1900, that employers were unwilling to engage apprenticed workers. While employment of Aboriginal servants in rural areas had been commonplace, many rural employers found the pool of casual labour already available to be quite suitable, even advantageous, as they were bound by no contract to wages or terms of employment.

Still, Aboriginal workers could, in some circumstances, demand wages that some employers found outrageous. The daughter of Henry Bate (a prominent townsman who had helped Ming's grandparents acquire their land at Wallaga Lake) wrote to her cousin in 1888, complaining that white 'female help is not to be had at any price':

> Wish you could send out a few Cumberland girls – we have to do all our own work, not even a washerwoman. We trained a half caste girl for six months. All she did was mind the baby about four hours a day and wash the dinner dishes, but she grew too fat and lazy for that at last and she had 8/- a week and only 14 years old.[15]

This was hardly exorbitant, being about half the rate commanded by a white housemaid in the city at the time. But this writer expressed her preference for unfree labour – 'Cumberland girls' being state wards. Indeed, when these rural employers realized that apprenticeship severely limited the wages of their employees, they were no doubt keen to participate. (Similarly, the Board made little effort to pursue defaulting employers.) The fact that the Board could simply take girls out of independent positions and place them in indentures would have also increased rural employer participation. In 1910, with its new legislative powers in place, the Board directed managers to furnish the particulars of 'respectable householders' in rural districts who might employ Aboriginal apprentices, and claimed that the supply of apprentices no longer equalled the demand. [16]

With the imposition of this system, Aboriginal girls were also and for the first time brought in numbers to work in urban households. But the wives of white-collar professionals raising families in the lush eastern and northern suburbs of Sydney would, in the normal course of things, have had no access to Aboriginal labour at all. Although they would have been attracted by the low wages in a time of chronic servant shortage, the Board did not advertise its apprenticeship scheme until 1940. My great-grandmother may well have been typical of urban employers in having the kind of rural connections to give her 'inside knowledge' of the system.

Yet, considering the prevailing discourse of the time which equated Aboriginality with disease, vice and racial degeneracy (something encouraged by the Board's own rhetoric), the decision of a respectable and aspiring middle-class suburban housewife to take a strange Aboriginal girl into her home to keep house and care for her children seems remarkable. They may well have felt themselves to be very progressive, tracing their interest in having a black servant, as Ming did, to a background where past relationships of benevolence were imagined, and constructing their decision as an act of kindness, even philanthropy. Certainly, the fact of being supplied with an Aboriginal apprentice was seen as recognition of their social status. The daughter of one Sydney employer (known personally to Ming), for instance, was adamant that the Board 'allowed' her mother to have two Aboriginal girls only 'because she had had them for so many years and cared for them'. Of such mistresses generally, the daughter asserted, 'their motives were of the highest ... it wasn't just to employ cheap labour for wealthy Sydney people'.[17]

The unspoken 'high motive' was the moral protection of these young girls. The apprenticeship policy had been explicitly formulated on the understanding that Aboriginal girls began reproducing at around 14 years of age, 'and so the thing went on year after year with the result that the half-caste and white population was increasing'. Service in good homes would prevent Aboriginal girls from having babies, unlike in their communities where, it was claimed, they 'never had a ghost of a chance to keep respectable'.[18] The outrageous premise that domestic service would prevent the continued 'breeding' of Aboriginal girls to white men could only be believable given the ubiquity of what has been called the 'goodfella missus' legend,[19] which was particularly attractive to middle-class urban women in the opening decades of the twentieth century.

The Protection Board had come into being just when a uniquely Australian identity was being constructed, catalysed by Federation in 1901. Urban soon-to-be Australians clung to a nostalgic identification with the receding bush. The dominant national mythology emerging from the 1890s posited the white pastoral worker as the national hero;

his casual sexual usage of Aboriginal women (and indeed of servants, or 'slaveys') was a snide 'boys' joke'.

Yet at the same time, an alternative tradition had grown up. In the colonialist culture of Australia, the widespread use of Aboriginal 'concubines' by white men on the frontier had been an issue of notoriety, being read as an index of colonial degeneracy. And so the white wife, for the good of Empire and Civilization, was expected to prevent her husband and sons from reproducing with Aboriginal women. When she arrived at the frontier the white woman was expected to displace Aboriginal women as the sexual partners of white men, transforming and limiting their role to domestic service proper.

In the masculinist tradition, however, such women were 'gin-shepherds', 'wowsers' and tyrants of petty irritation. A stock comparison of white women with Aboriginal women was increasingly satirized by turn-of-the-century popular cartoonists and writers as they engaged in the construction of a specifically Australian identity. The underlying target of perennially popular jokes depicting Aboriginal women affecting the airs of white women was the bourgeois white woman and her pretensions to equality with white men. This hostility was made explicit in a 1907 essay by the journalist George Taylor. Taylor presented the Aboriginal woman as 'the real Australian girl type' as opposed to the white woman, because her 'opinion on current politics isn't dished up for our breakfast every morning'. Although, 'I am sorry for this as her opinion on the present cry of "White Australia" should be interesting now she is passing into oblivion'.[20]

But even as Taylor griped about being forced to listen to white women's political views, the early feminists were making substantial achievements in this area, most notably the gaining of white female voting rights in the Federal parliament as well as the states (Victoria being the last in 1908). They did so by arguing the case of the sanctity of white motherhood.

Hand-in-hand with this went the construction of an exemplary white female pioneering past. The mythic 'goodfella missus' was formulated and popularized in a range of publications aimed at middle-class urban women and girls, the best known being Mrs Gunn's *The Little Black Princess* (1905, republished in a special school edition in 1924) and *We of the Never Never* (1908). In the place of the larrikin white nomad and 'Black Velvet', these works promoted the brave 'little Missus' and her cute child-servant 'Bett-Bett', the forlorn offspring of a white man and an Aboriginal woman. While the maternalism of Mrs Gunn masked the exploitation of black women's labour by white women and their husbands, it ascribed a virtuous and apparently powerful role for white elite women within the nation, and so provided a harmonious accompaniment to white women's political entry to federated Australia.

Against such a backdrop, well-to-do urban wives and mothers like Ming were called on to participate in public policy as maternalistic mistresses; and were asked to 'uplift' and 'protect' Aboriginal girls by taking them into their households as domestic servants. As mistresses, their role was to serve as conduits for the transmission of the values of working-class servility the Board hoped to instil in Aboriginal women. But such a role could almost as easily have been effected outside of the apprenticeship structure, given the intrinsically assimilationist and status-ridden nature of domestic service generally. As mistresses of *indentured* female labour, however, their participation enabled the state to maintain a high degree of control and surveillance over Aboriginal women and their offspring required for its programme for the destruction of their communities. By opening their households to Aboriginal apprentices, white mistresses, especially in the urban areas, provided the locale for their absorption under a bureaucratic social engineering scheme.

This was, of course, in complete contrast to the noble role for such women envisaged by themselves and in the rhetoric. In fact, white mistresses, being positioned between the state and the Aboriginal women, were intermediaries involved in an intimate, day-to-day experience of the practice of the state's Aboriginal policy. And as Ming's story shows, the contradictions within this policy between its rhetoric of maternalism and 'protection', and the reality of exploitation and abuse, could become apparent through the lens of private lives.

Part II
Alma

5
So desperately hard to understand

Two months after she had tried, unsuccessfully, to find Mary again, Ming advertised in the paper for a nursemaid. She had been unwell for some time; unbeknown to her, she had cervical cancer. Ordered by her doctor to go into hospital for another major operation, Ming needed someone to look after the children during her absence. The children were now aged twelve, ten and six years. This time the operation was a hysterectomy, a '*very* long and dreadfully agonising operation a most dangerous one also,' as Ming described it; she suffered complications and was in hospital for eight weeks. Once again, Norman was away, and once again, Ming apparently had little idea of what the doctors were doing to her. Her doctor wrote to Norman – not to her – to explain what the operation entailed, assuring him that his wife would still be capable and interested in 'conjugal relations' – though she would, of course, be infertile.[1]

In many respects Ming's situation was similar to the time when Mary had started working for her. But this time, in contrast, Ming was obviously unhappy with the woman she had hired, the only non-Aboriginal servant Ming would ever employ. She never recorded her name, describing her only once, abruptly, as 'a stranger, a woman I did not know'.[2]

Ming's dissatisfaction with this white servant probably had quite a lot to do with her decision to return to the Board to hire another Aboriginal apprentice the following year. But again, her female relatives were the main influence. In October 1931, Ming and the children had just returned from an extended holiday with Ming's sister Helen. Helen had married a Condobolin sheep farmer, and at the time had as a servant a 15-year-old Aboriginal apprentice she had hired through the Board. Ellen was originally from the Condobolin Aboriginal mission and returned there regularly between jobs. As a local girl she was familiar with her environment, and impressed young Narrelle no end by taking the children around the place and showing them the foods traditionally eaten by her people. Perhaps seeing Ellen with her children rekindled Ming's memories of Mary; perhaps Ming was reminded of her own childhood experiences wandering with the Yuin at Wallaga Lake. Back in Sydney, Ming found that her mother Isobel had taken on an Aboriginal apprentice, Annie, in August. Ming immediately applied to the Board to employ an Aboriginal apprentice herself.

* * *

If Ellen was the inspiration for Ming's decision, then the young woman who was signed over to her on 12 October 1931 must have been a disappointment. At the age of five Alma Worran had been placed in the Bomaderry Children's Home, a mission-run institution for Aboriginal children on the south coast, and had lived there ever since. Although now 18 years of age, she had never been out to service, and started with Ming on the rates of a first-year apprentice (£1 12s 6d, to be remitted quarterly to a trust fund, and 1 shilling a week pocket money). Not only did she have no experience in private domestic service, but Alma had had no opportunity to grow up on the land and in the culture of her people. There is every likelihood that she had no idea of where she came from or even who she was other than her name. The Board's ward register entry for her was extraordinarily vague: her place of birth, 'not known'; her father and mother, 'not known'; siblings and other relatives, 'not known'; not even her age was filled in. Apparently, all that was known about Alma's early life at the time she was registered in July 1927 was that she had been 'In Mother's care. Place unknown'.[3]

Seen through Ming's eyes, Alma appears only as a shadowy, insubstantial figure. It seems she made little impact on or connection with the family – my Gran today has only the vaguest recollection of her. Ming's rather limp description of her in later years was that she 'was a thoroughly good girl & we were very fond of her'.[4] Alma was mentioned only once in Ming's surviving diaries during her time with the Stracks, and this was merely an entry recording that Ming had paid for her shoes out of her housekeeping budget.

Admittedly the remaining diaries covering the period when Alma worked for Ming are extremely fragmentary. Ming was preoccupied throughout 1931 and 1932, the years Alma was with her, with a newly established paramilitary group, the New Guard. This, the most well known of the various ultra-right secret armies that sprang up in Australia during the Depression, was set up by a North Shore lawyer and ex-army lieutenant-colonel, Eric Campbell. The group aimed to overthrow the Australian Labor Party premier Jack Lang and his party, then in power in NSW. What was to follow was less certain, but as the New Guard despised both the democratic 'rule of the majority' and 'machine politics', and had a fervent hatred of organized labour, it presumably involved the installing of a leadership by a few select men considered to be of calibre (such as Campbell himself).

Norman's involvement appears to have been directly related to his difficulties in finding work in the early 1930s. The New Guard drew on middle-class war veterans like Strack, disaffected by their post-war experiences of unemployment, for both its 'commanders' (who retained the ranks they had held in the war) and its rank-and-file. The North Shore was where a substantial proportion of its members resided, and the Stracks were the custodians of the papers for 'Division 45', which covered the upper North Shore suburbs.

Gran, who was then eleven years old, remembers this as a thrilling time. New Guard meetings were held in the house and Norman kept all their papers in an incinerator, ready to be set alight if the police raided. She recalls being taken to see the men of the New Guard holding assemblies on cold mornings in a paddock at Frenchs Forest. Though in later years Ming would scoff at her husband's fondness for 'strid[ing] round in uniform',[5] and women were not, technically, allowed to be members of the New Guard, Ming it seems took a keen interest herself at the time. 'What are we going to do about the Bridge opening, plans are running apace,' she wrote excitedly in March 1932, days before the opening of the newly built Harbour Bridge by Premier Lang:

> We are ready & only await the word to begin operations, but & it is a very big '*but*' suppose we *do* remove Lang & his henchmen? What then? It will mean certain bloodshed, & that we believe is exactly what the Communists are waiting for, they are better equipped than we are & only want *us* to begin the fight, they will then have the opportunity, to come into the thing with arms & ammunition aplenty & so we are holding back as long as possible ...[6]

Ming was proud of the fact that it was she who handed Francis De Groot his sabre on the occasion of his cutting the opening ribbon on the bridge ahead of Lang.

While all this excitement was going on, Alma's life with the Strack family was uneventful for almost a year. Ming later wrote approvingly that 'she loved her church & Sunday School and went regularly'. Then, around September in 1932, she struck up an acquaintance with a local Chinese market gardener, who invited her to dinner and 'persuaded her to visit his garden'. Alma 'could see no wrong in this', but Ming was horrified.[7]

Ming would have been well aware of the contemporary eugenic notion that people of Asian-Aboriginal parentage were on the bottom rung of those judged 'unfit' by reason of their 'mixed-race' parentage. Pseudo-scientific theories of 'miscegenation' had combined easily with earlier stereotypes of lecherous, opium-plying Orientals in the popular imagination – to accuse any non-Asian woman of consorting with a 'Chinaman' was a common, and damaging, insult of the time. Ming's abhorrence of Alma's friendship with a man she described as 'this vile Chinaman' was due as much to his race as to the fact that he was married.

Ming forbade Alma from seeing the man. Alma resisted this interference in her personal life, and twice 'ran away' to visit her new friend. The second time she went, Ming was determined to put her foot down. She called the local police, who found Alma and brought her back to Ming in disgrace.

Ming asked if the police could remove the gardener from the area, 'but it was impossible without proof from Alma herself, & that she could not or would not give'. However, as they were required to do, the police automatically notified the Board's Secretary upon their 'capture' of Alma. The Board's Homefinder, Alice Lowe – the same whom Mary had cautioned Ming against years earlier – then paid a visit to Alma. The 'result of this visit was even worse, for Alma seemed almost distraught', wrote Ming, and no wonder, as Miss Lowe's less than gentle approach consisted of threatening to 'murder her if she went back to the garden'.[8] Stubborn Alma went once again to see her friend, was again collected by the police at Ming's request and was taken by them to a Shelter in town. From there the Board assumed control of Alma, stating on her record that she had 'absconded' and had been found by the police.[9]

Ming fully realized that by calling the police again she was effectively handing Alma over to the Board. She had the example of her mother's apprenticed worker Annie before her. Annie, also from Bomaderry, had been sent to a distant station under similar circumstances in April of that year.

Ming wrote a curious letter to her father in late September 1932, around the time she began arguing with Alma. Ming's sister Helen was in Sydney with her daughter Peggy, staying with their parents. Ming had long had a difficult and tormented relationship with her mother and her younger sister, and now was bitterly stung by her father's apparent 'siding' with them against her. Ming told her father that Annie had written her a 'long letter' before she had left Isobel's employ.

Annie had told her she had overheard Peggy regaling the dinner table with funny stories about Ming for the amusement of the rest of the family. She also reported to Ming various hurtful comments Ming's mother and sister had made about her in their conversations. 'It is most unwise to discuss these things in the hearing of one's domestics,' Ming wrote to her father angrily, 'but they could not be expected to know this.' Annie told Ming she had reprimanded Peggy in her defence (Ming claimed Annie described the child to her as 'a horrid brat') and that she was 'heartily sick of listening to them' and 'wanted very much to come to me!'[10]

If Annie's letter was genuine – it has not survived amongst Ming's papers, though that does not mean it was not genuine – it shows a remarkable affinity between Annie and Ming. Ming's letter to her father, however, shows clearly how Ming used her imagined relationships with her Aboriginal servants to define herself against her mother and sister. Ming did not mention Alma in the letter, even as she was struggling to exert her maternal authority over Alma at the same time, and her absence is resounding. Ironically, Board records suggest that Isobel and Annie might have been having similar problems. Annie was reportedly returned to the Board in April 1932 as 'unsuitable[,] getting out at night &c & being the subject of Inquiries by Police, who on one occasion returned her to Mrs Commons at 2 am after being out with men.'[11] Considering what was happening in both households, Ming's arch assertion of Annie's loyalty suggests that she was feeling defensive about Alma's challenge to her maternalistic authority. For Ming's vision of herself as a loving yet firm mistress depended on Alma's devotion and obedience.

Having called in the ultimate instrument of white authority, the police, to reinforce her power over Alma – taking, in fact, the same recourse as her mother – Ming attempted to regain some ground. She suggested to Miss Lowe that Alma should be sent back to the Bomaderry Home. She believed that Alma was 'passionately fond of [the Matron of Bomaderry] & the home & *never* should have been taken from it'. But the Homefinder 'informed me that she "loathed" these Missions where they spoilt the Natives and that she intended taking every girl from this home!'[12] Instead, Ming was told, Alma would be sent to Urunga, a small Aboriginal station on the North Coast. The Board had arranged for an escort to accompany Alma by rail from Sydney, and Ming went to meet her when they passed through Hornsby station.

Standing on the platform on the northern outskirts of Sydney, watching the trains arriving and departing through the different interchanges, Ming had the opportunity to think through what had happened. Dismayed at the unexpected outcome, she was disturbed by a sudden awareness of the role she had played in getting yet another Aboriginal girl banished to a distant and strange station. As the train pulled in and Alma alighted with Miss Rutter (the ex-matron of Cootamundra Home), Ming changed her mind about sending Alma away and told the escort she would take Alma back then and there. 'No, you cannot do that,' Miss Rutter replied, 'it is *never* wise to have them back':

> & so I let her go, foolishly I realise, but it is so desperately hard to understand at the time & she had run away so often for no known reason that it seemed useless to try & keep her ...[13]

Shortly after she arrived at Urunga, Alma wrote to Ming: 'I am awfully sorry I have given you all this trouble and I don't think I would be able to face you again,' she apologized. 'I don't know why I was tempted to do such a foolish thing but I know I won't do such foolish things again.' There was no need for Alma to write to Ming at all, but she did hint at her relief at having escaped domestic service. 'I am alright and I like [it] here very much,' she continued. 'The only work I do is to make my bed and scrub the room. Then I go down and play in the water and gather oysters. Or we either go to town or to the beach.' Perhaps Ming had written to Alma to ask her if she wanted to come back and work for her. In her next letter, Alma expressed the hope that 'it won't be long before you get another girl'.[14] Her initial apology is the only part of her writings that comes across as deferential. Overall, Alma's amiable tone indicates that she had been neither cowed by Ming nor resentful of her, and any regret Alma felt for her actions was a genuine remorse for, as she said, having given Ming 'all this trouble'.

* * *

Alma's nephew Herb remembers Alma being pointed out to him as his auntie when he was a child in the 1940s. It was on Burnt Bridge mission on the north coast on New South Wales, and she was with her husband.

Although the Board records were so scant, I discovered that they did have the details of a little girl who was Alma's half-sister, removed four years earlier. Through her, I traced Alma's family line, and eventually descendants from Alma's mother, who had lost contact with Alma altogether when she was removed. They directed me to Herb, an elder of his La Perouse community of Sydney, and related to Alma on her paternal line. He told me Alma married and had two children, but both apparently died childless. Going to visit Herb at the Aboriginal aged care complex where he lived, I found that he, too, had little re-collection of Alma. Later, I found an old photograph of someone I thought to be Alma, with her husband, and sent it to Herb. He and another elderly resident in the complex confirmed that it was her.

Herb provided me with an unusual insight into Alma's experience on several levels, however. Having himself grown up in institutions, at Bomaderry Children's Home from the age of three, then Kinchela Boys Home at Kempsey, remarkably Herb would go on to become the manager of the Aboriginal Boys Home at Kinchela, between 1967 and 1970. In the mid-1960s, he was appointed the researcher for Charles D. Rowley's ground-breaking study of Aboriginal communities around 'settled' Australia, entitled *Outcasts in White Australia*. Reading through my interpretation of Ming's sense of confusion about Alma's rebellious behaviour, which Ming saw as being so out of character with her sub-missive and obedient nature and her Christian faith, Herb wrote me long notes based on his own experiences and knowledge.

'I can understand Alma's difficulties in employment and her social behaviour, taking into account that 13 years of her life were spent in the Bomaderry Home,' Herb began. 'At Bomaderry (like many of the other children in this substitute care), Alma was given spiritual love and care by the Sisters in charge ... . In her sheltered life [at the Home] Alma would have received little or no instructions on sexual activities and control, and in her sexual desires would become interested in finding a partner.'[15]

Another former inmate, Jean Begg, was there in the 1940s (Alma was there in the 1920s). 'We were cut off from the rest of the world – we barely saw anybody – I think from birth till about 11 I must have saw about 12 grown-ups,' she recalled. The staff disciplined the children with crippling religious and racial fear:

I remember in the night I was terrified to go into the dark, because we was taught that Jesus was nailed to the cross, to cleanse us from our sins, so that we wouldn't be bad any more and we would know Him by the nail prints in His hands and I remember I was terrified of going into the dark. I was so scared that I would bump into Jesus and I would know Him by the nail prints in His hands. Besides that kind of religious fear, I had fear of Aborigines, knowing that they were evil, wicked and not understanding black, but only relating it to sin and drinking and cruelness.

All our identity was with those children in the homes .... . All we knew were our little friends in the home.[16]

Shadowy Alma had lived for 13 years in this institution, taught to fear her own people and her own self. Little wonder that Ming found her to be 'a good girl', and little wonder that both she and Annie seemed so innocent and vulnerable in the outside world.

Regarding the Board's insistence on sending Alma to a distant Aboriginal station, Herb wrote: 'It is generally accepted that we must all make our own way in life, but to send a person ... to live with people other than her own shows the lack of human understanding and tolerance of the Board.' As he had written some pages earlier: 'For the Board to claim that they did not have knowledge of Alma's background is absurd, especially when it becomes the role of the Manager of [the] Aboriginal Mission to maintain such records. To register details of one member of a family and not the other, is questionable.'

The Bomaderry Children's Home had catered mainly for infants and young children from the early 1900s. Run by the United Aborigines' Mission rather than the state, it was viewed as a potential threat to the authority of the Aborigines Protection Board. The Board set out to ensure that Bomaderry functioned not as a rival institution to the Cootamundra Home, but as an ancillary, and in 1930 directed that the age of all inmates be limited to a maximum of ten years. Miss Lowe was periodically to arrange the transfer of the older girls to Cootamundra Home or to domestic service situations. Alma and Annie were among the girls apprenticed from Bomaderry under the Board's authority the following year.

Theoretically, the Board did not have the legal power to indenture Alma, as she was 18 years of age. This was presumably the reason why the Board did not record her age (or Annie's), even though they certainly did know her details.

The Board had already registered both Alma and Annie as 'wards' of the Board in July 1927, in preparation for their placement in service. Although Alma was 14 at this time, the age the Board typically put girls into apprenticeships, both she and Annie had remained at the Bomaderry Home. I suspect that the staff may have refused to allow the transfer of the two girls at the time. Whatever the background to Alma's final removal from Bomaderry in 1930, it was inconceivable that the Board would return Alma to this institution.

'To want to re-employ Alma or have her sent back to Bomaderry, the place that she loved disclosed Ming's lack of knowledge of procedural policies and practices towards Aboriginals,' Herb continued in his notes to me. It seems 'there were lessons for her to learn in the whole process'.

Indeed, Ming's actions in Alma's case, and her hope that Alma could simply be returned to Bomaderry Home at her suggestion or released back to her at her whim, reveal a remarkable naivety on her part, as well as an ignorance of Board policy. Ming would come to learn, as Alma's nephew suggested, some hard lessons in the process of employing Aboriginal apprentices. As I struggled to make sense of what was going on, I also began to piece together a disturbing picture of the agenda behind the Aborigines Protection Board's apprenticeship policy, of which Ming – and presumably other employers of the time – were not altogether aware.

6
A better chance

The apprenticeship scheme for Aboriginal children drew on a 500-year tradition of forcing the children of the poor and itinerant into domestic 'apprenticeships' for which they received little or no wage. With the rapid upsurge of enclosures of the common land in England from the early eighteenth century, there was an equally rapid rise in rural dispossession and poverty. The system of Poor Relief became a customary source of cheap domestic labour as pauper children could be obtained as 'apprentices to Housewifery' at the cost of providing their lodgings, food and clothing, and the use of institutions and such apprenticeships in tandem provided the system for state and charitable care of destitute children. In the colony of New South Wales, where the assignment system represented the only source of domestic labour from the establishment of the colony in 1788 until well into the nineteenth century, the apprenticing of children from institutions was inevitable. Yet by the time the Board secured a legislative base to compel Aboriginal girls into service, the practice of institutionalization followed by apprenticeship had fallen into disfavour for the children of poor white people – and especially with regard to girls.

The Board was hardly unaware of the arguments about the 'moral dangers' of service for Aboriginal girls. Missionaries in 1882 had protested against the Victorian colonial government's proposed apprenticeship policy, arguing that in their experience servants had often returned to the stations pregnant to white men. In the parliamentary debates on the 1915 legislation, speakers against the proposed apprenticeship amendments pointed out that Aboriginal servants were particularly vulnerable due to their isolation from families and effective support. The 'problem' of indentured servants returning pregnant, and therefore 'useless', to the institutions from whence they came dated

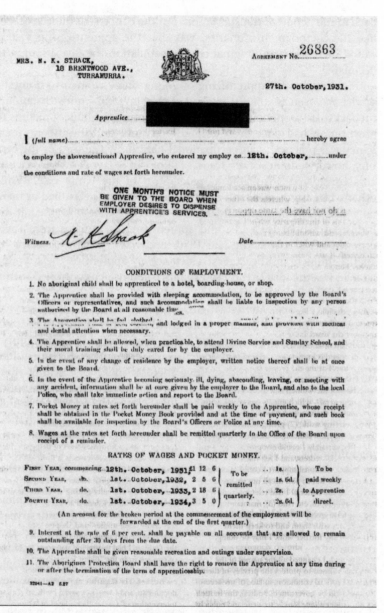

MRS. N. K. STRACK,
18 BRENTWOOD AVE.,
TURRAMURRA.

AGREEMENT No. 26863

27th. October, 1931.

Apprentice .... ██████████████

I *(full name)* .... hereby agree

to employ the abovementioned Apprentice, who entered my employ on 12th. October, ...under

the conditions and rate of wages set forth hereunder.

ONE MONTH'S NOTICE MUST
BE GIVEN TO THE BOARD WHEN
EMPLOYER DESIRES TO DISPENSE
WITH APPRENTICE'S SERVICES.

Witness ..... *N. K. Strack*   *Date* ....

CONDITIONS OF EMPLOYMENT.

1. No aboriginal child shall be apprenticed to a hotel, boarding-house, or shop.

2. The Apprentice shall be provided with sleeping accommodation, to be approved by the Board's Officers or representatives, and such accommodation shall be liable to inspection by any person authorised by the Board at all reasonable times.

3. The Apprentice shall be fed, clothed, ..., and lodged in a proper manner, and provided with medical and dental attention when necessary.

4. The Apprentice shall be allowed, when practicable, to attend Divine Service and Sunday School, and their moral training shall be duly cared for by the employer.

5. In the event of any change of residence by the employer, written notice thereof shall be at once given to the Board.

6. In the event of the Apprentice becoming seriously ill, dying, absconding, leaving, or meeting with any accident, information shall be at once given by the employer to the Board, and also to the local Police, who shall take immediate action and report to the Board.

7. Pocket Money at rates set forth hereunder shall be paid weekly to the Apprentice, whose receipt shall be obtained in the Pocket Money Book provided and at the time of payment, and such book shall be available for inspection by the Board's Officers or Police at any time.

8. Wages at the rates set forth hereunder shall be remitted quarterly to the Office of the Board upon receipt of a reminder.

RATES OF WAGES AND POCKET MONEY.

FIRST YEAR, commencing 12th. October, 1931,	£1 12 6		.. 1s.	To be
SECOND YEAR, do. 1st. October,1932,	2 5 6	To be remitted quarterly.	.. 1s. 6d.	paid weekly to Apprentice direct.
THIRD YEAR, do. 1st. October, 1933,	2 18 6		.. 2s.	
FOURTH YEAR, do. 1st. October, 1934,	3 5 0		.. 2s. 6d.	

(An account for the broken period at the commencement of the employment will be forwarded at the end of the first quarter.)

9. Interest at the rate of 6 per cent. shall be payable on all accounts that are allowed to remain outstanding after 30 days from the due date.

10. The Apprentice shall be given reasonable recreation and outings under supervision.

11. The Aborigines Protection Board shall have the right to remove the Apprentice at any time during or after the termination of the term of apprenticeship.

32041—A2 5.27

Figure 9 Ming's Aboriginal apprenticeship contract with the NSW Aborigines Protection Board, engaging Alma, 1933. Joan Kingsley-Strack Papers, NLA.

back to the period of transportation. But the concern of these speakers, like the Victorian missionaries, was that the apprenticeship system would increase the Aboriginal reserve population the Board sought to decimate.[1]

Traditionally, the apprenticing of young single women to domestic service was seen as an ideal method of moral reform – notwithstanding the fact that throughout the nineteenth century the bulk of recruits to prostitution had once been domestic servants, and illegitimate pregnancy was practically an occupational hazard. By the turn of the century, however, domestic service was falling out of favour for those white girls considered unsuitable as progenitors of the white race. While other white wards were still apprenticed, white girls classified as mentally, physically or, especially, morally defective were restrained at the Industrial School for Girls, and apprenticing of inmates from there dropped rapidly from the late 1880s and was 'virtually obsolete' by 1920.[2] Implicit in the state's reluctance to apprentice these young women was the idea that their sexuality could not be controlled within the context of domestic service.

At the same time Aboriginal girls were forced into domestic service. The policy, the Board argued, represented the 'only chance' these children had, to become 'decent and useful members of the community', by removing them from 'the vicious surroundings in which they find themselves'.[3] As usual the emotive rhetoric spoke of rescuing these 'almost white' girls from certain degradation, even though the policy would apply to girls of all shades of colour.[4] In their own communities, they 'never had a ghost of a chance to keep respectable'.[5] Despite these aspersions, the majority of girls on the Board's Ward Registers were institutionalized not on grounds of alleged 'immorality', but rather to be placed in apprenticeships. Even those removed ostensibly for other reasons were almost immediately sent out to service.

Despite the Board's claims of 'idleness' on reserves, domestic employment of Aboriginal women had been common since the earliest years of white settlement. As outside employment opportunities for men narrowed and the dependence of Aboriginal communities on rations increased under Board control, Aboriginal women's earnings would have become even more valuable to their communities and families. Providing an income while allowing for family obligations and some flexibility of choice, independent domestic work remained an option 'preferred' by young Aboriginal women under the Board. Parents also would find their daughters independent situations and may have had preferred to do so, if they knew the employers personally.

Now such arrangements could be, and were, cut short. Managers were instructed to arrange apprenticeships for young women already in service independently; indeed, a sizeable proportion of the recorded Cootamundra inmates had been in service locally *before* going into the Home, some for as many as four or five years.

Apprenticeship gave the Board maximum control, allowing it to place and transfer apprentices when and where it chose and to control their access to their home reserves. Although apprenticeships theoretically represented a four-year term of indenture, many women continued to work for years after that. The Board did not inform them that they were entitled to leave and it was an offence under the Act for any other person to 'entice' them to do so. Appeals by apprentices or their families to the Board for their return were treated with suspicion and often refused. Although the Board publicly stated its commitment to returning Aboriginal girls to their communities,[6] those who did return were frequently, and deliberately, sent to far off reserves rather than to their place of origin. In practice, many were returned to reserves only when they became a problem to the Board – particularly if they demanded the wages held for them in trust.

Apprenticeship also gave the Board unprecedented control over the girls' wages, both rates and disbursement – an important reason for its preference for apprenticeship. Aboriginal women would 'only waste the money buying rubbish' if they were allowed to handle their wages, the Board asserted, or 'some fellow' would try to get at them for it.[7] Apprentices needed the support of their employers to apply for any part of their wages (which they were expected to use for dental and medical expenses); former apprentices were obliged to apply to the manager or police for small sums of money for specific purposes. This ensured their ongoing submission to authorities, even as it allowed for the abuse of the system.

As it was, the wage rates were very low – lower than the rates for white wards in service and substantially lower than those earned by independent workers, which ranged from 10 to 20 shillings a week in 1910 to 20 to 25 shillings a week in 1920. From 1913 to the late 1930s, rates were 2s 6d a week for a first-year Aboriginal apprentice, 3s 6d for a second-year, 4s 6d for a third-year and 5 shillings a week for a fourth-year apprentice, out of which 'pocket money' (between 6d and 2s 6d a week) was allowed to the apprentice for her personal use. These rates were set in 1913 and, though raised minimally in the late 1930s, were not made equivalent to those paid to Child Welfare Department apprentices in NSW until 1941; the discrepancy between the rates by that time was to 'the extent of £1 per quarter for the younger children to £3 per quarter for youths and older girls 17 to 18 years of age'.[8] So apprentices accrued only meagre 'savings', even if they were able to access them. But many workers never received their trust monies at all and the question of what became of the Board's trust funds continues to be a vexed one. Together with the placement of Aboriginal workers, the control over their earnings represented the negation of any autonomy or indeed power young unmarried Aboriginal women might have had. It ensured their continued poverty and dependence, and the removal of their children in turn. Apprenticeship meant that the Aboriginal girls were denied to their communities as a resource – in terms of both their earning capacity and their reproductive capacity.

* * *

While the Board was explicit in its intention to use removal and apprenticeship as a method of 'absorption', what such 'absorption' meant in practice was not made clear. The original restriction on apprenticing particularly dark girls away from their communities was urged 'in view of the impossibility of [their being] merged into the white population',[9] the implicit assumption being that the girls in service would meet with and reproduce to non-Aboriginal partners. Marriage to an Aboriginal man was countenanced only as a last resort (in preference to seeing unattached Aboriginal women). In 1920 the Board directed station managers actively to organize marriages for Aboriginal apprentices 'holidaying' as the 'only solution' to the problem of the young women becoming restless and refusing to work after a period of four to six years. Like a recommendation endorsed the year before in direct response to protests against child removal at Cumeragunja station, that girls should be allowed to retrun at the age of 18 if they desired 'to marry an [A]boriginal man', it shows the Board prepared to concede such marriages only when it was expedient to do so.[10]

At the outset of gaining the 1915 amendment legislation, the Board had in fact recommended establishing a training home 'for lads', as well as 'facilities' for girls to meet and marry 'decent hard working young men of their own colour'.[11] And in 1918, having already noted some press criticism of their 'methods', the Board was stung to respond to an enquiry regarding two girl apprentices: 'Decided to fully set out the reasons for their removal ... and point out the policy of the Board was the uplifting of the girl by placing her in service with respectable families give [*sic*] them proper domestic training, making them useful citizens and wives for their [A]bor. Brother'.[12] But the Board was hardly making young Aboriginal *men* marriageable candidates, forcing them into casual labour and homelessness (indeed, the Boys' Home that was established eventually in 1924, would be imposed on what had been a flourishing independent Aboriginal farm).[13] It is hardly surprising that the girls in the Cootamundra Home awaiting their placement in service were actively encouraged to look forward to marrying a white man, and thus effect their own disappearance. They were told:

> There is a good chance that you will marry a white man and your children will be lighter and they will get caught up with a white man and their children will be lighter until they are completely white and that's how the Aborigine blood will be bred out. [14]

Yet only 15 of the girls on the *Ward Registers* ever married a white man.

By the mid-1920s the Board was subject to a barrage of media scrutiny of the apprenticeship policy. It was said that Aboriginal girls locked up in private households were being prevented from meeting and marrying potential husbands, thus 'making it difficult for many more to be born'. The Board was forced to defend itself; its aim was to prepare the girls for marriage to young Aboriginal men by giving them domestic training beforehand, and with a taste for a higher standard of living thus instilled, they would want to leave the reserves with their husbands when they did marry. The Board did admit that their marital prospects were 'reduced' by being in service, but argued they still 'had a better chance under the present system'. What exactly was meant by a 'better chance' is only hinted at by the concluding argument that 'extinction was ... inevitable'.[15]

In 1927, the year Mary was sent to Victoria, the Board intercepted a letter from the head of the Australian Aboriginal Progressive Association, Fred Maynard, to a 15-year-old apprentice. Maynard offered to help bring her rapist to justice, accusing the Board of failing to protect girls from 'these white Robbers of our Women's virtues' and aiming 'to exterminate the *Noble* and *Ancient* Race of Australia'. The Board forwarded Maynard's letter to the Premier, not to assist the young woman, but to alert him to the dangers of allowing an Aboriginal protest organization to exist. Its tacit sanction was demonstrated not only by its return of the assaulted girl to her employer after her newborn baby died. When she in turn died in an 'accident' within a few months, the same employer was soon able to acquire the services of at least another two apprentices, one of whom was also 'taken to Hospital'.[16]

'[L]isten, girlie, your case is one in Dozens with our girls, more is the pity,' Maynard had written:

> God forbid, these white Robbers of our woman virtues seem to do just as they like with down right impunity and, mind, you, my dear Girl, the law stands for it. There is no clause in our own Aboriginal Act, which stands for principles for our Girls, that is to say that any of these white fellows can take our girl down and laugh to scorn, yes with impunity that which they have been responsible for – they escape all their obligations every time. If a white girl get into trouble, by one of their own By laws they are immediately obliged to pay down [the] lump sum of £20 & then 12/6 when the child is born until that child is 14 years of age. What about our own poor Australian Aboriginal girls[?] Are they not worthy of protection, same as white girls[?] The Laws of the Aboriginal Act say not. ... I trust your case will be an eye opener to all of our sisters, throughout your district, as to the position of the White Man, under their so called civilized Methods of Rule, under Christianized Ideals, as they claim of Civilizing our people under the pretence of love ...[17]

The Board argued that Maynard's 'illogical views' were likely to 'disturb' the Aboriginal people.[18] But Maynard was only articulating the logical conclusion that the Board's failure to protect Aboriginal servants amounted to deliberate policy, a belief that was widely held by Aboriginal people. Aboriginal people on the reserves and stations could not fail to see that many of the women who had been sent into service returned with 'white' babies.[19] As one Aboriginal man explained in the 1980s:

> The hard part was that they didn't like *us* after the girls ... They'd come and get 'em and take 'em away. They'd have 'em down there for twelve months and they'd get 'em into trouble and they'd be comin' back with white babies. That's what we were up against. That's true that is ...[20]

And, in 1935, Koori activist Mrs Anna Morgan, from Cumeragunja:

> At the age of fourteen our girls [are] sent to work – poor illiterate trustful little girls to be gulled by the promises of unscrupulous white men. We all know the consequences. But, of course, one of the functions of the Aborigines' Protection Board is to build a white Australia.[21]

This construction was by no means far-fetched in the context of the times. From the late 1920s the Western Australian state government and the Commonwealth government in the Northern Territory had been pursuing policies of organizing marriages between fair-skinned Aboriginal women and white men as a way of 'breeding out' the dark colour.[22] Such policies also involved the institutionalization of young Aboriginal women and their placement as domestic servants. Here, as Russell MacGregor has argued, policy was initiated not by politicians but by senior bureaucrats; given rising public concern over the 'half-caste problem', politicians were circumspect about openly supporting such policies.[23] In fact, there were significant differences between the 'frontier' administrations controlling large Aboriginal populations and those of the more densely white-populated eastern states, despite there being a shared strategy of removing, institutionalizing and indenturing young Aboriginal women. Such overt controlled miscegenation practices were not an option in the south-eastern states, from which much feminist critique of Aboriginal administration on the frontier would emanate.[24] But they were well enough known to women's groups in south-eastern Australia by 1934 to account for the following racist response by several prominent conservative women's organizations in Victoria. The federal government had put up a proposal to put fair-skinned South Australian girls through the Victorian indenturing system. This was an 'insidious attempt', the women's groups argued in a joint statement, 'to mingle with the community women of illegitimate birth, tainted with [A]boriginal blood, the offspring of men of the lowest human type ...'.[25]

In 1937 Commonwealth and state Aboriginal authorities met at a conference to discuss their various policies and practices. Discussing the strategy of domestic service apprenticeships, the Victorian representative had stated that his Board's 'principal difficulty' was that girls in service returned pregnant or with children: 'The half-castes get into the hands of degenerate whites, and that is the end; they go on breeding in the same way,' he complained. Administrator A. O. Neville, acknowledging that they 'had much the same difficulty in Western Australia', reassured the eastern authorities that the policy of taking the apprentices' babies away neutralized the threat of an increasing Aboriginal population: 'these children grow up as whites ... [and] the mother goes back into service so it really does not matter if she has half a dozen children'.

The NSW authorities were much more reticent: 'We also have a system of taking girls in the early adolescent stage and training them for domestic service,' one Board member and bureaucrat E. B. Harkness told the other authorities. But in contrast to the girls of Western Australia and Victoria:

> These girls reach quite a high standard. Unfortunately, of course, if they go back to the old surroundings, they revert to old habits, and particularly to the lower moral standard, and become the mothers of illegitimate children early in life. ... I have taken a girl into domestic service. She is intelligent, industrious, and clean, and submits to reasonable discipline. I do not think if she were to go back to her station she would revert to the old standards, but, of course, one never knows.

Harkness referred his audience to the Board's Secretary, Alfred Pettitt, who, he said, would 'amplify' his statements. Pettitt, put on the spot, said somewhat offhandedly that 'statements' had been made 'from time to time about [A]boriginal girls in domestic service becoming pregnant'.

> In New South Wales, we throw the responsibility on the employer for the physical and moral well-being of the apprentices. As a matter of fact, the number of girls who get into trouble is negligible. We consider that if we can keep them away from the dangers of camp life until they reach the years of discretion we are doing good work. They are employed in the country and in the city, and we are very careful in the selection of the homes into which they are introduced. In the cities there is a constant demand for them from the best class of suburb, and we never have any difficulty in finding places for them.[26]

There is no doubt that the Board knew of the high rates of pregnancies to girls in service and was aware of cases of alleged sexual abuse and rape. The Board's *own* records (which we may consider an underestimation) show more than 10 per cent of the young women in service gave birth and the rate was notably higher among those who worked in Sydney, where the figure came closer to one in five.[27] We can compare this to the annual pregnancy rate for single white women generally in NSW, which was 1.4 per cent in 1911, 1.2 per cent in 1921 and 0.8 per cent in 1933;[28] or, even more damning, with the rate for white state wards in South Australia in the same period, which was 'less than 1 per cent'.[29]

These statistics, based on limited and inadequate records, are suggestive only. They do not account for girls taken before or after the years 1912 to 1928, and many girls apprenticed out directly from Aboriginal stations and even from Cootamundra Home were not recorded. They do not account for those who had miscarriages. Nor do they account for those engaged in sexual activity that did not culminate in pregnancy, but on the basis of these pregnancy rates we must assume that the incidence of sexual exploitation was also extraordinarily high. Indeed, the 1997 Human Rights and Equal Opportunity Inquiry found comparable rates nationally (17.5 per cent) for Aboriginal witnesses reporting sexual abuse following removal. [30] Clearly, Aboriginal girls in domestic service were at a remarkable risk of illegitimate pregnancy.

Despite existing legislation establishing a mother's right to support from the father of her child, the Board rarely mentioned paternity. Nor is there any evidence that it initiated any claim of maintenance against white fathers, although it had the mandate to lodge such claims itself under its own 1909 legislation, well in advance of the State Children's Department. As the controversial paternity legislation (introduced to prevent infanticide) of 1904 (the NSW Infant Protection Act) had been one of former Board member Ardill's initiatives, perhaps it accounted for the Board's abrupt decision in 1917 that his refuges – where the 'general rule' was that 'every effort' was made to locate fathers to claim support – were now considered 'undesirable'.[31] Immediately afterwards the Board's Secretary was directed to arrange an interview between the State Children's Board head Alfred Green (who was not yet a Board member) and the Protection Board's Chairman to discuss establishing a Home for girls 'unfit for domestic service'. Nothing further was heard of the matter.[32] The Board's inexplicable hostility to McKenzie-Hatton's Home for Aboriginal girls a few years later might be explained by her association with Fred Maynard's protest organization and presumed sympathy towards abused Aboriginal girls. Indeed, press criticism of the apprenticeship policy coincided with the functioning of her Home.[33] The Board resisted taking action against any white man who harassed, assaulted or impregnated an Aboriginal apprentice. The Board was not, however, above virtually profiteering from its pregnant charges, pocketing their £5 'baby bonuses', a national payment introduced in 1912 arising out of eugenic preoccupations and available to all Aboriginal mothers who did not have 'a preponderance of Aboriginal blood', where they could.[34]

In its first annual report after gaining its extraordinary powers to remove Aboriginal children in 1915, the Board had provided an unusually long statement concerning the 80 girls it had placed that year.

Some of them had 'made great improvement', it was reported, 'largely due to the strict supervision under which they are kept'. All 'in and around Sydney' had been visited at 'regular intervals', those showing a 'tendency to lapse into their old careless ways' being called on 'monthly'. The home of 'every applicant' for a servant had been inspected, and the reader was assured that the girls were 'employed by people who help to uplift them in every possible way'. Meanwhile, 'No complaint from either mistress or maid has ever been too trivial to be investigated, and the result has been a proper understanding on all sides.'[35]

But in the rural areas, Board inspections would be limited to occasional 'inquiries' by Board managers or police, if they happened to be in the vicinity of where the girl was working; and visits by the female 'Homefinder' to girls in Sydney were similarly sporadic and superficial. As for complaints made by 'either mistress or maid', in 1915 there is no record of any, but in September that year the Board responded to claims made by a station manager that Aborigines were being taken advantage of by employers in terms of their wages, and 'that a girl had been tampered with by an employer'. The wages issue was followed up, but regarding the claim of sexual abuse there was no further direct reference. In the next meeting, however, it was suggested that all girls in Cootamundra Home should be examined and provided with a certificate of health prior to being placed in service, the Health Department to 'facilitate the examination of girls brought straight to Sydney from reserves'. In 1916 a Board regulation made medical examination and a certificate 'as to their condition of health, and freedom from contagious or infectious diseases' mandatory for all girls before being placed in situations. Such examinations being code for pregnancy, venereal disease and even virginity checks, one might speculate that this precautionary measure – which protected employers and the Board rather than the girls – constituted the Board's singular response to any 'investigation' of the sex abuse claim that may have been made.[36]

The Board's standard and discreet removal of many of the apprentices' babies at birth was a tactic that Aboriginal women recognized as one to ensure that 'the white men in the house were not blamed'.[37] It also meant the Board could send the mother straight back into a white household, sometimes the same one. A state policy which condoned the impregnation of Aboriginal women by white men and the subsequent removal of their babies would have been entirely confounded by legal action being taken against the fathers and support given to the

Aboriginal mothers. The onus was on the white mistress and on her alone to ensure that the Aboriginal servant did not become pregnant.

* * *

'[A]s far as we could see all that was wrong with her,' recollected the daughter of a former white mistress, about a Sydney apprentice had been placed in a mental asylum by the Board, 'was that she didn't know how to say NO to the lowdown white men who wanted to take advantage of her'.[38] In the absence of a special Home for so-called 'incorrigible' girls, incarceration in a mental asylum was a not uncommon outcome for the apprentices, especially those less amenable than Alma. In fact, the ability of white women to protect their charges was limited, not least because of their difficulties in comprehending the extreme pressures on the young women in service.

White women of all classes attained the Federal vote arguably because the maternalist ideology espoused by the feminist campaigners had been successfully made compatible with the concerns of the modern state, particularly with regard to the eugenicists' call for state intervention in human reproduction. The falling white middle-class birth-rate, and the high rates of male desertion of dependent wives and children, ascribed directly by the women's movement to the failure of society to support white motherhood, were also high on the agenda of policy-makers. Not only white female suffrage, but the concurrent feminist campaigns for birth control, temperance and the raising of the age of consent from 14 to 16 years of age in NSW in 1910 were all couched in terms of the salvation of the white race and the strengthening of the nation.

While the celebration of motherhood provided the legitimation for the white woman's franchise, Aboriginal motherhood continued to be disparaged and denied. Many Australians (although not Board members or officials) apparently believed the increasing reserve populations were due to white fathers who refused or were unable to recognize their paternal responsibilities. Aboriginal women were characterized as defective single mothers or even 'prostitutes' likely to use their teenage daughters as 'assets' for their own 'immoral' lifestyles. Arguing that the nation had a claim on these 'almost white' children, the Board demanded that it should be placed 'in the position of parent to the children',[39] assuming the role abdicated by these irresponsible white fathers. In this context, white bourgeois women were called on to participate in public policy as, in effect, surrogate mothers.

And they were certainly willing. One of the main concerns of the conservative women's organizations of the time was to secure the more efficient and reliable supply of domestic servants. Privileged white women demanded support in their roles as wives and mothers in terms of the strengthening of the race, at the expense of those women judged less worthy to reproduce. Some went so far as to argue for compulsory domestic training and apprenticeships for all young women – excluding, one presumes, their own daughters. In this light elite women would indeed have welcomed the state's provision of 'trained' Aboriginal apprentices, but only as long as the Board was seen to have no other agenda than 'the uplifting of the girl', as it stated in 1918.[40]

There is no doubt that many mistresses were prepared to ignore the sexual abuse of their servants. White mistresses were themselves at times abusive and brutal towards their servants, and the imposition of bureaucratic control in place of parental authority did not protect Aboriginal girls from harsh employers. The records show that the Board consistently dismissed complaints by apprenticed workers, and even actively deterred police from following up allegations while refusing to permit parents to visit the victim.[41]

But a pregnant servant was a problem, not only because it meant she had to stop work, but because the pregnancy represented humiliating food for gossip and suggested the mistress's inability to restrain male household members. The Board's disinclination to identify and prosecute the father, instead, discreetly removing the apprentice, would have been quite a relief. Yet an earnest employer who did try to fulfil her maternal obligations to 'protect' and 'uplift' her servant could not expect to be supported by the Board – as Ming was discovering.

There was no support for Ming in her attempt to restrain what she considered to be the predations of Alma's unsuitable admirer. Rather, the Protection Board simply collected Alma and put her on a train for a distant mission. In dissuading Ming from her remorseful plea at the train station to take Alma back, the Board escort appealed to her good reason as a sensible and respectable woman. Ming's timorous and uncertain response reflects the pervasiveness of a discourse in which white women were the caring, but careful guardians, and black women irredeemable miscreants. Ming's will to try to continue to exercise moral guardianship over Alma was undermined; 'it seemed useless'. By invoking a sense of inevitable failure, Ming was given to understand that there was little any white mistress could do to control her servant's sexuality, beyond informing the Board when she 'fell'.

The police and Board response emphasized a lesson that Ming failed to learn from her experience with Mary, when she had ignored Mary's warning not to tell the Board. Taken aback to find once again that the Board had taken charge of her servant and arranged for her disposal, so to speak, in disregard of her stated preferences (let alone the interests of the young woman herself), Ming still could not grasp the fact that it was *she* who was intended to play the role of intermediary between the state and Aboriginal girls.

Under the Board's apprenticeship policy, Aboriginal women were deliberately and systematically disempowered, but Ming's story suggests that the apparent power of the maternalistic model conferred on their white female employers was illusory. Ming's failed attempt to play the role of maternal protector shows that the white woman's role was intended by the state to be subsidiary. Despite white women's involvement as mistresses, perhaps because of this involvement, white women were not permitted any voice whatsoever in the formulation of policy. It was a situation in direct contradiction to the stance taken by the women's organizations of the time and, by the late 1930s, there would be increasingly loud demands from the women's movement in NSW to secure a (white) female representative on the Board itself.

For Ming, the important realization that she was in fundamental conflict with the Board would not mature until she came into contact with yet another young Aboriginal servant. Her experience with Del would be the catalyst, and the beginning of Ming's determination to see that the Aborigines Protection Board was publicly challenged and exposed.

Part III
Del

7
Was fearfully shocked this afternoon

A couple of months after Alma's departure at the end of October 1932, the Stracks made plans to move once again. Because of this, and 'owing to a great deal of illness in the family', Ming had asked the Board's Homefinder if she could have Alma back to help her. Ming claimed that Alma herself wanted to return, but Miss Lowe refused, telling Ming it was Board policy to have such women married off. At this stage Ming still failed to understand the full implications of the Board's apprenticeship scheme and was simply aggravated by Miss Lowe's apparent perversity in refusing to allow her to take Alma back.[1] When Miss Lowe told her that 'she had a very good girl available – she was a particularly nice type of girl and would be able to help me in every way,' Ming immediately accepted her offer.[2]

The Stracks had been renting their comfortable house near Turramurra railway station from their friends the Knoxes, a Sydney family prominent in the establishment as well as in the New Guard. Now, as their involvement in the New Guard waned, the Stracks were moving to a more substantial residence in an adjoining suburb, Pymble. On a corner block, it was complete with an ornamental miniature turret, with long tiled verandahs all around, waxy-leafed, pink-flowered camellias at the corners and a couple of solid garden benches from which to enjoy the green, well-groomed lawn and spreading fig trees.

A publicity photograph of Ming, used in the programme for the British Empire pageant of 1933 (she was on the organizing committee), shows her, at 41 years of age, to be a poised and sophisticated woman. She wears her hair in the fashionable Wallis Simpson style, under an elegantly cocked little hat; that she was a little vain I can tell by the way she inexpertly doctored the photo to make her lips look

Figure 10　Joan Kingsley-Strack, 1933. Author's collection.

fuller. Always proud of her red-gold hair, as she grew older she had taken to dying it with henna. My Gran describes Ming's bright, safflower-blue eyes, which I cannot know from the old black-and-white photographs, nor from my own faded memories, but see in the face of my younger sister, who takes after her. She was compact, buxom and well-ordered, with shapely legs and small, high-arched feet. I remember now, even as an old lady, her neat stockinged legs and her little high-heeled court shoes.

Arrangements were made for Del's transfer to Ming's employment from a situation in the exclusive eastern suburbs of Sydney, in mid-January 1933. A wavy-haired, honey-skinned girl in her mid-teens (Ming was told she was 16), Del was close in age to Ming's three children – Peter being 15 going on 16, and Narrelle and Helen 13 and 9, respectively. Unlike Alma, although younger, Del was experienced in domestic service. She had worked as an apprentice in two separate situations since leaving Cootamundra Home in 1930, and she began at Ming's on a third-year apprentice's rates of 4s 6d a week.

Del's stay with the Stracks was only ever intended by Ming to be short-term, yet she stayed with Ming for almost two years, largely due to her own initiative in turning to her for assistance in escaping Board control. Del was the catalyst for Ming's eventual political opposition to the Board, as she brought Ming to an awareness of the exploitation and injustices inherent in the Board's policies. Through her personal relationship with Del, Ming came also to align her sympathies squarely with the Aboriginal workers and their families.

Only fragments of Ming's original diaries for 1933 and 1934 have survived, but those that do indicate that the typewritten manuscript diary she compiled as a record of Del's treatment by the Board was based on her personal diary entries from January 1933 onwards, probably with only minor reworking. I have used this manuscript diary for my reconstruction of Del's and Ming's story, in the main. The vividness of Ming's writing means I have little need for speculative imagination, and I feel confident that Ming did her best to document the scenes she describes as accurately as she could. 'I have been most careful to use Miss Lowe's own words in every sense and to keep strictly and exactly to the truth,' Ming prefaced this manuscript. 'I was so utterly amazed at the behaviour of this woman right through that I felt if I was to help Del at all I must keep a record of each incident as it took place.'

Having just moved, Ming had wanted 'to get help as soon as possible and just for a short period'. Del's current employer at Vaughn Park,[3] according to Miss Lowe, was going on holiday. Not wanting to take the servant with them, but hoping to retain her services when she returned, Del's temporary transfer to the Stracks for the duration of the vacation seemed convenient to everyone.

But it was clear that something was amiss even before Ming met Del. On 7 January 1933 Miss Lowe rang to say that Del had been sick and would be a few days late. Miss Lowe told Ming that they had had

Del examined by a doctor to check that she was not pregnant. 'Not because they thought for one moment that it was necessary,' she reassured Ming, 'but that she was a very attractive girl and she may have gone out at night, though of course no one had seen her, and she was *perfectly* all right.' Two days later, Miss Lowe rang again to tell Ming she could collect Del from the Board's office in the city that Friday, assuring her that Del's 'only problem' was that she had been dieting.

Ming's first sight of Del, however, did nothing to allay her reservations. 'Went to town to collect my charge today,' she recorded on 12 January,

> found the most unhappy little Half-caste I have ever seen sitting on a suit-case outside the door, with a large notice above her stating that *this* was the 'Aborigines *Protection* Board'! She was pale and her eyes were red with weeping; the girl looked downright ill and I hesitated to bring her home with me where there is so much work to do.

Miss Lowe appeared and proceeded to lecture Del, warning her that if she did not start eating, she would be sent to an 'Asylum'. Ming, taken aback, told Del she could 'eat just what she feels inclined to' while with her, and together they left the Board's office. That evening, however, Ming found herself nursing Del:

> Del spoke very little on the way home … . The children rushed out to meet us and adopted Del immediately. She is a gentle, lovable type of girl; all the children helped her to set the tables and do vegetables etc. Tonight I found Helen with her arms tightly around Del's neck and poor Del crying her eyes out. I put her to bed with a warm water bottle, but she was no sooner in than a violent attack of vomiting occurred. It was most distressing and continued till I went to bed. Have been up and down all night and cannot now sleep …
>
> Perhaps it is just the excitement which has upset her, though she does look ill.

But Del continued to be unwell, through January and well into February, when she developed a nasty ear infection. 'She is working all the time and never once complains though I often find her lying down now and crying,' wrote Ming. 'She said today "Oh, how *could* Miss Lowe send me to you and give you all this trouble. She knew I was sick before I came to you – I wish I was *dead*!"' With advice from a chemist and the public hospital, Ming treated Del's ear but found herself increasingly unable to cope with the 'awful discharge'. 'Very careful to use heaps of disinfectant and do not touch it with my hands. Burn everything and use only her own bathroom. Simply *must* get a Doctor as I do not know whether to put hot foments on it or syringe it – it is ghastly.' She found a private doctor in March who managed to cure the ear infection, but was unable to explain Del's general malaise.

By this point Ming was seriously considering sending Del back to the Board. 'Del won't allow me out of her sight for a moment,' she wrote, and went on to describe her phone call to the Homefinder, presumably made in Del's earshot. 'All this time Del was in a panic at the thought of going to Miss Lowe again and I hadn't the heart to send her, but was very indignant to think that they had palmed off a really sick girl onto me.' To her aggravation Miss Lowe had told her that it was the employer's responsibility to organize medical treatment.

> Poor Del ... What can it be? There is pain now in her side and queer muscular contractions of the stomach. I wonder what it can be.

Later that day, Del approached Ming. They were outside on one of the verandahs; Ming was trimming some flowers for the table, perhaps, or tending to some darning. Del was sweeping. 'Was fearfully shocked this afternoon,' Ming wrote in her diary. 'Del came to me and said "I'm so frightened, I'm afraid I'm going to have a baby. They told me I would. Oh, why can't I die?"' Stunned, Ming said nothing.

Del went on with her sweeping, then said:

> 'Ritchie Smith came to my room often and often and I used to hide in my wardrobe and hear him tell his mother that I was "out again". He would creep over and close the window and I was afraid to even breathe sometimes. I didn't know what to do. If I told his Mother she wouldn't believe me and Miss Lowe would have me sent to a reformatory without a chance to say a word. Sometimes I would pull my furniture up against the door so that he could not come in and once he told his mother and she said that I was mad and would be sent to an Asylum if I did that again. I didn't know how to stop him and very often he brought home things in silver paper called "Letters" and told me what they were for and where

babies came from! Oh, Mrs Strack, I did really think that babies came from heaven and I hated and hated him. I didn't want to hear and I tried not to listen. It made me feel very sick and hurt dreadfully. Often and often I was alone in the house with him and he used to put on his pyjamas and sit near the wireless and was in such a temper that I wouldn't come there too [and] it frightened me and I couldn't run away. Sometimes I just hid in the house and then he would tell his mother that I was out with a man all the time!

'One day I pretended that I went out with someone because I thought it might stop Ritchie if he thought I had a friend,' Del continued, 'but it did not stop him, he seemed to be quite mad and then when I was very sick he was frightened and said if I did not tell him the name of some other man he would have me sent to the police and to a reformatory.

'I was very frightened but I did not know anyone at all, only Hebe who worked near Mrs Smith and she did not know what to do – she was afraid of Miss Lowe too – we went to the Zoo together and I could hardly walk and felt very ill, and in pain; we had to come home and then Mrs Smith said: "Now Del, I am sure you are going to have a baby – let me look at your face – Oh yes, you are – and no one will have you and you might die – lots of people do and there will be no where for you to go!"'

'It was calculated cruelty, I consider,' Ming wrote in reflection.

Del told Ming that Mrs Smith instructed her to get a paper and pen and come to her room. Mrs Smith 'said that unless Del wrote exactly what she was told she would have her sent to gaol and Mrs Smith would just keep the letter to see if Del behaved herself'. She told Del to write that she had been 'out night after night' and must give the name of 'some man'. Del gave the name of the man one of her sisters in the country had married, the 'only name she could think of', although at that point she did not explain to Ming that she had made him up: 'She simply told it as though it had happened and left it at that.'

As Ming would later find out, Del had run away once before, from her first employer at Burrendah, but had been caught and transferred to an arguably even worse situation. By the time she came to Ming she was far too sick even to try to run away *and* believed that she was pregnant, and with no family contact, and her only friend Hebe (another Board apprentice) apparently unwilling to accompany her, completely isolated. It was a major decision to turn to Ming, though perhaps not so much a marker of the trust Ming inspired as it was of Del's utter desperation. Yet it is a heartening demonstration that Del's will to shape the direction of her own life had by no means been crushed out of her.

Del may just have hoped to stop Ming from sending her back to Miss Lowe or to her former employer. On hearing her story, however, Ming 'felt horrified & desperately sorry for this girl', and rang the Homefinder immediately, believing that the matter 'should be brought before the Board and the girl protected'. The following day Miss Lowe paid her a visit.

Ming recorded the events of that visit in great detail. To Ming's amazement, Del's fears of Miss Lowe's reaction were confirmed. Furious, Miss Lowe 'bounced about, opening and shutting doors and windows'.

'She is a brute. I *loathe* her,' she said. 'I wish I had never let you see her, she has a *terrible* record! She has lived with men before she was ten years old, that is why I took her away from Nortown!! She is a devil and will go to an *asylum* for this! She has a filthy mind, etc., etc., and these people are my *personal* friends and my oldest clients!!'

At last I said I suppose it does make a difference when they are your personal friends.

'Oh, no!' said Miss Lowe. 'They are too decent and he is not that sort of man. They are very well known and have lots of nice friends. I do not know how you could believe or *listen* to such a pack of lies,' said Miss Lowe. 'I am surprised at you. You will be in a libel action for this!'

Ming called in Del, who had been waiting at the door 'through this tirade', and told her to tell Miss Lowe herself:

I *insisted* upon the woman listening to the whole of the story without interruption, eventually. She then said, 'It is a pack of lies, but I insist upon a written statement from Del.' This the girl wrote out and handed to Miss Lowe.

She stood up and sat down and stamped her foot and glared at Del until I really thought she had lost her reason. She said, 'this girl must go, I will send her right away, I will never feel happy about leaving such a brute with your little children.' Imagine that!!

I said how dared you send a girl with such a record to me knowing that I had 'little children'?

I said, 'I do not believe you in any case, and I do believe that Del is telling the truth. She shall stay with me till this is proved one way or the other. The girl is ill and needs attention, and I believe that she is thoroughly good.'

Miss Lowe 'swelled visibly'. 'Why, have not I got a statement in my office files written by this girl giving the man's name, and has not she been out night after night with him and even been seen getting out her bedroom window?' Evidently, Mrs Smith had handed Del's damaging statement straight to the Homefinder, pre-empting any allegations by Del of sexual misconduct on the part of her son.

I said this utterly contradicts your first story to me and why, if you had all this information, was the matter not put into the hands of the police at once? She said 'Oh, we searched Vaughn Park for the man!!!! And you can't keep her, I'm sending her away to the home at once.' Her anxiety to get rid of Del at any cost was so apparent that I was determined to see that this girl had some semblance of justice first.

The Homefinder asked Ming for a bus timetable, and Ming left the room briefly to get it. On her return she found 'the scene had completely changed', the Homefinder 'red-faced but all smiles'.

She stood with her back to Del and making strange grimaces at me said, 'Del doesn't want me to use that letter now, Mrs Strack. She doesn't like being with you and wants to return to Mrs Smith, *don't* you Del? Yes, *yes!* Del!'
Del mumbled something, still staring at me, and I said, 'I'm afraid I don't understand you. Has Del said that that letter is untrue?'
'Oh, yes, it's all lies, isn't it, Del? *Yes*, Del.'
Del said, looking straight at me, '*No, NO*, I don't know what she means.'
'Oh, yes, you do, Del, you told me yourself not to use this letter! Now it will be quite all right; I won't use the letter but will treat the whole thing as a joke, and (aside to me) you don't know these brutes as I do! She says she hates being here, it is much too quiet. Just keep her for a month or two!'
'A month or two, Miss Lowe, after all you have said about her!' I simply gasped. It was too much for me to think out in a moment; however, after much more of this sort of thing Miss Lowe departed.

If Ming had not recently gone through that disturbing experience with Alma, she might have simply chosen to hand Del back to the 'care' of the Board as casually as she had cast off Alma, with scarcely a thought for the implications of such care. But Del's turning to Ming for protection against not only her former employer Mrs Smith, but more significantly against the Board, would have had a powerful psychological impact on a woman who was still smarting from the Board's perfunctory dismissal of her concerns over her previous servant. Ming was not one to stand back from a fight, not if her sense of justice was affronted. But in championing Del, Ming had the opportunity to alleviate her residual guilt over Mary and Alma, and at the same time the chance to show the Board that she was a force to be reckoned with. Even as Ming defended Del's rights to autonomy, she would struggle to contain Del within the mould of a helpless young girl in need of motherly protection.

* * *

The significance of Del's purported 'bad' record was not lost on Ming. Within a week of Miss Lowe's visit she asked for and received Del's own version of her childhood and removal, and gradually, as Del's confidence in her grew, Ming learnt more and more from Del about her initial removal and her experiences of institutionalization. In doing so, she provided Ming with a distressing insight into the reality of the lives of those children taken from their families and communities, supposedly for their own protection. Ming's dismayed diary entries at this time recall in tone the American slave mistress Mrs Shelby in *Uncle Tom's Cabin*. Here, Harriet Beecher Stowe presented her fictional white mistress realizing the hypocrisy of her efforts to give her slaves 'a condition better than freedom', when her husband overrode her Christian ideals by selling her maid's young child.[4] In Ming's case, it was the hostile intervention of the state rather than her husband which led her to fundamentally reassess her involvement in the apprenticeship system.

Del had in fact been removed under mainstream legislation, not the special legislation designed to target Aboriginal girls. Unlike Mary and Alma, and alone among the various apprentices engaged by Ming and other members of her family, Del was one of the minority of apprenticed workers who had been removed by court process rather than by the operation of the 1915 amendment to the Aborigines Protection Act.

In 1928, when Del was removed, she told Ming, her maternal aunt had been caring for her for the five years since her parents separated, and Del's mother moved away. When her aunt went off shearing with her husband, she left Del in the care of Del's grandmother. Around this time Del had begun, in her words, 'to play the wag from school & get my Aunty & Gran to write notes & friends and anyone who would'. They were sympathetic – they knew that Del had been harshly punished and was frightened to return. The previous headmaster at the local state school had been under departmental investigation for his mistreatment of children (especially of the 'senior girls'), and in the year Del began truanting, a distressed mother had lodged a formal complaint of abuse with the Education Department. A male teacher and the new headmaster had humiliated her daughter, and, more seriously, the teacher had broken the girl's hand caning her. The mother no longer wanted her daughter to attend the school, it being 'a misery for the child and myself'. Though these allegations were dismissed, Del's guardians were obviously not alone in the district among worried parents, willing to take their children out of school.[5]

Del told Ming that one day while she was playing in her 'cubbyhouse', 'a policeman rode up and told her she was to go away with him'. Del thought she had been reported by the local truancy inspector and was to be sent to Cootamundra Home. Instead, she was sent to a children's court and from there to the Parramatta reformatory, the Industrial School for Girls, the one remaining large-scale institution in NSW for girls committed by court to the care of the state. Although Del 'simply didn't know what it was all about' – 'I don't know what *I* done that was bad!!' – she blamed her friend May (who was actually related to Del), who was, according to this recounting of Del's story, a 'thief' – she 'collected coloured vases or pictures suitable for playthings' for their cubby-house, claimed Del. Apparently Del's family also blamed May, her aunt later telling Ming that 'poor little Del when she was sent away from here she was only a child and wouldn't attend to school her school mate was very determined and would always call for Del & they would not go to school so we thought they might get into mischief.' Del and May were both sent to the Parramatta reformatory and from there to Cootamundra Home. Del remained at Cootamundra Home for 'a year or two', then went to work in Burrendah in rural NSW, and later, to Sydney.[6]

The Board records corroborate the account given by Del and her aunt. She had been committed by court order for 'being uncontrollable refusing to attend school when sent by Guardian' and had been sent on to the Board by the Child Welfare Department. The unfortunate May, who never had the opportunity to defend herself, was committed on the same grounds.[7]

Yet, oddly enough, both May and Del's admission records at the Parramatta School state that their charge was simply 'Neglected: – Child had a dirty head' (i.e. had head lice). Their records stand out strikingly from the pages and pages of girls recorded committed for suspected sexual activity or for stealing.[8] It is remarkable that Del and May should have been admitted to the reformatory on these trivial grounds – especially when Del's family were under the impression she had been taken for truancy, or even theft, and that the Board records mention truancy. Truancy was a major preoccupation of the new child welfare bureaucracies of the 1920s, seen as a reliable indicator of parental neglect, which enabled the increasingly interventionist state to identify and take steps to reform potential young criminals. I can only conclude that both the report of her truancy and the policeman's allegation that he had found 'stolen property' were intended to intimidate Del's grandmother and aunt (who, living on an unmanaged Aboriginal reserve near a township, were possibly less amenable to Board interference) into not contesting her removal.

Furthermore, both girls were discharged from Parramatta School to the control of the Board a mere three weeks after their arrival, making theirs one of the shortest stays in the institution recorded. It would seem that their court committal was only ever intended to lend legitimacy to their removal to Cootamundra Home. There is evidence that the Aborigines Protection Board and the Child Welfare Department recorded acting in concert to secure committal of other Aboriginal children to Board control around the same time.[9]

The Protection Board had been closely connected with the then State Children's Relief Board (SCRB) since 1917, when the head, A. W. Green, had been appointed a member of the Protection Board. Green's original appointment to the Board was primarily to facilitate the transfer of fair-skinned Aboriginal children, removed under the 1915 Board legislation, to his department, minimizing inter-departmental conflict.[10]

Before 1927, however, only a small minority of the registered Aboriginal wards (usually boys) had been initially removed by the Child Welfare Department and then sent on to the Board. Although the Board threatened reluctant parents with proceedings under the 1905 Neglected Children legislation, Aboriginal children were usually removed under the Board's own legislative powers. Not until 1927 did the notation 'Committed by Children's Court' appear as a standard entry in the ward registers, although as the records stop at 1928, there is no way of knowing if this was a temporary aberration or the beginnings of a new pattern of child removal. The new use of the term 'committed by Children's Court' in 1927, however, can be explained as a response to public criticism. 1927 was a significant year for the Board in terms of its policies towards children. First, the Board was forced to confront calls from the recently established Australian Aborigines Progressive Association for the immediate cessation of the removal of Aboriginal children in 1925, and for a Royal Commission into Aboriginal affairs in 1927. The Board was put on the defensive, promptly registering its opposition to the proposal for a Royal Commission investigation.[11] Also in 1927, the Board and the Education Department had to address Aboriginal parents' protest against school segregation. At Bateman's Bay on the south coast, the Aboriginal community had mounted an organized campaign to resist the barring of their children from the local school. Aboriginal parents here (unlike at other places) won this particular battle, securing both access to education for their children and their continued residence on the town reserve.[12] So in Del's and May's cases in particular, the charge of truancy in their registration books can be seen as a way of recording the Board's determination to ensure the attendance of Aboriginal children at local public schools, and indeed of how Aboriginal parents were deficient even (and perhaps especially) where schooling was not segregated. Although Del was not the only child to be too frightened to go to school, she – and May – had the misfortune to be Aboriginal.

Neither Ming nor Del was aware of the discrepancy between Del's understanding of her removal and her admission record at the Parramatta School (and presumably, in the Children's Court). Nevertheless, Ming was startled by Del's account of being taken away for school truancy. For the first time she questioned the removal of the Aboriginal girls which was the foundation of the apprenticeship scheme. Del 'was like the rest of these girls, taken forcibly from her own people, under any pretext whatever,' she wrote.

If there was confusion in the official records, however, the story of Del's removal told by the Homefinder to Ming was a patent fabrication. Dreamed up to justify her refusal to countenance Del's allegations against the son of her previous employer, Miss Lowe would later circulate the dubious story of Del's removal in an attempt to forestall exposure of Del's maltreatment while in the care of the Board. And so the story of Del's removal, and not that of her rape, would become the issue.

8
A perfect farce

Clearly, Miss Lowe was not going to be content to leave Del in the Strack household. Until that point Del's previous employer would have been unaware that she had said anything to anybody, presumably secure in the assumption that she would be too frightened to do so. After all, Miss Lowe had in her possession, courtesy of Mrs Smith, Del's 'statement' about her supposed lover, she had had Del examined for (and cleared of) possible pregnancy, and transferring Del to another employer would have been an expedient solution to the whole crisis. By telling her new employer of the rape, Del had thrown a major spanner in a mechanism that probably had worked very successfully in similar cases. Ming's unexpected refusal to let Del go certainly changed everything.

Shortly after Miss Lowe's unpropitious visit to the Stracks' home, she rang to inform Ming that she 'insisted' that Del be sent back to the Board office the next week. Ming told Miss Lowe she would 'think the matter over in the next three or four days'.

> Del was still ill and implored me not to send her to Miss Lowe. I couldn't bring myself to do this, for a better girl never lived. She seemed to me to be a good girl in every way and appreciated every single thing we did for her. I should most thankfully have sent her away if these people had shown the least desire to help her in any way, but to have an innocent girl sent away as a criminal was more than I could stand, and so I decided to do what I could for her myself.[1]

Instead, five days, later Ming took Del to Sydney's Central Police Station. There they were met by Sergeant Armfield, a woman officer, who apparently had special responsibility for Aboriginal women in the city.[2] She told Ming – much to her astonishment – that the Board was indeed legally entitled to remove apprentices 'whenever they chose'. After taking a statement from Del, Armfield advised having her examined at the Royal North Shore Hospital; if she was pregnant, then legal action could be taken.

Del was seen by a gynaecologist that afternoon. He found she was not pregnant, but opined she was suffering a hysterical pregnancy, brought on by 'nervous shock'. He told them both to stop worrying about it. Ming was sceptical, noting that the pain was so bad that Del 'even cried with it' at times. They returned home, where Del was violently sick as soon as they arrived and all that night, with 'fits of severe trembling'.

The policewoman had also suggested that Ming approach the Child Welfare Department to see if she could send Del 'to her own people for at least a holiday'; but on ringing the next day Ming was told that they could do nothing and that she should speak to the Secretary of the Aborigines Board.

Alfred Pettitt was the Board's first full-time, salaried Secretary when he was appointed in 1909, fresh out of high school and having completed his Public Service Board exam.[3] The Board had just gained its first legislative powers, and Pettitt was appointed to act as the administrator by the Chief Secretary. Apart from the years of the First World War when he enlisted, Pettitt had overseen the day-to-day running of Board business – including the apprenticeship system – ever since.

Pettitt told Ming to bring Del in to see him. Ming agreed on the condition that Del would get a fair hearing and be allowed to return home with her. It was on this day, 16 March 1933, that Ming made a careful written account of Del's own version of her removal, obviously in preparation for the interview.[4] Before going to the Board the next day, Ming, with Del, stopped at the Legal Aid department, where Ming was told she should have another witness with her, 'a Member of Parliament preferably'.

'I could just see myself inviting Sir Thomas Bavin to accompany me to the meeting!' Ming wrote.

> Good heavens, the idea! They read the act to me and it was the same as before. The Board had complete control, and if I refused to let her go I would be liable for a 'Civil action', or something like that. It sounded dreadful, but not quite hopeless. There was still half an hour before the meeting, but what to do, I wondered!

Ming decided to call in on the offices of her solicitor friend Eric Campbell. Although the New Guard leader was away in Europe at the time, Ming was able to see his brother, the other Campbell of the firm Campbell & Campbell. Initially warning Ming that she should 'have nothing to do with the thing at all – it wasn't quite nice and I wouldn't like to be mixed up with this sort of thing', Campbell advised that Del should refuse to deny her statement, should sign nothing *but* the statement, and that if the Board attempted to keep her, Ming should threaten to go at once to Mr Parkhill. Ming seemed to know who he was. The federal member for the northern Sydney shire of Warringah, Parkhill was quite possibly connected with the New Guard, being also an avowed anti-communist, an ultra-nationalist and a supporter of returned soldiers' demands.

'This sounded very simple and off we went,' wrote Ming. 'He [Campbell] also said that if I wanted him for anything to ring and he would come to the Board, which was very comforting to know.'

Pettitt met Del and Ming at the Board office, where an official transcriber took Del's statement, which Del told exactly as she had told Ming. (At first, to Ming's dismay, Pettitt asked Del only about the first statement she had made, for Mrs Smith. At this point Ming was still unaware that Del had made up the name of her supposed lover under duress. Ming then told Pettitt he 'had better ask her' about the later statement.) 'Del stuck to her story right through just as she had told me, but it was dreadfully difficult for her to do so with the fixed stare of these people upon her. I felt terribly sorry for her,' she wrote. The transcriber then left, and 'in stalked Mrs Smith and Miss Lowe'.

We were amazed, and poor Del sat up and simply stared. What a mean, contemptible thing to do to the girl. It was an awful shock. However, it had to be faced, and I sat close beside Del to help her. Mrs Smith simply screamed at the girl and said she hoped that *I* would suffer for taking Del's part. To my surprise nothing they could say could shake Del from her story. They vied with each other in terrible and vile untruths about this girl, until at last she broke down, saying to me, 'It's *not* true, oh, it's *not true.*'

After each tirade Mrs Smith would say to me, '*Now*, do you believe her? Well, will you believe *this* ...'

I said, 'Yes, I believe Del in spite of you all.'

They then said, 'Are you trying to imply that we are *liars*?'

I simply said, 'I believe Del absolutely; you may put any construction on that you like.'

Mrs Smith, 'Well, she's a sexual maniac, isn't she, Miss Lowe?'

'Yes,' said Miss Lowe.

'Yes,' said Mr Pettitt.

I said, 'How *dare* you say that, you will prove it.' And they all sat up and said 'Oh well, not *exactly* a sexual maniac!!'

Miss Lowe, 'She has lived with dozens of men. Now will you take her back?'

They said she had threatened to kill someone with a tomahawk, and was mad. She had even put her bedroom furniture against her door to prevent Mrs Smith from entering.

They said I was hysterical and refused to discuss the matter with me! That Del had become remarkably intelligent since being with me!! I simply said 'Naturally.' Mrs Smith put her head back and roared with laughter.

She then did her level best to terrify Del and to shake her from her true story, but though Del wept bitterly she still stuck to it.

It was horrible and dreadful, and they finally said, 'She shall stay here. Ring for the police, Mr Pettitt.'

But he hesitated and I said, 'Do that and I shall take this whole matter to Mr Parkhill.'

This had, in Ming's word, 'a magic effect'; Miss Lowe immediately backed down, saying that if Ming wished to keep Del despite everything that had been said, she could – 'for a time'.

It turns out that Parkhill was an extremely powerful politician of the time, and indeed many expected him to become Deputy Prime Minister. Prime Minister Lyons had rewarded him with the plum position of Postmaster-General for his prompt and politically astute handling of an investigation of allegations of mistreatment of Aborigines in Northern Territory (NT) whilst Minister for the Interior in 1932. He was known as 'Bulldog' Parkhill because 'once he gets his teeth into anything he never lets go', and wielded formidable influence which would explain the Board officers' sudden capitulation. Yet Parkhill's report on the NT Aborigines' alleged maltreatment had hardly been sympathetic. He found no evidence for serious allegations of abuse and assault and explicitly blamed Aboriginal women for the 'problem' of their 'moral welfare', arguing that the solution was to remove their children at as early an age as possible, literally from their mothers' breast.[5] Considering this, the Board officers must have believed that their actions in Del's case could not be so easily dismissed or explained away; or perhaps they feared

Parkhill's intervention might set in train an official investigation into the administration of the Board in general.

Mrs Smith was agitated about this sudden reversal and tried to insist that she get Del back right away as Miss Lowe had promised. She had to be content with the reassurance that she 'needn't worry. Mr Pettitt would see that it didn't go any further!' Ming was incensed:

> I stood up then and said, 'You are a perfect farce. This Board is paid to protect these girls and you all sit there laughing at this defenceless girl. She has the right to appeal to this Board for protection and *this* is what she gets. You ask why I am interfering, that is the reason! If Del had even one member of this Board that she could appeal to it would not be necessary for me to intervene, but there is not a soul. She is alone, and I *will* help her. It is disgraceful and shameful. Once before you took from me the most devoted little half-caste I have ever known and sent her without money or clothes and with a small baby to Victoria. There was only slow starvation for her, and you try to do the same thing again. It is time the whole matter is shown up and it shall be if I can do it.'

There was 'a chorus of grunts'. As Ming took Del's arm to go out the door, an undignified scene took place:

> ... Miss Lowe rushed over and tried to shake hands! I put my hand behind my back but she still shook it!
>
> Del didn't wait for any more, but made for the stairs and freedom. She said to Mrs Smith, just at the last, 'Ritchie is a coward and a mongrel. No [A]boriginal man would treat a white girl as he treated me!' It was the first and only time I have ever heard Del raise her voice or show any sign whatever of temper and she had suffered more than she could possibly stand.
>
> They all looked very nervous, then Mrs Smith said, 'You were *never* alone in the house, Del.' And Miss Lowe said, 'No, Mrs Smith paid a woman 30/- a week to just be in the house with Del!'
>
> I asked what was her name? And they looked blankly at me. I said 'Have you many more stories like that?'
>
> Del said there was never any woman there, and night after night they went to the pictures, Ritchie coming in just as they were leaving and saying that he was tired, or would not have time to dress, and remaining at home.

I simply said, 'You utter frauds, you will be forced to protect these girls from this sort of thing before very long,' and we left. Del sobbed all the way home and was so upset that I sent her straight to bed.

The fact alone that the Board administrators actually brought in Del's ex-employer in an attempt to intimidate Del into retracting her allegations – which were surely serious enough to warrant investigation – suggests a significant degree of collusion between Miss Lowe and Mrs Smith in trying to silence Del and Ming. But even the personal friendship between Miss Lowe and the Smith family does not adequately explain why the Board so blatantly favoured Mrs Smith's position. And to argue that Miss Lowe and Pettitt genuinely could not conceive of the possibility of an Aboriginal servant being raped by a respectable white youth would presume a staggering ignorance on the part of two of the longest-serving officers of the Board.

The reason why the Board sacrificed its obligation to protect Del and instead shielded her alleged attacker was because Del's individual case had the potential to expose the broader pattern of sexual abuse and Board inaction intrinsic to the policy of removing and apprenticing out young Aboriginal women in white households. Brought in to confront Ming personally, mistress against mistress, Mrs Smith's role was to split the dangerous alliance between employer and worker against the Board – for Del's protest would have been entirely ineffectual had she not secured the support of a white mistress.

That Mrs Smith had no further recourse once Ming threatened political intervention is further evidence that the balance of power between the Board and employers (however friendly the relationship) was firmly weighted towards the Board. In the interests of protecting the Board, rather than Mrs Smith, the administrators were obliged to let Del go and consider other alternatives.

* * *

The Monday following this harrowing interview, Del collapsed. Ming had left her in bed while she started the washing, but Del 'crept out and was in the middle of it when I made a cup of tea and Del staggered in. She looked at me dumbly then fell to the floor with blood running from her mouth. She was quite unconscious and looked a very strange colour, then became fearfully pallid.' Del was taken by ambulance to the Royal North Shore Hospital.

For ten days, according to Ming, they 'could not move her'; then they took an X-ray and found 'nothing wrong'. The next day Ming attempted to see the Police Commissioner and Board Chairman, W. H. Childs, but he was away. Deputy Police Commissioner W. J. Mackay saw her instead, giving 'us good advice but could do nothing as it was Mr Childs' business'.[6] Ming called on Del in hospital and found her 'crying bitterly because she cannot come home':

> Is afraid Miss Lowe will take her away. I do wish they would do something definite. The suspense is wearing us out.

Ming brought Del home five days later, the hospital having concluded there was 'nothing the matter with her'. But that night Del was vomiting blood.

Ten days later Ming wrote in her diary that Del had 'vomited incessantly since coming home from Hospital and always blood'. 'It is terrifying,' she wrote. 'I cannot stand much more of it; am afraid she will bleed to death.'

'[S]he might die ... . It is very serious – why can't these fools do something to find out [?]' Ming rang Sergeant Armfield, who 'most patiently' listened to her 'tale of woe'. Then she wrote to Mr Childs, to arrange an interview. Not having heard anything further from the Board since the interview, Ming also wrote to the Board's office, telling them that she intended to nurse Del until she was well enough to return to her people, and 'told them they could pay the Hospital Bill!'

Two days later, Ming called on Mr Childs with Del in tow (she 'was very weak, can only just walk'). A police orderly, taking their names and business, refused them admittance. 'He insisted upon ringing Mr Pettitt of the blessed Board again. Oh dear, I was sick of that man's name, and it was so useless – he thought Del probably had T.B.!!' (Ming's altercation with the officious policeman would become a point of contention, as when Ming later saw B. C. Harkness, a Board member, Pettitt presented a letter from Mr Childs' office, which claimed that Ming had refused to go in when she called on the Chairman. According to Ming's account, she had been so offended by the police orderly's attitude that she had gone back alone that same afternoon to castigate him for his 'disgraceful' behaviour – whereupon he had told her that she could see Childs immediately. Ming said that it would be 'pointless without Del' and left.)

Pettitt arranged for Del to see Dr Booth, a tuberculosis specialist and the Inspector-General of Health, straight away, he insisted, and meeting Ming and Del at the Board's office, he accompanied them to the doctor. Dr Booth's attitude was alarmingly hostile. 'Now, we are going to find out all about you, young woman! You won't like that will you? All the things you are trying to hide from us will be discovered now,' he said, and when Ming protested, he turned on her, insinuating that Ming was frightened that Del had become pregnant whilst in *her* employ. After Ming told him how the hospital had been unable to find out what Del's problem was, the doctor said, 'Oh, they knew what was the matter with her, and in fact the more they knew the less they would be likely to tell *you!*' Ming was disturbed by his hostility and also by the fact that he had greeted Pettitt as his 'old friend'. 'They are all friends and work in with each other,' she wrote later. 'Mr Pettitt must have told the doctor things about Del; how else would he have spoken as he did. Surely he does not treat all his T.B. patients in this manner.'

Dr Booth sent them to the Rachel Foster hospital to see yet another doctor friend of his, but fortunately, a female doctor, who seemed kind and sympathetic, examined Del there. This doctor's examination corroborated Del's allegations – yes, Del 'had been interfered with', she told Ming, 'and it was probably as Del said herself, a very unpleasant business and causing great pain'. For Del's chronic vomiting, the doctor diagnosed a possible gastric ulcer and sent her away with 'powders and a mixture to take'. This diagnosis was communicated to the Board through Dr Booth.[7] Though Del's illness remains a mystery, the doctor's treatment seemed to help as her vomiting gradually eased over the next few weeks.

* * *

However, throughout the following month, May 1933, a series of alarming incidents targeting Del started up at the Stracks' new residence at Pymble. First, while the family was out leaving Del at home alone, a man came to the door asking to use the telephone, and, when Del refused, he 'held her tightly and kissed her' before departing 'hurriedly'. The Stracks returned to find her in 'a poor huddled heap'. Two nights later, when Ming and her husband were out and Del was with the children at home, a brick was thrown through the glass door. A week later, Del was alone in the house during the morning. When Ming returned she found Del 'in a fearful state' with a swollen and bleeding lip. Del said the same man had come to the back door and 'grabbed' her as soon as she opened it.

Del told Ming she had called the police, and later, two plain-clothes police arrived, a Detective-Sergeant Todd and another officer. (Police officers had also interviewed Del after the brick-throwing incident.) The attitude of the senior police officer was remarkably unsympathetic. Todd told Ming that he did not believe Del and said, inexplicably, 'we had this trouble before'. Todd told her there was 'only one thing to do, get rid of her', or at least have her 'mentally examined'. A few days later, Ming took Del to the Pymble police station where Del made a statement to two women police officers – Ming was not allowed to be present.

After this, Ming recorded that everyone had been away from the house for 'an hour or two' one day and returned to find 'all the verandah beds had been unmade, and dragged about the floor. Del's bedding was thrown over the railing into the garden, and her blanket stolen'. The final incident Ming recorded occurred late one night, when she was in the kitchen at the back of the house. Ming heard a sound outside and, seeing a shadow 'close into the wall', threw a teapot of cold tea at it. 'It rose suddenly and departed, much to my surprise. I am sorry the tea was not hot,' she wrote. 'I do so hope that this is the last of it. We will all be nervous wrecks at this rate.'

Indeed, there were no further incidents after this. They seem completely bizarre and there is no way of knowing if they were connected in any way to the struggle with the Board or with Del's allegations against her employer's son. Ming had suspicions that they were in fact connected and the assault by the 'strange man' in particular a tactic to give Del 'a bad name'. Todd's response was odd, and as it turned out later he had been privy to the false record constructed by Miss Lowe. It does seem sinister that the attacks ended abruptly after Ming herself witnessed something – perhaps they were indeed being arranged to create the impression that Del was mentally unbalanced.

* * *

Then, hard on the heels of these attacks, the Board's Secretary suddenly took an interest in the wages Ming owed to the Board's trust fund. Pettitt had apparently failed to take note of the fact that Ming had paid *no* wages for Del since her arrival. The day Pettitt had taken Ming and Del over to Dr Booth, Mrs Smith forwarded a part-payment to Del's account making up the last of her wages owing; no further payments were recorded.[8] Almost certainly Lowe or Pettitt advised Mrs Smith to make up this payment (covering a two-week period) so that they could comfortably proceed against Ming's arrears. On 8 June, Miss Lowe called on Ming to get Del's 'pocket money book' back. This was a record held by the apprentice of receipts for their 'pocket money', a small sum (in Del's case – being a third-year apprentice, while with Ming – 2 shillings a week) which their employer was supposed to give them directly. Ming refused to return the pocket money book and in fact it remains amongst her papers, and shows that Del had signed for receipt of her weekly allowance up to 16 June 1933.

It seems the Board intended to use Ming's non-payment of Del's wages as a further tactic to force her to return her. However the Board's intervention now antagonized Ming further. At this point she made a definite decision that she would not make any payments into the Board's trust account for Del, on the grounds that they would not release this money to her, or to any other apprentice.[9]

Ming had made what appears to be a handwritten copy of Del's letter to the Board, sent some time around June or July:

> Dear Mr Pettitt,
>   I have been out at Service for some years now & I have been very ill. The things that Miss Lowe & Mrs Smith accused me of were untrue, & they know it. I was very ill when I came to Mrs Strack & now I need a number of things & want half my money to get them with. I intend to spend it just how I like the money is mine. I want to spend it at once, & please let me know exactly how much I have as I may be going to Nortown for a holiday soon.
>   Yours sincerely
>   Del Malloy
> P.S. I will put the money in the bank at Pymble & have my own book & take it out when I want to.[10]

Pettitt did not bother to reply to Del, instead sending a coldly polite letter to Ming, requesting that she 'kindly advise me as to what purchases she [Del] intends making, and whether, in your opinion, they are necessary', and reminding Ming that she owed £5 9s 3d for Del's unpaid wages.[11]

A reminder notice to Ming followed in early October, her arrears now totalling £8 7s 9d. The day after Pettitt sent this, he must have realized that the Board had failed to get Ming's signature on her initial contract for Del's indenture (made in January) and sent her the agreement form to sign and return.[12] Without it, it would be impossible for the Board to successfully sue Ming for Del's wages.

Ming wrote a furious reply, telling Pettitt that she and Del had not forgotten the Board's response to Del's allegations. She intended to keep Del with her until Del had 'every penny that is owing her by the Board', and she would then return her to Nortown, 'where her own family will afford her a measure of protection':

> I have interested every organisation in Sydney in this case, also the 'Press' & Members of parliament as I said I would do and will not

now or at any time pay one penny to the Abo. Board for Del Malloy – but any money which she considers oweing [sic] by us shall be paid into her *own* account where it will be safe. I shall not give you any detailed account of what Del Malloy wishes to buy or to spend her money upon. She is quite capable of spending it wisely – the money is her own & she has a perfect right to do with it as she pleases. Mainly she wants peace & happiness and 'Protection' which I intend to see that she gets at any cost …

'Del will expect her money immediately,' she concluded.[13] Pettitt's response was curt; a form letter headed 'Kind Request' asking her once again to return the agreement form.[14] Ming did not respond. She was busy preparing for a public and legal battle with the Board.

Six months earlier, in July 1933, the journalist A. J. Vogan, a friend of her mother, had introduced Ming to the Bryces, a couple who lived in nearby Killara and who were members of the philanthropic Association for the Protection of Native Races (APNR).[15] Vogan had been a harsh critic of the treatment of Aborigines since the late nineteenth century, when he had published *The Black Police*, a sensational account of the Native Police in Queensland, and he disliked intensely the colonial practice of using Aboriginal children for labour. In 1911 Vogan was one of the founding members of the APNR. Now no longer a member (having withdrawn in 1919), he was happy to put Ming in contact with the Bryces. Mr Bryce took Ming to a meeting of the APNR in October 1933.[16]

The Bryces were very sympathetic. They had also clashed with the Board, over the reimbursement of wages to a former apprentice, Katie, whom they had employed as a servant in the mid-1920s. Katie had applied for her trust monies after coming to work for them to pay for dental work and to buy 'Xmas things', but her request had been refused. The Bryces had brought her case to the APNR and it may be that this experience had served as their introduction to the APNR as well. (They were apparently unsuccessful, Katie being taken from them by the Board and no record to show she ever did receive her money.)[17] Ming met at around the same time – possibly through the Bryces – an estate agent named Watson, who told her that he had taken the Board to court to get wages owing to an apprentice called Sarah, employed by his wife. He had 'got the money for Sarah and had the girl freed from the Board'. The Watsons' example caused Ming to reflect regretfully, 'I only wished that I could have done likewise with Mary, but we could not afford it at the time', and hardened her resolve that she should 'never part with [Del] until she received [the money the Board owed her] – what dishonest people they are – one can only despise them'. Had she known that the Board had secured a 'confidential police report' on Mr Watson's 'business character and financial standing' at the time of the girl's application, she would have been even more disgusted.[18]

So by the time Pettitt wrote to Ming to ask her what Del wanted her money for, Ming had, as she had said, approached the press (*Smith's Weekly*, a popular and rather sensationalist news magazine) and various organizations with her 'bundle of notes re Del'. It was from this point that she began transcribing her diaries dating back to Del's arrival and compiling a public narrative of Del's mistreatment, which she could give to others – including the APNR – to read.

9
She loves pretty things and knows how to wear them

Del's story is an indictment of the authorities' attitude and behaviour towards the girls in their charge. Yet publishing her story requires an alertness to the position of Aboriginal people today. As Ming would come to realize, Del was repeatedly interrogated, compelled to give evidence that was then turned against her and used to consolidate and perpetuate her victimization. She was in a position in which colonized and enslaved people find themselves throughout history to the present day, and her story can be 'heard' in different and not altogether sympathetic ways even now. Del was caught between the need to tell her story in order to seek justice and the framework of dominance in which her telling took place.

Like most non-Aboriginal Australians at the time, when I first found Ming's papers, I had no idea that past governments had carried out systematic policies of removing Aboriginal children – mostly girls – and placing them in what amounted to forced labour. Nor did I comprehend how malevolent in both intention and practice these policies were. Like Ming, I too was sickened and outraged, and I hoped that I might yet realize Ming's hope of exposing the Aborigines Protection Board.

Sitting in my Gran's downstairs 'granddaughter' flat, surrounded by piles of dusty, torn and stained papers, piecing together this terrible legacy, I heard on the news that a Human Rights and Equal Opportunities Commission of Enquiry had been set up to investigate past practices of removing Indigenous children from their families. And when the enquiry came to the North Coast region to hear evidence, I made sure I attended the hearings.

It was an intensely disturbing experience. I sat on a hard, uncomfortable chair at the back of a small room, staring out at the bright sunshine outside, listening to elderly Aboriginal men and women, voices tearing raggedly as they described their own painful experiences – experiences they had borne for decades as their private, individual shame, now presented for public judgement. Asked by a lawyer to read out a statement written by an Aboriginal man who could not attend, I pleaded the inappropriateness of such an action and managed to find a (white) man to read it to the Hearing instead. Mortified, I stood outside and watched as a younger woman tried unsuccessfully to persuade her frail, elderly mother to give evidence. 'We come all this way to be here,' she said to me over her mother's shoulder, 'and now she won't talk!'

I had an overwhelming sense of invasion, exacerbated by what I was doing at my Gran's – deciphering these old diaries and papers, most of them obviously not written for public consumption. I was painfully aware of the witnesses' absolute dependence on the willingness of non-Aboriginal Australians to listen sympathetically and respectfully. They had no guarantee of this, let alone of any redress. But without the willingness of Aboriginal people to testify, this history would remain buried.

Having traced the families of all four women who had worked for Ming, I had discovered, to my surprise, that all the Aboriginal women, like Ming, had chosen not to talk of their experiences to their children or extended family members. I had in effect forced each woman (including Ming) to speak to their families, who themselves have then had to come to terms with these often painful revelations. It was an awkward position to be in.

In Del's case the issue was particularly pointed. Although she had not told her family of her experiences, of the four women, Del had been the most outspoken in her own lifetime, the most determined not to bear the burden of her oppression in silence. As a result her family had some inkling of what was to come as they ushered me through to the backyard of their home in a harsh, dry, outback town, and waited to hear what I had to say. From the outset they were understandably reserved and on guard, although I did not know why for some time. It came back to that manuscript diary that Ming had compiled as a record of Del's treatment by the Board.

Ming first began keeping a regular diary, as far as I can work out, in the early 1930s – like many female diarists of her time, she needed to wait until the children were out of babyhood. Writing at night, after the rest of the household was asleep, was a safety valve, a release for the daily frustrations of a life she felt obliged to hide from friends and family. 'I write because I cannot speak about it & it relieves my shattered feelings,' she reflected. 'It seems a harmless sort of relief.' That entry was made about six months before she met Del. When Del came along, her purpose shifted.

Having painstakingly transcribed her diaries into a manuscript documenting the Board's actions, Ming intended to use this manuscript as a legal document, if necessary, an affidavit. What had been a source of private relief had now become a very important activity to her in terms of its public use. It was a testimony of truth, intended to be used in court as evidence.

Eventually, a copy of the manuscript was deposited in the archives of the anthropologist Professor A. P. Elkin, who acquired it through the Association for the Protection of Native Races (APNR) when he took over as Secretary in 1939. That year, Ming would attempt to recover the diary from Elkin, regarding it as 'dangerous' to herself – she was by that time active in the political movement for Aboriginal rights. She was not successful in getting it returned, however,[1] and it was through this document, one of the few remaining public records of Ming's activities, that a handful of researchers and historians uncovered Del's story. At least one researcher had already contacted Del's family seeking permission to access her records, and, unwittingly offending the shocked family, had been denied. Now here I was, the proverbial bright-eyed and bushy-tailed university student, on their doorstep.

Much to my relief, the ice was broken by Del's eldest son, Bob, I felt, when I mentioned a toy train that Ming had sent him when he was a baby. He remembered it with fondness and softened towards me. In the end, after much discussion, he agreed to give his permission to let me look at the official records – a lengthy, awkward and embarrassing process as it turned out, as the red tape involved was considerable. But at that stage Bob did not want me to make the story of his mother public. Reluctantly, I agreed to leave Del's story where it lay.

Discussing this impasse with Bob and other family members over the years, I would come to a more thoughtful awareness of the complexity of such a situation. There is a powerful reverberation in the way that, in the process of transformation from private diary to public document, Ming's testimony came to occupy unstable, 'dangerous' ground. Like the testimonies of the Aboriginal witnesses for the Stolen Generations Enquiry, presented for consumption, indeed judgement, by 'the colonizer', there is always the danger that instead of finding rehabilitation or restitution, the Aboriginal people will only expose themselves to more odium, more opprobrium, more evidence against themselves.

Several years later, I spoke to Bob on the telephone. 'I've been thinking about your book,' he said, in his gruff way. He seemed to be having a change of heart and asked me to come out to see him to discuss it. Sadly, I could not get to see him before he died soon afterwards.

Bob's family referred me to Del's next eldest son, Jack. He was quite relaxed about Del's and Ming's story being published, and interested as well. So, finally, the story can come out. But I feel Bob's anxious presence at my shoulder. His concern highlights how important it is not to take for granted the voices of those who suffered humiliation and abuse – these stories are not offered lightly, and they have repercussions to which non-Aboriginal Australians might be altogether deaf.

* * *

Del's forthright demand to Pettitt for her wages practically amounted to a challenge to the Board. The Board Secretary evidently suspected Ming's influence, just as Miss Lowe and Dr Booth had insinuated that Ming had somehow put Del up to making her allegations against the Smith boy. But although the sole copy of Del's letter that remains is in Ming's handwriting, its tone and language indicate that it was an authentic reflection of Del's own words and her view of her position. Perhaps Del dictated the letter to Ming in the first place, and indeed Del may well have initiated it.

All through the public narrative Ming compiled out of her diaries, Del herself barely emerges as an active participant. Her image of humble submission to her fate, head bowed and tongue tied as the battle for her future raged around her, reflected the way Ming saw her. Such a representation of Del's passivity suited Ming's purposes as much as it did the Board's, though for different reasons. Emphasizing Del's helplessness and vulnerability allowed Ming to assume the role of Del's defender and would also have helped Ming to persuade others in her social circle to assist. But Del's personality and the nature of her relationship with Ming are revealed much more vividly through her private conversations with Ming, recorded by Ming almost as essays, with painstaking attention to the idiom and inflection of Del's speech. Out of these echoes, Del emerges as an exceptionally strong and determined character.

Throughout a life of privations, punctuated by episodes of betrayal and brutality, Del refused to be cowed or to accept unfair treatment. She showed no signs of anything but hatred and outrage towards those whom she believed had acted cruelly and unjustly, and only compassion for those on the receiving end of such actions, including herself.

Her refusal to be intimidated into submission was symbolized in the way she described her attempted escape from 'gaol' (as she, like other Aboriginal girls, termed the Parramatta Home), which ended in her capture by another inmate, who warned her to acquiesce:

> Del: Mis Strack! You ever bin in gaol?
>
> Mrs S: No, Del. Why?
>
> D: Oh cos it's *awful*! *Gee* it's awful – those *walls*! They shut you right *in* & you can't see anything at all. Yer always saying to yerself – I'll *run* away right away if I could only see out – I must & I *must*. Till at last you talk to another girl about it & she says she will run too, & then when we're out for a walk in the Park, with crowd of people all *round* you, (looking after you!) you suddenly dig a girl in the side & tear for your very life. Oh *gee*! We did run & they chased us, but *no* one could catch *me* when I start. I don't *see* things, only just leap & bound along till I'm safe from them all. [B]ut at last I stopped. A girl *did* catch me this time! & she said quickly before the others came up, 'Del don't be *silly* it will only be *worse* for you now – don't ever try to run away – *I* did once!'

Del's captor was right – Del 'was flogged terribly hard' on her return and then confined alone in a small, dark room.[2] But there is nothing in her recollection to suggest she ever regretted her attempt, despite the harshness of her punishment. Del was always defiant, fiercely assured of her absolute prerogative to exercise her own judgement and will.

Only a glimmer of this persona shows through in Ming's 'public narrative' – when Del told Mrs Smith that her son was 'a coward and a mongrel'. Yet in light of the Del who emerges from the conversations recorded by Ming, this blunt assertiveness was entirely characteristic. Del deliberately chose to appeal to Ming for alliance in her battle to be freed from her old employer and from the Board's control; indeed Ming's position enabled her to challenge the Board in a way impossible for Del.

That Del was not drawn into the fray by Ming, but rather the other way around, can be read between the lines of Ming's narrative and becomes explicit in her later letters to Ming, written from Nortown. Not only did Del report showing no hesitation in rebuking Pettitt, but in another, earlier letter, she complained to Ming about having to explain what she wanted to spend her money on when she applied for it. '[A]ny one with comon sense would know what I wont it for,' she wrote.' [A]ny how its my money and I should get it with out telling them anything.'[3] The similarity in tone and style between Del's original letter to Pettitt in 1933 and these later writings indicates that the letter was in fact written in her own words and expressed her own feelings.

It was Del who opened Ming's eyes to the fact that Aboriginal girls were taken 'under any pretext' whatsoever; and it was Del who enlightened Ming as to the experiences of the girls in Cootamundra Home, where she had lived between 1928 and 1930. Ming's shock, registered in her careful recording of Del's stories, indicates that she had never heard (and probably never asked for) Mary's story of her time at the Home, twelve years earlier. She was certainly not alone; even the most kindly of employers of Aboriginal apprentices would later profess to knowing nothing of the 'baby-snatching' of Aboriginal children and their treatment in Cootamundra Home.[4] No matter how emotionally reliant a mistress might have been on her servant, in the typical domestic service relationship the servant's required invisibility and silence, her 'non-person status', usually prevented her from revealing her innermost feelings to her employer.[5]

The rapport between Ming and Del was not immediate. Del's difficulty in expressing herself initially was reflected in the way that she continued to sweep, rather than sitting or standing directly before Ming, when telling Ming about the abuse she suffered at the hands of Ritchie Smith. In contrast, her later approaches to Ming were more confident and direct, 'putting her head round the door' to tell Ming why she never put butter on her bread (because they never had it at the Cootamundra Home), or gently correcting Ming 'with a laugh and big black eyes fixed with shining intensity upon my face' as she explained the reason for the harsh treatment she and others received in Parramatta and Cootamundra – 'Because that's *prison*'.[6] Del had probably been extremely relieved by Ming's reaction to her original disclosure, and having breached such a formidable barrier between herself and her new mistress, she released a flood of other distressing personal memories. She would also have realized that by opening up in this way, she not only maintained and increased Ming's sympathies, but was providing Ming with ammunition for their battle with the Board.

Del described a life of deprivations and suffering in the Home, of how the meals were inadequate and 'the girls were all skinny & always getting sick. They were always hungry. We used to go to bed hungry & cold & shivering.' She described how 'their feet were cracked with chilblains in the winter & all night long they cried & whined at the pain of stone bruises'.[7] She also told Ming of how the girls tried various ruses to escape the constant regime of work:

Sometimes those poor little kids would say they was sick & stay in bed & I used to bathe them & take their temperatures & I thought they must be very tired & wanted a rest so made the thermometer go up by shaking it! & then show it to Matron! Once a girl lay in the sun & was very sick & had sunstroke & had to go to bed & have the Dr. & the next morning they were all crawling out of bed early to lie in the sun! & they all came in saying they felt sick & wanted to go to bed ... one day I saw a girl climb onto a tank & drop in through a hole in the top. After a bit she called loudly for help but I didn't go, & Matron came running out & got a ladder. I was laughing round the corner of the house as she climbed up & rescued the drowning? child! She was brought in & put to bed & had a lovely time! I wished I could think of something to do too ...[8]

Many of Del's recollections involved her concern for the younger children. In the Home the older girls were expected to take charge of them, but Del's accounts suggest that that they also supplied the small girls with their only source of affection. This would have particularly appealed to Ming's maternalism and certainly increased her sense of dismay and growing outrage at the practice of Board 'protection'. 'They were so *little* it used to make me cry,' Del told Ming. '*Gee* Mrs Strack, I could have *killed* that woman [the Matron] – & when they were all sent to bed cold & shivering & I wanted to go & tuck them in, she used to make me stand behind her chair & brush her hair & comb it. I would have liked to pull it as hard as I could ...' The Matron 'beat them with sticks & whips & blackened their eyes', Del told Ming, and once the cook had gone to the police because she thought the Matron was killing a child. '[T]hat old Matron was *cruel*. *Gee* she was a cruel woman, we hated her.'[9]

Claims of excessive violence by Matron Lamont (appointed in 1919) had been made by a white woman, Mrs Curry, who had begun working at Cootamundra as an assistant matron just prior to Del's arrival. She was almost certainly the 'cook' Del recalled, as it was the assistant matron's responsibility to train the girls in the kitchen. In May 1928 – a few days before Del was admitted to the Home – Mrs Curry had been to the Board to complain that

the children were 'flogged', 'slashed with a cane across the shoulders', and generally treated with undue severity and lack of sympathy, the use of the cane being a daily occurrence

among other physical abuses not recorded by the Board. The Board first tried to brush her aside with a note 'to inform her that her allegations were thoroughly investigated and found to be baseless', but was forced to grant her a hearing with the Chairman, Mr Childs. Having heard her, the Chairman 'informed Mrs Curry that as her statements lacked corroboration they must be regarded as unfounded and unjust. Mrs Curry then withdrew', and that was the end of the matter as far as the Board was concerned. Mrs Curry was promptly replaced by a Miss Tomkins. By the Board's inaction, the Cootamundra girls had to endure the Matron's sadism for another two years, until she resigned in 1930.[10]

Understandably, Del was cynical about the 'advantages' the girls were told they had:

> sometimes Miss Lowe came to stay with the Matron & would tell us how lucky we were to have such a 'kind Matron & such a lovely Home'!! She [i.e. the Matron] used to sit us all round & tell us that we had to be good [illegible] Jesus wanted us to be! & we wouldn't go to heaven if we weren't good either. We didn't *want* to go to heaven if she was going to be there. ... We hated to hear her talk about 'Jesus' too, cause next minute she was belting us. They used to have Guides & Brownies too (no wonder they called *us* 'Brownies'![)] We hated it. We used to make up a 'good deed' to tell the Lady, cause she was angry with us if we didn't tell her *something*![11]

The contrast between how she relayed Del's and Alma's experiences of institutionalization was dramatic. Ming's attitude underwent a fundamental shift in accepting and sympathizing with Del's disdain for Christian piety and menial work. Ming's awareness of Del as a separate individual with her own needs, desires and experiences was crucial in enabling her to feel, for the first time, a concern and indeed empathy for her worker, that were not based directly on her own interests and experiences. Her consciousness of Del as a unique individual only grew as Del revealed more and more to her.

Del disarmed Ming with candid disclosures – telling her of her dreams, for example, or of how she resented her mother for leaving her – and hilarious accounts of incidents in her life around the house, and even at the Cootamundra Home. Read aloud, stories such as the time Del took off on an uncontrollable motorbike incautiously left near the Cootamundra Home, scattering children, and eventually riding round and round a tree until the petrol ran out, capture a sense of her irrepressible good humour. Ming was captivated by Del's prettiness and vivacity. Though she had photographed Mary on a number of occasions, Ming never described Mary's physical appearance (nor Alma's) at all; now she began to pay increasing attention to detail in describing Del's manner and looks. In one particularly long entry she affectionately described how the light played on Del's face and the endearing (if stereotypically 'native') way she stood as she talked – 'one hand gracefully resting upon the mantelpiece, she balanced upon one foot the other being tucked up under the knee'.[12]

Many of Ming's private writings about Del demonstrate her motherly affection for her. Significantly, of the four servants who worked for Ming, only Del ate with the family on a regular basis. However, Del resisted Ming's attempts to treat her as 'her little girl', telling Ming to not to buy her gifts but to get something for her own daughters, for instance; insisting on replacing a jug she had broken[13] – even though the age difference between them would have made a maternalistic relationship relatively realistic. While Ming admired Del's defiant spirit, Del forced her to relate to her as a full and complex person with her own mind, and not as a humble and acquiescent maid.

* * *

From mid-1933, as Del's health improved, personal tensions were developing between the two women, revolving around Ming's increasing worries about her ability to protect Del and to monitor her relations with white men.

In July 1933, after the cessation of the mysterious harassment at the Pymble house, Del had begun seeing the local grocer's boy, the young fellow who delivered the Stracks' fruit and vegetables. He was 'quite decent', wrote Ming, 'he came to me quite openly and straightforwardly and asked my permission (after the first time) to see her' and Del 'was quite happy and contented'. Ming did make a point of explaining to him that Del was 'a half-caste'. White men who became involved with Aboriginal women at this time in Australian history were considered 'degenerates' in the harsh racial ideology of eugenics to which Ming and many others subscribed. Because the young man seemed polite and respectable, Ming assumed that he must have not realized that Del was Aboriginal. 'Cabbages', as Narrelle uncharitably nicknamed him, visited Del at Ming's house for 'a month or two' before leaving the district. Ming felt sorry for Del. 'Poor old Del,' she wrote, 'she craves companionship[;] she is forbidden to speak to other native girls on this line [i.e. other apprentices on the North Shore] and they to her and her loneliness almost amounts to pain'. Del's stomach complaint returned after her boyfriend left and Ming put her back on a 'milk diet'. She was not much help in the house, to Ming's frustration. 'I dare not let her do any heavy work – or any work at all in fact it is most distressing,' she wrote. 'How I wish that Board would pay the girl[;] how much longer must we wait?'

At this point in August 1933, the Stracks again moved house and returned to Turramurra. Here Ming became alarmed by the reaction of young men in the area to Del: 'People will talk to Del everywhere she goes, these larrikins speak to her and try to make appointments she has just told me of two I am afraid that any day they may succeed in getting her away.' Indeed, it seems that Del was being subjected to quite intense sexual harassment from certain local boys. 'Night after night,' bemoaned Ming in September of that year, 'I have found these degenerates standing at our gate and several times right in the garden, they whistle to her continuously Have even turned the hose upon them.' Some months later, Ming would record in her diary that a 'youth' rang Del from a public phone box. She had said, in exasperation, 'Haven't you learnt *yet* that you must not speak to this girl.' 'The reply came instantly, 'Oh yeah.' 'What can I do to protect this girl?' Ming asked herself. She had appealed to the police for help but was told 'it was not actually an offence'. Ming's fears that Del would be taken from her by these predatory white males reflected her own racist ideas of Aboriginal women's sexuality. She believed that Del would be easily 'tempted', not only because of her loneliness, but because Ming supposed her to have 'the strongest primitive instincts which are easily aroused'.

In December 1933, Del wanted Ming to go out for an evening walk with her. Ming, being 'irritable', refused to go and told Del she was not to go out alone. They argued, and Ming, now 'really angry', 'spanked her with my open hand' (my guess is that she slapped Del's face). At this Del left the house then rang the police, who accompanied her back to the Stracks. Del may have been fearful of Ming's reaction on her return – this was Ming's interpretation – but, even if the police themselves saw their role as only returning a miscreant servant, in going to the police Del sent a clear message that she would not accept abuse even from her. While Ming was confronted by Del's assertiveness, at the same time Del did win a new, albeit grudging, respect.

'She is a very gentle type of girl an unusual type,' Ming summed up Del's character, having described their argument, 'much more spirited than most Aboriginals and quite intelligent up to a point and with a very good memory she loves pretty things and knows how to wear them …'.

Because Del challenged Ming's assumptions of innate racial superiority, she depicted Del as an aberration. Ming's condescension to

'Aboriginal spirit' and, by implication, Aboriginal 'intelligence', is at least as revealing of her racism as it is of the strength of Del's response to Ming. Her musings on Del's 'love' of 'pretty things', and indeed her discussion of her as a 'type of girl' (both being signifiers of the mistress's position, standard to domestic service discourse), can be read as a way of reinforcing the hierarchy of class. While Ming was not averse to slapping her own daughters when they misbehaved, maintaining such class and race boundaries appears to have been a defence to the challenge Del posed to Ming's identity as a benevolent white mistress at this time. Significantly, Ming excised this entry from her own copy of the manuscript diary (it remains in the APNR copy held in the Sydney University archives) – an indication of how disturbing Ming found the incident in her own construction of her relationship with Del.

Ming's aggressive reaction to Del, and the whole excess of the argument itself, was no doubt related to the tension of waiting for the Board to take action on the wages issue. Pettitt had reiterated his demand that she complete the apprenticeship application form that same month. In January 1934, Ming received another reminder notice, informing her that she was now in arrears for £11 12s 9d, and threatening legal action.[14] Again, Ming did not respond, confident that should the Board attempt to prosecute her for non-payment of wages, she would not only be able to get Del's trust monies returned to her, but she would also be able to expose it publicly. Before she heard again from the Board, however, Del was once again involved in an unpleasant incident which confirmed Ming's misgivings about her ability to 'protect' her, and galvanized her into stepping up her protest against the Board.

10
You must not go against these people

At midnight, on 23 February 1934, Ming and Norman were woken by a phone call from the Hornsby police. Del had been seriously 'roughed up' by some youths, she had given the police their names and her attackers would be picked up within an hour. At the police station, Del told Ming that she had gone out earlier that night to meet a youth named Andrews. He had taken her to the local park,

> and as soon as they got inside the gate two other youths attacked her – they kicked her when she turned her back and punched her when she faced them – two of these fellows held her down on an 'ants' nest' ... she fought hard too and she certainly looked like it – they told her she was in a certain condition! and called her some dreadful names ...

The police had to wait for Detective-Sergeant Todd to arrive before they could bring the youths in for questioning, but when Todd did arrive he said, as he had done before, that Del was a 'liar', and again that 'she'll have to be got rid of! she's got to be mentally examined!' He added that she was a 'public nuisance' and he was 'going to hand her over to the Board's control'.

Todd told Ming that he knew 'all about' Del, having 'been to the Aborigines Board. I've got all her record from them.' He refused to authorize the Hornsby police to bring the youths Del had named in for questioning (despite the sergeant-in-charge's wishes) and asked Ming if she was 'game' to take Del to a public hospital to be examined. The Stracks drove Del to the hospital, Todd following in a police car. At the hospital a 'feeble looking lady Doctor' refused point blank to conduct a clinical examination of Del; the detective told her then to look at her for external bruising, which she did 'hurriedly', finding 'several sore spots' where Del had been punched or kicked in the stomach. Todd told Ming that two women police would take a statement from Del, and Ming told him that she had 'heard enough tonight' to convince her that the police and the Board were 'in league against this girl'. They got home at five o'clock in the morning when Ming made these entries in her diary.

The women police did not arrive. Norman wrote to Todd demanding to know what action he intended to take in regard to the assault and telling him he was forwarding a copy to Deputy Police Superintendent Mackay.[1] The next Monday Ming went to see Mackay, who said 'the matter would be investigated this time'. On the advice of Mrs Bryce, Ming called on the Vice-President of the APNR, David Stead; he advised her to go straight to Mr E. B. Harkness, Under-Secretary to the Colonial Secretary, and, having been first appointed in April 1916, the longest-serving member of the Board. Ming went straight to Harkness and, mentioning Stead's name, was ushered in to his office.

Harkness seemed 'very interested' in what she had to say and asked Ming was she thought of Miss Lowe. Ming 'described her with much gusto!' Then Harkness told her that, while he had not personally met Miss Lowe, he 'had felt for some time that possibly she was not the best one to be in this position and that quite a lot had come to his ears from time to time from "outside"'. 'I replied,' Ming recorded in her manuscript diary,[2]

> that we thought and the Public did generally that Miss Lowe *was* the Board! [W]e knew that Mr Childs was the chairman but had never heard of anyone else. Miss Lowe simply informs the girls and the employers that all [A]boriginals belong to her – no one else has anything to do with them. [T]hey are terrified of her. She is like a fearful 'Ogre' who rules their poor miserable little li[v]es and they become perfectly dumb in her presence ...

Harkness listened, then said, 'I am a member of this Board you know and it looks to me as tho' there was a bit of dictatorship going on here. I think I'll send for Pettitt – you don't mind do you?' Ming replied, 'Not at all, of course' (she 'was extremely glad, really').

Pettitt duly arrived, looking 'somewhat green' according to Ming, and clutching several bundles of documents.

Harkness demanded to know if Pettitt considered Miss Lowe a 'suitable person' to be employed by the Board. 'Yes, sir,' Pettitt replied, and told Harkness that she had held the position for over 20 years.

'That does not say she is a suitable person,' replied Harkness. Did Pettitt see that she 'did her job properly', as was his 'duty'?

'Oh yes. She always gives them [the Aboriginal apprentices] the opportunity to speak to her alone.'

'How do you know? Do you go with her yourself when she visits the girls?'

'No.'

'Look here, Pettitt. I think – to use the vulgar language of the street – that Miss Lowe has you in the bog.'

Pettitt was affronted. 'That's a nice thing to say to a man, sir!'

'Well, Pettitt, I'm going to talk straight to you and I don't think Miss Lowe *is* treating these girls in the humane and kindly manner that they have the right to expect from the employees of the Board. I hear things you know and sometimes I listen and I am very interested also. I happen to know all about a certain woman at Vaughn Park. Del's previous employer –'

'She was Miss Lowe's friend and Mr Pettitt's personal friend Mr Harkness!' Ming piped up. Harkness ignored her.

'She is absolutely unfit to have a native girl in her employ. I am being perfectly open with you Pettitt, and you mark my words I know what I am saying. Is there an Aboriginal girl there now?'

Pettitt, after a moment's thought, said no – although, as Ming wrote and the Board records confirm, 'Miss Lowe had told Del and I that this woman *had* another girl.'

Pettitt took from his papers a letter from Mr Childs' office and handed it to Harkness. It was the letter claiming that Ming had refused to go to Childs' office. Ming then went through the entire story of *that* encounter for Harkness, describing how the police orderly had bullied them into going to see Pettitt to arrange the appointment with Dr Booth. In the telling she managed to describe Pettitt as an 'earthworm or a doormat', as well as how dreadfully ill Del had been.

'Well really,' said Harkness. 'If this is true there is room for investigation here.'

Ming explained that she had no intention of returning Del to the Board as directed. 'All the girl has wanted for months past was peace and companionship and protection none of which she can ever have [here] – I want to send her to Nortown to her own people whom she would love to see and I must first get her money from the Board, they will not pay her.'

Harkness turned again to the Board Secretary. 'Now Pettitt, is there any reason why Mrs Strack should be treated in this extraordinary manner? Have you anything against her?'

'No, sir.'

'Well, it will be quite all right to do as Mrs Strack asks with the girl. She can go to Nortown for a holiday and return later and you can pay her some of her money – she would like some pretty things to take home – a pair of stockings for her mother, perhaps. Is that all right, Pettitt?'

'No,' said Pettitt. 'The police went won't let her go to Nortown.'

'Why not? You will write at once to Nortown, Pettitt, and let me know. You should have a reply in the next few days – and if she can't go there, I suggest Quirindi as I know the manager there and he's a very fine man. Will that suit you, Mrs Strack?'

'Yes,' Ming replied. 'That will do splendidly, except that I want her to have *all* her money.'

'Oh now, come, Mrs Strack, you know quite well we couldn't pay this in a lump as someone would instantly hear about it and get it from them.'

'I can't see there is any difference between someone else getting it and the Board sticking to it – when do they get the rest?'

'Well,' Harkness replied. '*Some* time, they get paid.'

Ming was scathing. 'Do you mean that someone goes round the country rounding up the girls who have not received their money and who are afraid to ask for it? I consider that it is pure exploitation, Mr Harkness.'

'Oh no,' he said. 'Not exploitation – they *are* paid some time.'

'They are *not* paid and it *is* exploitation,' insisted Ming.

Harkness sighed. 'Well don't worry about it any more, Mrs Strack. I'll do what I can and Pettitt will enquire about Nortown – I'll let you know within the next few days.'

Ming departed 'feeling much happier on Del's behalf'. She told Del when she got back home that she would 'soon have her money or some of it' and they would have a day in town shopping. Del 'was delighted at the thought of seeing her people again,' Ming wrote.

Having told Ming he would get back to her in a few days, Ming waited a week before hearing from Harkness, but his news was only a brief message that Del would have to pay her fare home out of her own money. Another week passed without event. Then, on 16 March 1934, two police officers came to the Stracks' door while they were having dinner. They had come to take Del, they said, she was to go on the mail train that night for Nortown.

Claiming to have a warrant, they presented a letter marked 'Urgent Matter' in red, signed by Pettitt, instructing them to remove Del and put her on the train, making her fare payable to the Board. Detective Todd had written across the top to notify the Nortown police. The Stracks were 'perfectly dumbfounded', then Norman pointed out that this was not a warrant.

'Well she will not be going with you tonight or at any time,' said Ming to the police, 'they won't get her from my hands until her record is cleared and she receives her money from this Board.'

My great-aunt Helen, then ten years old, remembers vividly and with great pride the sight of Ming, small and furious, standing between Del and the police. Taking Pettitt's letter from them, Ming went to the phone and rang Harkness.

Harkness now denied knowing anything about Pettitt's letter. 'I'm just about to have my dinner and I don't know what they have been doing this week – I've been away ill.' Ming pleaded with him to do something.

'I'm sorry, Mrs Strack, I can't do anything – you must not go against these people,' he warned her. 'Now be sensible or you will be in serious trouble. You had better let her go.' Harkness told her he had only spoken to her because Mr Childs was away, and that she had better speak to him. Ming rang off, disgusted ('what a man') and returned to the police 'very crestfallen but still determined not to part with Del'. She sent the police away after a lecture '– they went at last, were quite friendly and feeling uncomfortable I think. I felt rather sorry for them on thinking the matter over – for they are all being made fools of – by this Board.' Then she rang Eric Campbell, who was now back from his overseas trip.

The New Guard leader told Norman and Ming to come and see him at his home at once. From there Campbell rang Todd and advised him to do nothing further until Campbell himself had seen Mr Childs and the Colonial Secretary, the Hon. F. Chaffey.

* * *

What Ming did not know was that two months prior to her interview with Harkness, the Board had approved a draft of proposed amendments to the Aborigines' Protection legislation. These directly related to cases such as Del's, where an Aboriginal worker had managed to evade Board control by taking refuge in the household of a sympathetic employer. The Board proposed the insertion of clauses to the section dealing with apprenticeships, giving the Board the authority to terminate such employment and to 'remove the Aborigine concerned to such Reserve, Home or other place as it may direct'. Another two new clauses related to the payment and recovery of wages. One enabled the Board, at its discretion, to direct *any* employer to pay the worker's wages to the Board's Secretary; the other enabled an officer of the Board, or a police officer, or any other person authorized by the Board, to institute and carry out proceedings against any employer who refused such direction for the recovery of the wages. These three clauses, which had been circulated amongst the Board members in December 1933, effectively covered Del's case. If enacted in legislation, they would have allowed the Board to enforce Del's removal and to act against Ming for non-payment of wages into Del's trust account, even though she had not signed the contract for Del's indenture.

It seems highly likely that Del's case (among others perhaps, such as the Bryces' worker) was uppermost in the mind of Commissioner Childs, and no doubt of Pettitt also, who as Secretary had had a major role in drawing up the proposed amendments. And Harkness would have been aware of the direction in which the Board was heading at the time that he interviewed Ming, not just because he was a Board member, but because, as Under-Secretary to the Colonial Secretary, it was his responsibility to ensure that the draft amendments were presented to the Colonial Secretary.[3] One can only assume that Harkness had failed to make the connection between Ming's story and the proposed amendments (which were eventually enacted in 1936, by which time Mackay had taken over from Childs as both Police Commissioner and Board Chairman) and it must have been his turn to look 'somewhat green' when Childs returned. That is, if the whole thing were not an elaborate charade played out by these two most powerful figures on the Board.

Childs' secretary at the Police Department rang Ming the next day (a Saturday) to say that Childs wanted to interview her *or* her husband in his office on Monday morning. When Ming asked if he had spoken to Campbell, she was put on hold; the secretary returning to say that Childs had just spoken with her solicitor, and the Commissioner suggested that she see Campbell before the appointment with Childs. Ming replied that that was 'exactly what we intended to do and I hoped that our previous treatment upon visiting Mr Childs would not be repeated', to which the secretary said, 'Perhaps *Mr* Strack had better come'. Shortly afterwards, Campbell rang to tell Ming that

Childs 'had some evidence from local youths which gave the girl a very bad character'.

* * *

Considering Campbell's position as New Guard leader, his intervention with the Police Commissioner on Ming's behalf is worthy of comment. There is no suggestion that the New Guard movement ever took any interest (positive or negative) in Aboriginal issues. The New Guard was still functioning at this time, although its significance as a political force had waned somewhat following the dismissal of NSW Labor Premier Lang in May 1932 and the installment of the United Australia Party–Country Coalition under Premier Stevens in his place.

Back in 1931, at the peak of the New Guard's activities, the 'peculiar inaction' of Childs in dealing with the New Guard had impelled Premier Lang to send him on long-service leave. Acting in Childs' place, Police Superintendent Mackay had managed to infiltrate the New Guard, enabling the NSW Police Department to begin preparing a charge of seditious conspiracy against Campbell and six other prominent New Guard members. (He had also passed on his detectives' reports on the organization to the Sydney *Smith's Weekly*, allowing that paper to publish a comprehensive list of the New Guard's members in October 1931, so blowing their secrecy.) The Lang Labor government announced it would be holding a commission of inquiry into the New Guard's activities, while the Federal government announced its intentions to hold a Royal Commission into allegations associating the New Guard with the Defence Department. But the proposed Royal Commission had been shelved after Lang's controversial dismissal, as were the New Guard's plans for a revolutionary uprising. The Federal United Australia Party Lyons ministry represented a new, conservative party that had come to power in 1932 against an incumbent Labor government (and would eventually become today's Australian Liberal Party) whose ties to the ultra-right militias were, if not visible, certainly plausible. (Ming, for her part, considered Lyons and especially the new UAP leader in New South Wales B. S. B. Stevens to be politically sympathetic.) Stevens' government, which took over from Lang in New South Wales, allegedly issued a cabinet minute to the Police Department directing the police to discontinue all investigations into the New Guard. According to the foremost historian of the New Guard movement, the Police Department, 'under Mackay's direction, clearly wished to proceed with the conspiracy charge irrespective of Lang's dismissal', but the Stevens government intervened to protect the New Guard in return for their support for the UAP.[4] So it would appear that at the time Ming approached Campbell, Childs, and especially his deputy Mackay, were his traditional enemies, and furthermore, that Campbell had shown himself to be more politically astute than they.

However, going by Campbell's own account, his relationship with the police authorities – in particular with Mackay, whom he characterized as 'the dominant personality in the force' – was somewhat more complex. 'The strange thing,' Campbell later wrote, 'was that in spite of now all too frequent brushes, we not only avoided being personally hostile but actually became, under the surface, quite good friends and on a Christian name basis.' He even claimed to have personally persuaded Mackay on one occasion to release eight New Guard members who had been arrested for putting up billposters.[5] Even allowing for Campbell's tendency to self-aggrandizement, it does seem that he enjoyed a cordial relationship with the Commissioner and Superintendent, particularly after two years of Stevens' government.

Probably, Campbell thought it a fairly harmless yet kindly exercise to help one of his members' 'womenfolk', as he termed them, to gain an interview with them. His intervention was not seen by Police Commissioner Childs as a threat – he went so far as to advise Ming and Norman to see Campbell before going to the Police Department. As it turned out, Campbell tried to talk Ming out of her involvement.

* * *

On the Monday, Campbell told the Stracks that Childs had statements from some youths that Del was 'a prostitute and has been soliciting and charging 1/-'. These statements were almost certainly taken from her attackers when the police investigated the assault and, combined with the statement Del had made about going to the park to meet her boyfriend, were now being used *against* her. Ming was not having it – if Del had been soliciting as alleged, she said, then the youths involved were guilty of an offence and should be charged. 'Well,' conceded Campbell, 'it opens up a good many points of law.' Indeed, the charge could also be used to protect Del's attackers from any future claims for maintenance should she in fact be pregnant. Under the 1909 Aborigines Protection Act, claims for child support from the father of a child by an Aboriginal apprentice could not be made if the court was 'satisfied that at the time the child was begotten the mother was a common prostitute'. Then Campbell told Ming that Childs had told him that neither the Board nor the police had jurisdiction over Del as she was *eighteen*. This must have certainly come as a surprise to Ming, but she quickly pointed out:

> In spite of *this* they tried to take her and send her penniless to Nortown 12 hours previously. Surely Mr Campbell something can be done to protect this girl – with such a record as they have given her and without money clothes or even food it would only be a matter of an hour perhaps before the police at Nortown (if they did really intend sending her there?) would find grounds for arresting her ...

'When I read in Pettitt's letter [the one the police produced as a warrant] that her "mother" would meet her,' Ming continued, 'it seemed to me that there was a deliberate attempt to mislead the police and me since Del has no mother and she told Constable Walsh this herself.' (Del's mother was alive, as Ming knew, so presumably she meant that Del – who had confided in Ming her resentment of her mother – did not recognize her mother as such.) Campbell agreed that it did 'on the face of it look strange'. 'Anyhow,' he said, 'go along to Mr Childs and talk the whole matter over.'

Campbell warned Ming, somewhat tentatively, as they were leaving that he thought that Childs 'wanted to see *Mr* Strack', and sure enough when they arrived at Childs' office, they were once again refused admission by the police orderly. As the Chairman of the Aborigines Protection Board, Childs' repeated avoidance of Ming and Del was significant.

Deputy Commissioner Mackay then came out, saying that Childs was busy and going out, and that he had been sent to interview them instead. Childs could not 'waste his time over trivial matters of this kind'. When Ming protested that this was a 'very serious matter', involving 'scandalous' behaviour by the Board, Mackay told her that she 'was not to come there making wild statements and imagining that I could hold up the entire police force when they had important matter[s] to attend to ... and they have had some evidence against this girl which settles the matter.'

'I said,' wrote Ming, 'Mr Mackay would you rely upon the evidence of degenerates? These low type whites have not only [called] night after night but have come right into the garden to get Del to go away with them. I have driven them off myself, doesn't this make a difference?'

Mackay, offended, rose in his chair. 'How *dare* you say the Police are liars to me, Mrs Strack?' he 'bellowed and roared'. 'I refuse to discuss this with you'.

'I reminded him that we had not asked to discuss this with *him* but with Mr Childs,' wrote Ming, 'and he sat down and would not speak to me at all but asked Mr Strack to tell him what we wanted'. Norman then asked 'why the police allowed themselves to be made fools of by the employees of the Board and a number of other things and that it was Mr Childs' duty as chairman of the Board to inquire into this matter. It was illegal for the police to enter our home without a warrant and that Del Malloy had no mother. Mr Mackay said what else?'

'I insist …,' began Ming.

'Don't you come here *insisting* upon anything.'

It was 'horrible and most humiliating for us both,' wrote Ming. Norman 'wanted to drop the whole matter, he is disgusted. I tried again':

'But I don't want to make more trouble just to …'

'Am I speaking or are you?'

The interview continued to spiral into a shouting match 'and we were all saying anything but what we intended to say'. Eventually, Ming asked 'humbly and meekly' if she might tell him of what Mr Harkness had said, 'naturally I would not and could not speak of this anywhere else but I thought he should know,' she demurred. Mackay listened as Ming told him what Harkness had said to her in front of Pettitt, concerning Mrs Smith being 'unfit to have a native girl in her employ'. 'Does this not put a somewhat different complexion upon the terrible record these people have [given] this girl, Mr Mackay?'

Mackay changed tack:

'Now Mrs Strack, do let this matter drop, don't worry about it anymore, you will be losing your health over it and Mr Strack will be ill too. You've got this thing on your mind and can speak and think of nothing else, it's not fair to Mr Strack to give him Aboriginals for "breakfast, dinner, and tea" – I wouldn't allow my wife to do it.'

'But you won't understand,' Ming protested. 'The girl who I believe is innocent is simply doomed if I cannot clear her name somehow. She is so utterly alone[,] cannot you do something about it? We have always been told that she must make these statements and now it is simply evidence against herself – the Board should be made to do likewise.'

'No they shouldn't and you can't go back over a year to things that happened then, there's a law that prevents that and you will be in a libel action if you do,' said Mackay. 'People have been in here complaining about your statements to me.'

'I *will* protect and defend her,' Ming retorted fiercely, '… *no* one has ever been punished for injuring Del, *she* is always the guilty one, yet nothing has ever been proved against her till now. [I]nstead of punishing these degenerate renegades your men take statements which out all the blame upon her once more. ... I shall go right to the bitter end with this matter.'

Mackay just laughed, asking if she had she any money, and saying, 'I think you have been reading a nice Detective story now haven't you?'

Mackay's contempt reveals the way in which the authorities at the time saw those women who employed apprentices as subordinate to the control of their husbands, who were expected to silence their wives firmly should they become overly and outspokenly concerned with the welfare of their Aboriginal charges. It was undoubtedly this that explained the insistence that Norman, rather than Ming, should be received by the Chairman. Describing her feelings afterwards, Ming wrote that while she felt humiliated and 'thoroughly crushed' by Mackay; she was nevertheless 'very glad' that she had accompanied her husband. In his 'present mood they would have had little trouble convincing him that he was up against a wall and that it was not nice to be mixed up in a matter of this kind'. Ming apparently saw Norman as the weaker party, continuing that *she* remained determined to fight: 'I cannot give in now[;] it may save some other poor little native girl from unhappiness if it cannot save Del.' In fact, Norman's support for Ming throughout her battle so far on Del's behalf was quite remarkable. But the effect of Campbell's and Mackay's comments seemed to have considerably dampened his enthusiasm, as Ming does not mention his further involvement in Del's case.

By this point it was obvious that they *were* 'up against a wall', the combined forces of the Board's Chairman and Police Commissioner, the Deputy Police Commissioner, the Board's Secretary and 'Home-finder', and influential police and medical authorities. Del's initial opponents, Mrs Smith and her son, had receded into the background; the issue of her rape had been completely sidelined. In fact, no action of any kind would ever be taken against the young man who had raped Del, nor was any action ever taken against the Board, or the government, for their fraudulent and corrupt actions.

By now a successful prosecution of Ritchie Smith was virtually impossible, with Del's two conflicting statements, her fabricated 'bad record' and the latest 'evidence' in the Chairman's hands. It is unlikely that the Board was at all concerned about it. What remained a problem was the potential damage to the Board arising from Ming's public exposure of maladministration by salaried employees – her 'wild statements' concerning the lack of adequate 'protection' from abuse of Aboriginal women in service, and the irregularities and lack of accountability in the management of the trust fund system. Ming was far from being intimidated by what appeared to be a cover-up between Board members, the administration and the police. Rather, it served only to strengthen her conviction that there was something drastically amiss in the policies of the NSW state towards Aboriginal people, and that she *had* to do something about it.

11

There is a lot of dark girls that went through it

On 27 March 1934, just one week after the meeting with Mackay, Ming gave an informal talk at a prominent, Sydney-based women's organization, the Feminist Club. 'The Aborigines Protection Board,' Ming told her audience,

> deals wholesalely with young [A]boriginal girls. They are taken from their natural protectors, their parents, to work in homes in the suburbs of Sydney and elsewhere. Any degenerate white renegade can prey on them and escape the law, while the unfortunate girl, instead of receiving protection from the Aborigines Board, is dubbed a devil, a fiend and a liar.
>
> When an [A]boriginal girl gets into trouble, or summons enough courage to ask the Board for the money she has earned, and which is held in trust for her, she is sent for a 'holiday'. And she never comes back.[1]

Ming's decision to go to the women's movement for help in her defence of Del marked a significant shift in terms of her seeking broader support. In the first instance, she had simply brought the matter to the Board; the hostility she encountered there took her to the police, and then the Police Commissioner himself, with a consummate lack of success. Now, she went to the contemporary feminist movement. Perhaps Mackay's response as much as anything had sent Ming in this direction.

Back in July 1933, when Ming had first begun making approaches to various individuals and groups on Del's behalf, she had received an assurance from the president of the Feminist Club, Millicent Preston-Stanley, that she was 'ready to do anything to help'. Ming was a personal friend of Preston-Stanley ('I love & admire her,' she wrote on another occasion), and in 1933 she was Preston-Stanley's 'Social Secretary' for her British Empire pageant.

Ming was not a member of the Feminist Club, though she had been invited to join in 1923. Instead, she was connected with another elite women's organization, Adela Pankhurst Walsh's Australian Women's Guild of Empire, having being the instigator of the formation of a Pymble branch in the mid-1920s. Ming withdrew her membership of the Guild in June 1933, just days before Miss Lowe's visit to retrieve Del's pocket money book. Though the Guild leader's husband had been an early member of the New Guard movement who then denounced that organization as 'fascist', the timing of Ming's departure leads me to believe her decision was due to a conflict between her association with the Guild and the support Preston-Stanley was willing to offer. Adela Pankhurst Walsh had opposed the campaign for reform of the custody laws in January 1933, and as this was Preston-Stanley's preoccupation at the time, she would certainly have wanted Ming to disassociate herself from the Guild. There is no evidence that Ming ever approached the Guild for support for Del; her withdrawal was on the grounds that she had 'invalids' in the family and was too busy.[2]

At her talk at the Feminist Club Ming presented Del to the members, apparently purely as an exhibit, for it does not seem that Del herself spoke to the meeting. 'I took Del with me to the F. Club,' Ming noted, 'introducing her *after* the talk to the audience as "The fearful little criminal" who was so young when taken to the [Parramatta] Reformatory that she did not understand a thing about it ...'[3]

Just before displaying Del to the audience, Ming set the mood with a story Del had told her about how the attendants at the Parramatta Reformatory 'had lifted her upon the table asking her to put her arms around the one she loved best!'[4] Ming represented Del as she wished Del to be seen – an ill-treated, artlessly child-like victim of the Board's machinations – and represented herself as Del's untiring, self-sacrificing champion, the only one who stood between her and her bitterest enemies. Del was undeniably ill-treated, and equally undeniably in no position to challenge the Board single-handed. But it must be kept in mind that it was Del's initiative from the outset to approach Ming, and it was Del who had managed to convince Ming to keep her from the Board when Ming's every inclination was to send her back. One must not make the mistake of construing Del as a passive object in the whole drama simply because her voice is barely audible behind Ming's strident demand for her redress. If she was indeed as silent throughout the confrontation with the Board as Ming describes her, this was almost certainly because she recognized that such discretion was in her best interests.

Indeed, it seems that Del's humble demeanour at the meeting invoked the Club members' sympathies. 'Many of the people who were there that day had never seen a half-cast[e] or an Aboriginal!' Ming wrote afterwards, 'and they were full of pity for these people'.[5] A resolution was passed that the Club would 'stand behind any organization or society for the Protection of Native Races'; other women's organizations would be asked to cooperate and hold a public protest meeting. Ming was overwhelmed by the positive response they received and took heart:

> [T]hey showed such intense interest and were so horrified at the cruelty of our present system in regard to the Aboriginals and half-castes especially women that I feel if we could only follow this up with other meetings and protests from all the Societies who have the real welfare of these people at heart some notice would be taken of it … . We could easily get the other women's Clubs or organizations to join forces[;] it is only that people have not known about these things before and I feel sure that we will succeed in getting an enquiry into the infamous behaviour of the so called Aborigines Protection Board and its handling of the trust funds now – there were several reporters present at the Feminist Club and I told these as much as I safely could about Del's treatment etc.[6]

On this note Ming concluded the manuscript diary she had been compiling and sent it to Reverend Morley, Secretary of the Association for the Protection of Native Races. In a covering letter she informed him that she now paid Del's wages into a joint account in both their names because 'the Aborigines Board is untrustworthy and money paid *in* does *not* come *out* again – and I wish the girl to have her earnings she is *not* a slave'.[7] By this time the APNR was pressing for an investigation into the mismanagement of Aboriginal trust fund monies in Queensland, and Ming had realistic hopes the same might be achieved in NSW.

* * *

It was Morley who first suggested that Ming make her manuscript diary an affidavit, saying he would then organize a small APNR deputation to approach 'the authorities'. Despite Ming's enthusiasm for raising public awareness in order to bring about pressure for an enquiry into the Board, Morley cautioned her against 'widening the circle of those actively moving in the matter at present, and especially we ought to avoid, at the present stage, any newspaper publicity which might easily cause embarrassment'.[8]

Ming chose to ignore his advice and delivered a copy of her diary at the *Smith's Weekly* office in the 'middle of April' 1934. The news editor was excited and wrote up a version of the story himself, 'but at the last minute we found we could not run it, for some reason or other, (it's all bona fide I suppose?)'.[9] His response suggests some form of intervention; and in the article *Smith's Weekly* eventually published, in October (quoting Ming's speech to the Feminist Club), the writer mentioned that a Board official, when approached, had 'emphatically denied the charges made by Mrs. Strack',[10] which may have been related to the editor's withdrawal in April. (It is interesting to find that Ming had apparently hired Campbell 'to attend on' the Board's Secretary Pettitt in March and April, though she made no mention of this in her manuscript diary.[11]) Such a scandalous story would have made 'splendid reading', as the editor told Ming, but it could also have placed the paper in danger of offending powerful interests – including the NSW Police Commissioner.

On 17 April 1934, Ming attended an APNR executive meeting, at which a sub-committee was appointed to investigate Del's case. It consisted of the Bryces, a Salvation Army officer, Lieutenant-Colonel Howard, and Mr J. T. Beckett, the former Protector of Aborigines in Queensland (the latter two having been recently appointed executive members of the APNR). Ming attended a meeting of this sub-committee held on 26 April, where she told the 'whole story', leaving them each with a copy of her manuscript to 'peruse'. A fortnight later, Beckett wrote to her about preparing the diary as an affidavit, saying that he felt, on the basis of his Queensland experience, 'it is mainly, probably entirely correct'. Before going any further, however, he told Ming he would ask a Mr T. E. Roth to read it, forwarding it to Roth the same day with a letter advising that he found it 'most convincing'.[12]

The identity of Roth, addressed by Beckett as a 'worker in the same cause', is not clear. He was certainly not the former Chief Protector of Aborigines in Queensland, W. E. Roth, whom Beckett probably knew personally. W. E. Roth had died the previous year. Beckett probably meant the influential Sydney solicitor, financier and philanthropist, T. E. Rofe. An executive member of the APNR, Rofe was in attendance at the next APNR meeting on 15 May; when Ming attended another meeting of the sub-committee the following day, she found this now included Rofe, 'a solicitor', as a member. Rofe appears to have been the

APNR's adviser on politically sensitive matters in NSW.[13] As no letters from Rofe have been located, his opinion on the manuscript diary's legal worth is unknown, but Ming found that now he was involved, the sub-committee were 'a little afraid of the libel', although they assured her that they were 'going into Del's case thoroughly'.[14]

Meanwhile, Mrs Bryce had received a reply from Captain Couglan, a Salvation Army officer at Nortown, who had, he said, interviewed Del's grandmother, mother and aunt. Del 'had no bad record apart from would not go to school', he reported, and also gave the information that Del had been taken by the Nortown Sergeant of Police, with the consent of her grandmother, at the age of 13, giving a birth date for her. The date differs so slightly from the one recorded by the Board – the omission of one numeral for the day she was born – that it was probably a typographical error.[15]

What is curious is that this same Salvation Army officer, writing to Howard several months later in response to a request from *him* for information on Del's family, said that he had not found out Del's age because he had not yet spoken to 'her people'.[16] Presumably, then, the information he gave Mrs Bryce at this point was from another source – either the police or the Board itself.

Ming had suggested in her covering letter to Morley that the APNR find out Del's age and the circumstances of her childhood, possibly from her relatives at Nortown. Del's age was an important issue, given the Board Chairman's claim to Ming's lawyer that she was out of Board jurisdiction, yet, as Ming pointed out, the Board had attempted to remove her with police intervention *and* were still claiming that Ming owed wages to Del's trust account. Del herself was vague about her age, having told Ming she thought she was about nine or ten years old when first removed, which would have made her about 15 at the time Childs claimed she was 18.

Morley was actually in the midst of his correspondence with Del's first employer, Mrs Young of Burrendah, in northwestern NSW, and his own inquiries to her included the question of Del's age. He had written to Mrs Young's mother-in-law, listed by the Board as Del's employer between October 1930 and January 1932, prior to her transfer to the Smiths at Vaughn Park, but she had forwarded Morley's letter to her daughter-in-law, for whom Del had actually worked. It must therefore be conjectured that Morley had first approached the Board for information about Del, and had been advised – perhaps by Alice Lowe – to contact her old employer.

Just as there was collusion between the Board and Del's former employer Mrs Smith, it seems that there was some degree of collaboration between Del's first employer and the administration in attempting to silence Del and Ming. Mrs Young Jr. wrote a remarkably hostile letter to Morley in which it was evident that she had been informed in part of Del's supposed 'bad record'. 'Del was neither truthful nor trustworthy,' she wrote, '& it was not for a childish offence that Del & her cousin May had to be sent away from Nortown, for there [*sic*] behaviour was so bad, that had they not been sent to an Institution the would have been put in prison ...' Not only could Mrs Young recall the family relationship and even the church affiliation of the two girls (particularly remarkable in the case of May, who never worked for her), but this vague hint of the girls' unsavoury past strongly suggests that she had been in communication with Miss Lowe. Yet, despite her intimate knowledge of Del's background, Mrs Young was unable to answer the one question the APNR was particularly concerned with: she had 'forgotten' Del's age.[17] One might construe that the Board had asked her not to supply this crucial detail, as it in fact had recorded a birth date for Del. In effect, therefore, the Board was withholding this important information – indeed, one expects Morley would have inquired this of the Board originally.

The Board's own record, apparently made when Del was transferred to Cootamundra Home in May 1928, had her down as having just turned 13 at the time of her removal. The Child Welfare department on her admission to Parramatta reformatory recorded the same birth date. This would have made Del 18 in May 1933.

This conflicts with Del's own belief that she was removed when she was nine or ten. Confusingly, the not always reliable *NSW Pioneers Index* of births gives yet another birth year for Del (1916), making her twelve at removal, and 16 going on 17 when she began working for Ming. But the birth year calculated from her age as recorded on her death certificate, 1918, shows that Del consistently believed herself to be about ten when she was removed. Indeed, if Del had in fact just turned ten, rather than thirteen or even twelve, at the time she was removed, this makes the memory she told Ming, of being placed on a table by the attendants at Parramatta Reformatory, credible. It is also more consistent with Miss Lowe's original claim that Del had 'lived with men before she was ten years old, that is why I took her away from Nortown!!' – a claim that appears glaringly inconsistent if the Board did not remove her until she was some years older.

May's age was also obscure, although she was supposed to have been a year younger than Del. If the Board officials had decided to raise the girls' ages by a year or two in order to have them apprenticed out early (the age of apprenticeship being 14, not twelve or eleven), one might speculate that neither they nor the Board itself wished this to be exposed. Conversely, if they stuck to the story that Del had been apprenticed at 14, so turning 18 in 1933, there was no justification for their actions, as she was indeed out of their jurisdiction.

Del's former employer strenuously defended the Board's apprentice-ship policy, admonishing Morley for his remark that the Cootamundra girls were sent to the city unprepared for 'its dangers'. '[I]nstead of people being against the Board,' she asserted, 'they should do all in their power to help them. I write from experience with these girls as I have had them for years ...'[18] Mrs Young obviously had an interest in keeping in the Board's good books. She and her mother-in-law had worked out a smoothly functioning relationship with the Homefinder, which assured them a constant supply of servants. In fact, Miss Lowe had arranged Del's first indenture, to the mother-in-law in 1930, and so may well have falsified Del's age to do so.[19] Furthermore, as Mrs Young's own treatment of the young women who worked for her was exces-sively violent and abusive, it is not surprising she should want to brand Del as 'untruthful' and 'untrustworthy' just in case Del said anything against her.

Del had been 13 years old, as far as *she* knew, when she started work-ing at Burrendah. She joined Alice, recorded as 15, who had been work-ing there for over a year before Del's arrival. Another girl had been working with Alice five months earlier. This remarkably brave young woman had stood up to the younger Mrs Young when she tried to flog her with a stock whip, as she regularly did to the more timid Alice. 'Yes, you just hit me with that, but you see these pots: they'll go, I'll let everything go at you,' the girl had said. She was promptly transferred.[20] Del replaced yet another apprentice who was transferred the day after Del arrived: 'most unsatisfactory', the Board noted disapprovingly.[21] Del would have known both Alice and her two predecessors, as they had been at Cootamundra Home at the same time she was.

Del told Ming about the time she and Alice were 'inspected' by a local policeman:

> Mrs Young was all smiles & stood looking hard at them when he asked (before her) if they were quite happy there. Del said, *how* could we say 'she was an old devil to us & flogged Alice till she nearly died

– we were too frightened, *poor* girls.' We often wanted to run away &
did once.[22]

Del's aunt's impression of the treatment Del received at Burrendah was
far from favourable. Writing to Ming in September 1934, she told her:

> Myself & husband happened to be working not far from the Youngs
> home I heard Del was there I rang her up on the phone & was speak-
> ing to her for a few minuits I knew they were not treating her well I
> wanted to see her but I was told I could not see her a few days after
> my husband wanted to have a word with Del & Mr Young came to
> the phone he said to my husband what the Hell did he want to speak
> to Del for I heard from a girl after I left that they treated Del very
> cruel so that is the sort of people these poor unfortunate dark girls
> get sent to to get thrashed about with them there is a lot of dark girls
> up this way that went through it ...[23]

The abusive and hostile behaviour of Del's Burrendah employer was
indeed by no means unusual under the apprenticeship scheme, as
numerous oral histories from former apprentices attest. This pattern
of violence meant in effect the maintenance and continuation of the
apprenticeship system, such employers colluding with the Board in preventing their own exposure. While Ming's story shows that apprentices
and mistresses could work together against the Board, the Mrs Youngs
(and indeed Mrs Smith) demonstrate that the structure made alliances
between Board and mistress more likely. But as we shall see, the com-
pliant attitude taken by the APNR also prevented such public exposure
by the one body that was in a position to do so.

12

& so we are 'slave-owners'

In May 1934, Ming was thrilled to be introduced to a real flesh-and-blood 'little Missus'. She was at a fund-raising bridge party for the Sane Democracy Association, a right-wing, anti-Communist group. An elderly woman, Mrs Tenny, had previously lived in the Northern Territory – 'the only white woman for hundreds of miles'. Having 'at once asked [her] about my beloved Aborigines' and expecting an equally fond rejoinder, Ming was shocked by Mrs Tenny's response. Mrs Tenny's husband had been the manager of a Bovril meat works, and she told Ming that 'we always had them working on our Stations ... . We had a string of Stations from the Territory to Adelaide & they worked for us in hundreds'.

'I said, "I suppose you could hardly have done without them?"

"No," replied this lady, "& it made me mad, after my husband died I went to London for a trip & *there* would you believe it, people actually had the audacity to stand up at drawing room meetings & others & say that we were '*Slave* owners'."

I said, "& so we *are*! just exactly *that*, we take these tiny black children from half-starved parents to lonely 'Homes' later to exploit them."'

To Mrs Tenny's disbelieving reply – 'Oh I've never heard of *that*, I'm sure we *don't*' – Ming told her of how she was unable to get Del's wages paid out by the Board. Mrs Tenny had heard of the APNR though, and went on to ridicule the claim made by Morley (probably in the London drawing room) that 'natives' in Australia were forced to work at gunpoint:

'"What *nonsense*, there are so many of them *wanting* to work that you can't give it to them all, but they all *live* on the Station & we feed them."

'I said, "did you always pay them or pay the Board?" The reply was "no we didn't *pay* them! 'Money' was no good to them!"'

'This is *one* way in which to make money – no wonder the Bovril firm had accumulated wealth!!' thought Ming to herself.

'I said "I think that a good deal of the trouble in the North has been caused by foreigners, they come out to the sacred land of the natives & steal their 'lubras' [women] –"

"Pooh!" said Mrs T. "They don't need to *steal* them[,] the men *give* them away! anyone can have a lubra for a small gift or two! They often have competitions with the pick of a lubra as a prize!"'[1]

'Oh how unbearably wicked it all is,' Ming reflected in her diary, '& so hopeless to make these people feel shame.' Mrs Tenny went on to quiz Ming about the 'boards', of which she also had not heard. 'I told her that *these* were the slave owners & exploiters, far more so than the man on the land who, to a certain extent, was forced to get the natives' assistance, but surely they had the right to *some* compensation for their lost & sacred land & tribal ground?'[2]

Ming's conversation with this woman, who represented her counterpart 'on the frontier', was quite significant at this juncture in her life. Challenged by all that she was learning from Del, Ming was developing an articulate construction of her image of the 'good fella missus' on which she modelled herself; and she was devouring the APNR material that the Bryces passed on to her about the mistreatment of Aboriginal people in the Northern Territory.

Two things had just happened in May 1934 that were of great personal significance to Ming. First, her grandmother, Maggie Hobbes, now living in Sydney, took to her deathbed. Ming set up a vigil, reminiscing over the remarkable stories the old lady had told her and her family of her life, especially of her relationships with the Yuin.[3] Indeed Ming wrote her 'little Missus' entry two days after meeting Mrs Tenny.[4] Second, two days *earlier*, Ming had found Mary again.

'I have written to her,' Ming wrote in her diary, 'dear old Mary! How I should love to see her ...'[5] Almost certainly Ming had tried to contact Mary in order to help her in her campaign against the Board, especially as she had contacted Mary's solicitor at Bairnsdale at the same time. The manager at Lake Tyers Aboriginal mission had responded to her query, informing her Mary was back at Brungle station in NSW with her husband. Convinced now that the Board had exiled Mary to avoid paying out her trust fund, and regretting having not taken the Board to court herself, in Brisbane,[6] Ming was also anxious to reaffirm her sentimental view of the mistress–servant relationship.

Now, by comparing herself as an employer under the Board to a mistress whose employment of Aboriginal workers was independent of government intervention, she was able to distance herself from her ironic self-inclusion as a 'slave owner'. Instead she cast the Board as the agent of exploitation, but Mrs Tenny's refusal to admit her duty as an employer to pay wages, and her condoning of the casual sexual usage of Aboriginal women, was a rude confrontation of her idealized image of the white woman employer.

It is interesting that Ming's response was to point out the obligations white landowners owed to the Aboriginal people for their dispossession. This was the first instance I have found of Ming mentioning the alienation of Aboriginal people from their land and one wonders how she would have incorporated this into her view of her grandparents. The implication is that she believed that white landowners were morally bound to provide paid employment and protection (for women) from sexual abuse in compensation for the loss of their land.

However, she did not discuss her grandmother with Mrs Tenny, turning instead to the subject of Daisy Bates, a writer on Aborigines and a woman whom Ming fervently admired, who had recently been honoured by an audience with King George V and. As it turned out, Mrs Tenny knew Daisy Bates, having employed Bates' husband 'Dick'[7] as a stockman on her property. '[S]he's an awful woman,' Mrs Tenny told Ming, '... everyone was sorry for old Dick, fancy having a wife who "went Black"!'

Ming was outraged, but her admiration for Bates was increased. Daisy Bates was a 'brave woman', Ming concluded in her diary, who had 'the courage to fight for a defenceless people, in spite of the objections & obstacles put in her way by *her* husband & *his* employers who naturally did not wish to be deprived of their unpaid labour!'[8] Ming was clearly shifting in her identification with the privileged respectable 'missus' towards the rather more ambiguous white female role model of Daisy Bates. Even as she was lauded in the popular press at the time, Bates' decision to live alone among the Aboriginal people challenged colonial and patriarchal restraints on white women's role and activities. One also detects a faint hint of dissatisfaction with her own husband in Ming's reference to Dick Bates.

Indeed, Ming was becoming increasingly frustrated by the 'objections & obstacles' placed in *her* way, and particularly with the APNR's inaction: '[A]m in a predicament about Del too,' she wrote in her diary towards the end of May 1934, 'they are so slow in their investigation & I *cannot* afford to keep her on & on like this'.[9] Norman was having difficulty, he said, getting enough business in his freelance advertising work to pay the rent on their Turramurra house, and had told her that they would have to move. He insisted they take up a friend's offer for Ming and the girls to live rent-free in a cottage at Blackheath in the Blue Mountains, west of Sydney.[10] In early June Ming wrote a letter to Rofe urging him to speed up the investigation; she had not yet been told what the Salvation Army report contained.[11] Ten days later, Norman deposited Ming, Del, Narrelle and Helen at Blackheath, and returned to Sydney with Peter to stay with Ming's parents.

Although Rofe it seems did not reply to Ming's letter, Beckett reported to her towards the end of the month, after the next meeting of the APNR (which Ming did not attend), that a deputation was to visit the Chief Secretary Chaffey. Beckett was not optimistic about their chances – 'one cannot hope for very much for cold-blooded bureaucracy seems to dominate the situation' – and he told her that Del would not be able to sue the Board for her wages as she was under 21.[12] The will of the APNR to deal with Del's case seemed paralysed at this time. In fact, unbeknown to Ming, the only object of the deputation was to ask that an APNR representative and 'a lady member' should be added to the Board membership;[13] there would be no further reference to Del in the APNR's minutes over the next four months.

Ming's prospects of exposing the Board's malpractice and mismanagement seemed increasingly bleak. But as she waited impatiently, Ming was moving to the view that Aboriginal women did not want or need the protection of white mistresses, but rather the right to remain within their own families and communities. This view would become more sharply focused as she encountered extraordinary difficulties getting Del returned to her people.

* * *

As Ming prepared to leave Sydney with her daughters and Del in mid-1934, her relationship with Del was suffering under the strain of constant waiting. Following the assault in February 1934, Ming had redoubled her efforts to exercise constant vigilance over Del, writing of how Del was 'living the life of a prisoner'. And the harassment Del was suffering had recently extended to the youngest member of the Strack family. While out with Del, nine-year-old Helen was slapped in the face and called a 'bloody nigger' by a brother or friend of one of Del's attackers. Ming, already feeling guilty about the effect on her children of her campaign to get justice for Del, was extremely upset to find her own daughter subjected to racist abuse and 'decided at once that Del must go' – it was this incident that had prompted the letter to Rofe:

> Del also was weeping & said 'I know, it's all my fault, they always say those things to me when I am out with Helen & she tried to stop them! it doesn't matter for *me* I *am* a "nigger", but how *dare* they do it to Helen.'[14]

Del's sudden tearful capitulation averted Ming's obviously hitherto repressed hostility towards her, but evidently, at the back of Ming's mind, she blamed Del for what had happened in February, and resented her.

The following weekend, Ming, Del and the two girls moved to the Blue Mountains. There, Ming's freshly expressed anger towards Del continued to spill over in the pages of her diary. '[T]oday I feel too tired even to get up,' she wrote three days after their arrival:

> will have a well earned rest I think & let Del do the work[;] she is big & strong now, & I have nursed her long enough. She is in a curious mood today, is getting restless, hates Blackheath & wants to get out of the house. She cannot do this without me – owing mainly to her own stupidity. She will only be here a short time now I hope ...[15]

As it turned out it would be another four months before Del returned to Nortown. According to Ming, she refused to allow Del even to step out of the house for three of those months, and then only in her company.[16]

However, Ming had left Del essentially to her own devices, minding Narrelle, for three weeks during July while she was in Sydney with Helen – a not inconsiderable responsibility, although Ming asked the nuns from a convent next door to keep an eye out for them. (Helen was in hospital in Sydney for an appendix operation.[17]) Del wrote cheery letters to them both from Blackheath, assuring Ming she was doing lots of housework and going to bed early.[18] Narrelle, now 14 years old, was enjoying having Del all to herself – and Del was too, judging by the humorous cartoons she drew at the time, depicting the girls reading in bed together in front of the fire, cooking and doing 'slimming exercise'.[19] Narrelle wrote to ask Ming if she could stay home from school on the Friday (Ming had enrolled her and Helen at the convent school[20]) 'because if Del is going to clean the house out and make a cake, I could help her. Will we make a rainbow cake or a sponge ...'[21] Ming apparently wrote to Narrelle suggesting that she would arrange for someone to come and stay with them, whereupon Narrelle replied hastily there was no need: 'Del and I are very quiet, and don't run around outside ... . Del keeps the house nice and clean ... and there [is] enough bread to do us for a year.'[22] Ming was very pleased with Del when she returned, gratified that she had been so 'absolutely good & reliable' in her absence.[23] Del told her that she had had two letters from her family while Ming was away and they were getting ready for her return.[24]

Bettune Bryce wrote to Ming in August, reporting that she had brought up Del's case again at the APNR meeting that month. 'Our only plan at the moment,' she admitted, 'was to see Chaffey questioning the suitability of Miss Lowe ... . They will ask what qualification she had for the job etc.'[25] Ming decided to write to a United Australia Party politician, Joseph Jackson, the minister for local government. She outlined what had happened since Del was with her, and asked him if he would put the question in Parliament 'why the Abo. Board is permitted to bring these children to the cities, where they do *not* receive protection & where they have difficulty in obtaining the money which is theirs – it is pure exploitation'.

'The right place for these children,' she went on, 'is with their own parents or relatives & where they are not exposed to every white degenerate who cares to have dealings with them.' She also asked if he could procure a concession railway pass for Del and if he could also ask in Parliament if the Board invested the trust funds, and 'whether the people employed by the Board and the Board members themselves, have the necessary qualifications for this position. We would very much like to know, in fact we have *the right* to know, how & *why* they are elected.'[26]

In turning to a politician for help, Ming began to reflect upon her political allegiances and the role she played as a woman and as a voter. As a 'staunch U.A.P. follower' it was natural for Ming to appeal to a UAP politician. However, she went on to say that if he could not help her,

> I must go to a Labor member, who's sympathy is all with these defenceless people .... I am determined to obtain justice for this girl & her people & will go to 'Jock Garden' [a Labor politician who was the target of the fiercest denunciations and attack by the New Guard] rather than be beaten, for these men will take up a cause of this kind & carry it through, and they are wise enough to realise that *women* swing the votes & are always listened to and encouraged by Labor men, which is causing the Public to say, 'if you want anything *done* and you are a woman – go to a Labor member!!' I do not think that our men quite realise how much this is going to mean to us.[27]

Despite her bravado, it seems she did not impress Jackson, who wrote her a brief note in reply telling her that he had requested the Board to furnish him with a concession pass for Del, but making no mention of raising questions in Parliament.[28]

A few days later Del received a letter from her aunt at Nortown. '[D]o you really want to come home [?] if you do let me know', her aunt wrote. 'You dont want to let them put anything over you. You are your boss & can leave when you like ... . So now del rite straight back & let me know as we will all be glad to see you.'[29] This letter suggests that Del was perhaps being rather ambiguous in her communication to her family on her planned return.

Del left a note to Narrelle about the time that she received this letter, telling her that she had collected the mail that morning and that there were two letters for Narrelle also, 'so I'm quight [*sic*] please aren't you [?]'. It would appear, however, that Del was feeling a little woebegone at the prospect of leaving. 'Well theres not much news to tell you this time,' she wrote, 'but keep this letter allways because this will remind you of me when I'm gone so don't tere it out please will you and I'll say good by forever.' Del even signed this note formally, with her full name.[30]

But Ming was convinced that Del's return home was indeed what she really wanted. '[I must get her] back to her people where she will be happy – poor little beggar,' Ming wrote in her diary one night, Del having suddenly and unexpectedly burst into tears, crying 'brokenheartedly', during a picnic that day:

> I suppose that it is the inborn love of their sacred home land, the land from which all their social and moral codes have sprung, the land which they would cheerfully die for ... . I couldn't help wondering, if perhaps Del was feeling the call of some long dead spirit people, who lived & loved in this very spot in the dim past. Perhaps she felt a sudden wild call from her people, & could not explain her weeping but there is no doubt that the great Mountain Tribesmen *did* wander & camp along the crest of this range where we are settled now – perhaps just on these very stones some sacred ceremony took place, or was it a Trysting place for dusky lovers? or the tearful farewell of a slender Aboriginal girl and her warrior who may never have returned from the hunt. May-be she came each evening to perform the sacrificial rites of her people to old Bolooloo (Golden Moon) ... in the hope that it would compensate the Moon Goddess & she would then return her brown man to her arms once more.

Whatever the cause, Del, looking sadly round about her suddenly burst into wild weeping. We could do nothing to soothe her .... She told me afterwards that a dreadful loneliness suddenly came over her, she felt frantic & wanted to run from this unhappiness but felt rooted to the spot, it is all very strange – poor lonely souls ...[31]

Ming was projecting her own 'dreadful loneliness' onto Del. Isolated from her Sydney friends and in the bitter cold of a late Mountains winter, Ming may well have wondered why Norman rarely came to see them. Writing later that year reflecting on her own feelings at the time, she confessed that she herself had been 'feeling very unhappy and *very* lonely',

> for I had no one to converse with but the children and Del on the mountains ... I couldn't help myself drifting into an atmosphere of make-believe & imaginings where I could live with my dream people & extract a little happiness from them. I dont think we ever realise how much we want happiness & understanding until we are alone on a mountain top ...[32]

* * *

Del had written to her aunt and her aunt in turn wrote directly to Ming in mid-September, informing her that 'Del likes you She tells me in her letters how you are so good to her.' She went on flatteringly, 'I am pleased poor Del [h]as one good friend to stick to her the poor dear must have had a rough time sence she left home it grieve me to think they are saying such nasty things about her Any how,' she reminded Ming, 'Del is a young wom[a]n now, if Del wants to come home send her to Nortown & I will meet her ...'[33] Without knowing the contents of Del's letter to her aunt, it seems Del was still unclear about whether or not she really wanted to go home. But by now events had taken on a momentum of their own, and what Del wanted was becoming irrelevant.

13
It makes me *rage*

By the time Ming received Del's aunt's letter, one pass, covering Del's trip from Blackheath to Sydney, had been given to Ming by the local police at Blackheath on 10 September – thanks to Jackson's intervention. A separate rail pass for Sydney to Nortown had to be picked up from the Board's offices in the company of a police escort. Ming refused to accept this condition, 'in view of certain happenings during the last year'. Mrs Bryce wrote to Ming again on 19 September reporting on the APNR's meeting that day. The 'upshot' was that Morley and Salvation Army officer Howard were going to call on Pettitt to ask for Del's Nortown pass to be sent to Blackheath also and 'to demand her money'. She told Ming that Morley had been 'shelving' the case so far.[1]

It seems Morley distrusted Ming, or at least was concerned about getting entangled in anything that might, as he had put it to Ming, 'cause embarrassment' to his organization. A week after that meeting, Morley had directed Howard to make enquiries at Nortown 'as to the fitness of the home there and the general conditions of it, and as what parents or guardians would be there', before 'taking further steps in the matter of the railway pass'. Some days before they received the Nortown Salvation Army officer's reply, in October, however, the two men had gone to Pettitt. Immediately after this interview, on the same day, 4 October 1934, Howard wrote a curt letter to Ming. He had the rail pass for Del for Sydney to Nortown, and he told her to place Del on the 9.45 a.m. train from Blackheath the next Monday (8 October). A Salvation Army officer would meet her at Central, and this officer would collect 'some money for Del as pocket money' from the Board. 'It will thus be seen that there is now absolutely nothing in the way of Del going to her folk,' Howard wrote, 'and having what I am sure we all hope will be a very happy holiday.'[2]

Ming replied telling Howard she would not send Del as she was sick in bed with the 'flu. And 'in any case' she wanted to know about Del's trust money and the false record the Board had given Del, 'since *this* was my sole reason for keeping her for so long'.[3] She offered instead to take her to Sydney the following Monday (15 October), then changed her mind and rang the APNR to say Del would be staying another week.

With her return imminent, Del now began to openly assert that she did *not* want to leave. It should be remembered that she had never herself asked to be sent home – only that she should not be sent back to the Smith household or to the Board's control. It was Ming's idea from the outset. On 11 October, having agreed to put Del on the train for Nortown on the next Monday (15 October), Ming wrote in her diary that 'Del is worrying about leaving me – she says she doesn't *want* to go now'. Del engaged Ming's need to be loved, while pragmatically pointing out how much hard work there would be for Ming without her around. 'Can't bear to leave us,' Ming reflected on Del's state of mind, '& her affection is genuine I know. She says that I can never manage to do all the work & will be too tired, & she *knows* I always be forgetting about the fire & it will go out! which is just about what *will* happen!' Ming was made suddenly aware of how much she depended on Del's labour, and what would happen once she had to cope alone:

> I must shake myself up I can see & *remember* the blessed fire and the everlasting cooking & washing up, the washing & ironing, cleaning, sewing etc. etc. etc. etc. it fairly makes me shudder at the moment. I've *got* to cope with it & thats all about it, theres no money for anything else ...

It was this appeal that successfully delayed Del's departure for another week.

Del *did* finally leave the following Monday, 22 October, after Ming, by her own account, spent the week feverishly sewing clothes for her. It had been a traumatic week, with all in the household still laid low with 'flu:

> I *must* set Del up since I cannot give much money ... . I have remade a number of my items of wearing apparel for D., am simply too tired to sleep, but *must* make everything possible instead of buying. Oh *how* my head aches – would give *any*thing for a day in bed! ... I had hoped to get Del to help me to clean out the house thoroughly before she left, but she was too ill poor girl – I did a very *large* wash

on Wednesday & am suffering a recovery! poor little Narrelle tried to help but was terribly tired ...

One might hazard that Ming had not been paying Del much, if at all (especially considering their joint bank account was at Pymble), nor clothing her very adequately, and this frantic rush to get her a wardrobe was an attempt to compensate. Del refused to accept Ming's efforts graciously, resentful that she was being sent away in spite of her appeals. In two separate letters written after her departure, Ming commented on how in the last fortnight Del became 'sullen' and 'did not care about her appearance',[4] which presumably referred to her lack of enthusiasm over the outfits Ming was making. It appears that Del really did *not* want to go back to Nortown at this point and must have been upset with Ming for forcing her to do so.

Without any words on the subject from Del herself, there is no way of knowing why she did not want to go home – if this was indeed the case. The only clue to her feelings comes from a rather odd letter she wrote to an unknown recipient (possibly one of her sisters), which Ming copied. Probably written around the time Del heard from her family in July 1934, the letter does provide an insight into some of the trepidation Del felt about returning:

Hows Nortown looking now? Well I think I'll be home for Xmas so I'll be quite *divergent* after all these years. I bet I won't be able to pick you out. I have forgotten [e]very thing about you all, suppose you have the same. Where does Nance live? is she up there or as she gone away[?], why doesn't she get married, if I want to get married have I got to ask Mum or have I to please myself, did you? I'm realy getting married to this man he goes about with a walking stick and he has a beard and a mustarsh and has bald and his back is bent with age, so you no how old he is ...[5]

The letter continued on in Del's characteristically jocular story-telling style, giving a self-deprecatory anecdote about herself and her aged suitor in what was almost certainly a comic fiction constructed by Del to amuse her reader. (They paraded in his sulky at the Sydney Show, thinking they would win 'first prize', because 'we looked so beautiful' – only Del fell out while bowing to the crowd and 'made myself silly as a rabbit'.) Despite the humour, it hints at Del's fears she would be forced into an arranged marriage (by the mother she had not seen for so long) and that she might possibly prefer not to return if she could not 'please myself'. Having spent so many years away from her community, Del seemed to have had doubts about how she would fit in on her return.

The night before Del left, she and Ming argued, Ming having discovered that Del had 'been having night visi[ts]' from 'white devils' – 'she is a great disappointment to me after all that I have been through on her account,' Ming wrote angrily. Whatever the truth behind this mysterious and abrupt diary entry, Ming made a big point in her later letter to Morley of how she *had* to send Del back, in spite of her protestations, because of the sexual menace looming. Ming never had any plans to keep Del with her indefinitely (as she had with Mary) and confronted with Del's appeals to let her stay, this was the only way that Ming could reconcile putting her aside with her conscience:

> She wept & begged me to keep her but I did not *dare* take any further risks & so we packed her suitcases (of which the straps had mysteriously disappeared overnight & she had to tie them up with string). I am sure that she did not really believe that I *would* take her away, & I hated doing it ...[6]

Del's chagrin was evident on the morning of her departure. Ming's hope to send her off fitted out in her new clothes was thwarted by Del's refusal to give her this satisfaction. 'Del couldn't wear her pretty cream frock & cream hat, & white shoes, said she was cold & wore her old winter things which looked very dowdy, her heel had come off the new white shoes!' Ming complained in her diary. 'I feel disg[usted] It has cost me so much to obtain these things – however!'

Del's refusal to make this concession can be seen as a final gesture of self-assertion: she was not a doll to be dressed by another woman, but would dress as it suited her. No doubt Ming, smarting with a sense of personal betrayal, tried to hurt her in return by holding the clothes she had made for Del over her head, as the embodiment of the obligation she felt Del owed to her. By spurning Ming's new clothes on the day she left in favour of her dowdy worn ones, Del was symbolically rejecting Ming's claim that she owed her anything, even to the extent of reminding Ming that, until now, she had been forced to wear shabby old clothes.

Ming took Del directly to the Salvation Army's head office. There they met Howard, who left them with a female officer, saying that he was going to call the Board to tell them the officer would be along to collect Del's money. Ming asked if it was necessary that Del go in person to the Board, to which the reply was 'Yes', but it was unnecessary for Ming to go. Nevertheless, when Howard returned, telling them Del was to catch the evening train to Nortown, Ming insisted on accompanying Del and the officer to the Board's office:

> I knew it would probably annoy Col. Howard but I felt that these two old men [Howard and Morley] had not played the game & had simply sent the peremptory letter telling me to put D. on the train. I feel that I am entitled to know what took place at the Bd. & should not have to request some sort of statement from Col. Howard or Rev. Morley. It seems to me that they have merely looked upon this whole matter as a nuisance, & have simply taken the easiest way out of it by practically handing Del back into the hands of that scoundrel Pettit.[7]

Pettitt was, according to Ming, 'somewhat taken a-back' to see her there. She then learned that the arrangements for Del's return to Nortown by train that evening had been made by the Board Secretary himself, and he had notified the Nortown police and Del's mother (surprisingly, if Pettitt was telling the truth) of her imminent arrival. Ming was furious at his interference, especially as Del's aunt had arranged to meet her. The reason for Pettitt and Howard's reluctance to allow her to accompany Del became clear when Pettitt handed Del a mere £1. Ming's temper was not at all improved, but there was nothing much more she could do, and she eventually left Del at the Salvation Army and took a train back to Blackheath.

Ming was utterly distraught at the outcome. '[I]t was nothing but base pandering to officialdom & a pathetic anxiety to please the miserable Pettit that has resulted in all *my* efforts going for *nothing*,' she raged in her diary that night. Ming realized that she could have collected Del's pass to Nortown herself at Central, and could have put her on the afternoon train herself, without either of them having to go near the Board again; but she had believed that Del would be given a reasonable sum of her money:

> She was given £1-0-0! ... It has just simply disgusted me & all my efforts have been perfectly futile. Oh *damn* these spineless jellyfish who put politeness before *truth* & say as the dear little S.A. officer said to me 'I could *sense* a feeling of dislike between you & *Mr* Pettit – *but* (and *this* is the crux of the whole position) – He has always been very *nice* to *us* and I couldn't do other than treat him in the same way!!' What he did to the poor miserable wretches of

Aboriginals simply did not come *into* the picture! There is no red blood in some of us. No sincerity no enthusiasm nothing to *make* the Governments listen – they know that a milk & water 'Association' is perfectly harmless, & so they answer their letters 'politely' and smile smug smiles up their sleeves & forget it. It makes me *rage* inwardly & outwardly ...

The next day she wrote a recriminatory letter to Morley, accusing the APNR of betraying Del, that they had 'simply handed her over to her bitterest enemies just to be rid of the whole business'.[8] She was quite right.

* * *

Morley and Howard's report on their interview with Pettitt in early October, which Ming did not see, is revealing. Ming had requested they 'find out how much money she [Del] would receive and whether any apology was forthcoming for their libelous statements'.[9] A memo written by Morley (perhaps for the sake of Ming's friend Bettune Bryce) showed that they had intended to ask various ticklish questions of Pettitt, including the age Board jurisdiction ceased, whether Del's family at Nortown had written previously to the Board 'in their anxiety to find her' and received no reply, and why the Board had not compelled Ming to pay Del's wages to her trust account.[10] But their report did not indicate whether such questions had indeed been asked. Instead, their irritation with Ming is suggested by the way they dwelt on Pettitt's affability and cooperation. He 'readily' handed Howard the pass from Sydney to Nortown, and 'readily' agreed she be escorted to the railway by an officer of the Salvation Army instead of a police officer. Pettitt then suggested that if they were still unsatisfied, he would accompany them to visit Childs, who had 'expressed his willingness to receive representatives of the A.P.N.R.'. Morley and Howard decided that this 'was not considered necessary'.[11] It is obvious that they took no genuine interest in Del's case whatsoever.

In fact, the rather awkward report on Del's family circumstances that came in from the Salvation Army officer at Nortown a few days after Morley and Howard met Pettitt was disregarded. This officer reported he had heard that 'several white men' regularly visited Del's grandmother's house and 'they have a pianola and dance till the early hours of the morning and take drink there so you can imagine what would be the result of such behaviour'. He admitted that his information was not 'first-hand' (this was the same officer who had earlier supplied

background information on Del that almost certainly obtained from
the local police or the Board itself), but implied that Del should not be
allowed to return there. Despite such an unfavourable report, Howard
forwarded this letter to Morley with the comment that 'my own feeling
is in favour of Del's going home. It will break the Strack spell, which
might be good.' Del's stay with her family would only be brief, Howard
wrote, as there was a domestic situation awaiting her there.[12] It is evident from this correspondence that both Morley and Howard were
hostile to Ming. They were concerned, not with Del's welfare (being
prepared to send her to what they saw as an undesirable and dangerous
environment), but with separating her from Ming and getting this
troublesome case off their agenda. They had of course already accepted
the rail pass from Pettitt on Del's behalf, and informed Ming, but
Howard's snide comment on 'the Strack spell' was a telling indication
of the way these men viewed the relationship between Ming and Del,
and Ming herself.

* * *

Writing in hindsight in the weeks following Del's departure, Ming
struggled not only with her failure to defend Del, but also to come to
grips with her discovery that Del had been having 'night visits'. She
clearly felt that Del was at least partly responsible, and was disturbed by
the threat to the norms on which her own sexual identity was built,
which this implied. Sexuality for Ming was a painful and difficult issue,
especially as there was considerable tension in her sexual relationship
with her husband. To Ming, her own body was the site of a series of life-
threatening pregnancies and of little understood, frightening and
painful operations. Yet having feared abandonment by Norman from
the earliest days of their marriage, she was always concerned that she
would lose him to the sexual charms of another woman. For Ming such
women were simply 'prostitutes', after the support he could offer –
untrammelled sexual desire in women was a concept barely conceiv-
able to her, although she implicitly accepted its existence in men. In
Ming's society, the penalties for sexual activity were so much higher for
women than for men. Pregnancy spelt social disgrace and poverty for
unmarried women, but even married Australian women, being in effect
their husband's property – as were their children – had no legal recourse
against conjugal rape, and only attained equal rights with the father to
guardianship of their children in May 1934, after a long campaign by
Preston-Stanley, which Ming followed with interest.[13] The intensity of
Ming's desire to shield Del from white male sexuality almost certainly

derived from her own intense feelings of vulnerability and injustice; for this reason she had the greatest difficulty with Del's flouting of her 'protection'.

Utterly and sincerely aghast at Miss Lowe's accusation that Del was a 'sexual maniac', Ming resorted to an absurd and insultingly racist cari-cature of Aboriginal sexuality to defend her action in sending Del home against her wishes. Although Del had 'been goodness itself' and 'she *did* try ... to keep her promise', she was overcome by her animalistic nature, wrote Ming. It was 'springtime and she, like all her people, have only one instinct at this time of year, to find a mate – it is the primitive longing so deeply rooted in them'.[14] And so Ming construct-ed herself as fighting a losing battle, not simply against the indifference of the authorities and the base lusts of exploitative men, but against Aboriginal nature itself. In doing so she failed to see how untenable Del's situation was – a bright young woman, yet denied any aspirations for a partner and children whatsoever.

But in calmer moments, Ming concluded that Del's isolation from her family and her own people was the main cause of her supposed vulnerability to temptation. In June 1933, Ming had recognized Del's loneliness and explained it as the unhappy consequence of the policy of removal and apprenticeship. Having been 'taken forcibly from her own people' and 'forbidden to see or correspond with' them for years, she was then 'sent away to Sydney':

She was now to be exposed to every possible evil ... because they are alone, always lonely. There is not a single little niche wherein they can find security and love and companionship which is life to them.[15]

It occurred to Ming that women like herself might play a more useful role, not as mistresses, but as members of the Protection Board itself. A few weeks after Del left, she wrote a letter to the press demanding that any vacancies on the Board should be immediately filled by women, 'since there is not *one* on the Bd.'. Indeed two or three women should be installed on the Board, 'they would need to be pretty courageous ones too!'[16] Her stance was clearly influenced not only by her firsthand experience of the uselessness of the 'old men' of the APNR, but also by her experience working with the campaigners from the elite women's movement. Ming was not yet ready to argue that state control over Aboriginal people should be dispensed with altogether. But she was moving to a position where she saw feminism, as in the appointment of middle- and upper-class white women to positions of public power, as being a way to administer Aboriginal policy in a more humane and positive direction. And she was impatient to take up political action to this end.

It was at this time that Ming began to revive her relationship with the person who represented both how much she gained from the policy of Aboriginal child removal, and how much she owed.

14
A devotion I hope I may fully repay

Having made no further mention of Mary in her diary after May 1934, when she found Mary's address at Brungle Aboriginal Station, it seems that Ming did indeed get in touch with Mary again. In early January 1935 Mary wrote to Narrelle and Helen, thanking them for the Christmas presents they had sent her: 'it makes me think of home when you used to give me a lot of nice things like that'.[1] The resumption of Ming and Mary's relationship after a break of five years was consolidated by the giving of 'parcels' of old clothes and the like to Mary. Such one-directional giving has been described as the 'ubiquitous expression of maternalism' within the domestic service relationship, a ritual serving to 'reify the differences between the women'.[2] Its continuation years after Mary's departure highlights the continuing obligations both women felt Ming owed Mary, and must be seen in the context of what was happening in both women's lives at the time.

Ming's emotional investment in this was all the more telling, given that she was hardly in a position to distribute largesse at this period in her life. It is hard to imagine that Ming had had an excess of wearable secondhand clothes since Del's departure in October, when she fretted in her diary, 'We have all allowed ourselves to get into a deplorable state simply because there was never a farthing to spend on clothes.' Although the Depression, which had begun in 1929, had not initially been too hard on the Stracks, as it deepened Norman was facing increasing difficulties finding work as a freelance advertising agent and accountant. Just before Christmas, in December 1934, at Norman's insistence, Ming had reluctantly moved from Blackheath with her girls to live rent-free at her parents' place at Davistown on the central coast. Peter, now 17, stayed with her parents at Pymble to finish his high school matriculation. There she found herself neighbour to a community of unemployed people which had sprung up in the vicinity during the Depression. It was her first direct contact with poverty, and she was naively impressed by the communal spirit she witnessed, writing of how 'These poor "dole" people are anxious to lend me all they possess ... and yet they have so little'. She became enthusiastically embroiled in political arguments with her neighbours, many of whom she considered 'staunch upholders of Communism'. 'I *long* to help them,' she wrote in her diary after one such discussion:

> I don't wonder that the man who has *nothing* yet who *wants* work urgently, should feel that the 'System' is wrong. We *know* it is – yet so far have not found anything but Communism to take its place. We finally agreed that we are all trying to find a way out in all our own particular manner & that our aim is much the same, whether we be Communist, or Christian ... we want to make the world clean & straight & fair again & safe for our children ...

The radical views of Ming's new neighbours challenged but did not shake her reactionary political beliefs. Ming saw money, in the form of charity, as the obvious solution to the current economic and social crisis. 'Those who *make* money are making it for *others* – how ever *they* looks at it it comes up the same,' she ruminated:

> – if they are mean & hard they horde it up, for others after they have gone – if they are generous they make it & have the huge wonderful pleasure of giving to others – *no* one on this mortal coil can use more than he *can* so what's left goes to the next fellow, & what is squandered goes also *to others* ...
>
> We go hungry to bed & with an empty stomach & a full head, one is liable to see *red*. & the outcome is Bolshevism, & the *cure* is generosity, in the shape of *food* & square deals, it spells contentment.
>
> to give money is easy & means nothing, but to give thought backed up by notes, means a happy world, free from rancour ... It is the man *with money* who can do this for us, & he only, if he would not be so blind, he would see that it would only improve his business & bring real happiness, where as at present, our only hope is unionism & force.

I can't help notice the change in Ming's voice in her diary entries during this period, but she could not genuinely shift from her sense of herself as part of society's elite. Although Ming identified herself here with those who 'go hungry to bed', she clearly wanted the 'huge wonderful pleasure of giving to others' for herself. '*How* I would *love* to be able to give that man £50-0-0,' she wrote of one of her avowedly Communist neighbours. 'What untold joy it would bring & how he would eke it out. It would mean a new life to he & his brave little wife .... . I long to just *help* them all, if I *only* could, with money it would be so easy.' Ming's charitable maternalism towards Mary at this time must be seen in the context of these political beliefs and attitudes, as being motivated by a sense of duty as well as the more pleasurable desire to assist one less fortunate than herself.

Much had changed in Mary's life also; she had had four children with her husband, as well as her first child, who was still with her. The Depression was taking a deep hold everywhere, but for Aboriginal people, paid work was now altogether impossible to find, and pressure on the Aboriginal reserves had increased dramatically. Not surprisingly, the correspondence that now opened up between the two women revolved quite explicitly, from Mary's side, around her needs. Significantly, Mary reverted to the use of the submissive 'My Dear Mistress' and made her more assertive requests through Ming's daughters, rather than to Ming herself. So, in her letter to Helen, she added in a postscript, 'ask mother has she got some old clothes to give away. Tell her the other old clothes she sent me, I wore them out.' 'Tell her to send me some old clothes and old shoes and hats,' Mary instructed Narrelle. 'Tell her that I am running about with no shoes on and I don't like [it], makes my feet very sore.' [3]

For Ming, recoiling from what she had learned of the apprenticeship experience from Del, her gifts to Mary may well have provided reassurance that *her* involvement in the system had not been 'dishonourable', by reaffirming those bonds which signified Ming as the caring mother-employer and Mary as the faithful daughter-servant. Having found Mary again, she was anxious to restore her rose-tinted, comforting view of their past relationship.

Mary suggested to both girls that she might be able to visit them soon in Sydney. 'I might be down for a holiday to see you all if I could get some money together for my train fare,' she had written to Narrelle. 'I would love to see you all again.'[4] This may well have been unthinkable while Ming was living at Davistown in the midst of an unemployed camp, but Ming's position there was essentially that of an observer. In December 1934 Ming returned to her parents' house in Sydney, for Christmas presumably. Peter was due to start university the next year and, according to Ming, her mother now told her she refused to house him any longer. Ming began house-hunting on the North Shore in the new year, and Norman managed to find regular work with an advertising company. Having found a small house for rent at Roseville and moving in at the end of January 1935, tentative arrangements were made for Mary and her children to visit the family.

For Mary, too, there may have been a genuine desire to return to a more comfortable and safer time. It is striking that after so many years Mary could still speak of Ming's household as 'home'. But the plan was for Mary to have a 'holiday' with Ming – not to return to work for her. This suggests a possible change in the way that both women viewed their relationship; while perhaps still not a 'friendship' as such, the dynamic evidently had shifted away from that of a labour exchange. Potentially, a genuine and ongoing familial connection may well have developed. Such an outcome depended however on Ming's ability and willingness to assist financially. Apparently, Ming offered to pay Mary's fare (no mention of her children) to Sydney, but failed to make good her promise, much to Mary's disappointment. 'When I got this last letter from you I thought it was money [you] said that you was going to send me for my trip to Sydney,' Mary wrote in June.

> I was so disappointed when I opened the letter. I am getting two suitcases in town next week in case you send my fare this time. I would love to come down for a holiday just to see you all again … . don't forget to send me my fare down. I will love to see Miss Helen and Miss Narrelle and Master Peter, also all the rest of your people and all … . I am getting my clothes washed up [?] next week in case you send my fare. Try and send my fare if you can manage. Oh the last letter you wrote to [me] I thought it was the money when I see it R from Roseville I was glad you sent the money. Oh well I must stop now …[5]

But Mary never did visit. There is nothing in Ming's papers to explain why; indeed, there was no mention of Mary at all in Ming's diaries, prolific and tear-stained as they are, from that point on.

* * *

Having confided in her diary prior to moving back to Sydney that she could 'not *bear* the thought of being cooped up in a little house with N. again, now will drive me *mad*', Ming was shocked and hurt to find on her return that Norman wanted a divorce. Her parents persuaded him to 'wait', perhaps hoping they would sort out their problems once they were in their own home. But Norman began staying away three nights of the week, although his father (whom Ming detested), visiting from England, was staying with them from February to September 1935. Her conflicts with Norman escalated rapidly. 'Hating' his job, Ming recorded in September that he came home with the sour news that he had been fired, and they had had a particularly fierce fight in which he had slapped her across the face and had to be restrained by Peter. Norman soon found work again, but almost immediately began to work late, and throughout the latter months of 1935 Ming was obsessed with the suspicion he was having an affair.

One afternoon in November, she decided to meet Norman after work. They walked in stony silence to a park. '[D]own the grassy bank were a man & woman caressing, kissing, fondling one another while *we* sat as far away from each other as we could get!' Ming wrote in her diary.

'What is the matter with you – or with us?'

Norman answered, in a sudden rush of fury, '*We've* got nothing in common – *you* like ethereal things, culture, *art*, I hate the very sound of the name. I *hate* the things *you* think are beautiful – I'm earthy. I *like* worldly things & I goin' to have them. We're getting further & further apart. I'm not going to spoil *my* life, I'm going to have the things *I* want. *You* don't get any pleasure out of *my* sort of enjoyment & I *loathe your* kind – so what's the good a-wasting *my* life – I tell yer I'm *through!*'

Later that night, after the couple went home, fighting all the way, Ming finally had her suspicions confirmed. Norman admitted he had been having an affair for the past three years.

I just sat there, for, to really *know* this thing, even tho I *said* I'd rather know than suffer the uncertainty any longer, was too horrible for words. What was I to do now? He went on, 'When a man is nearing forty he always feels the need of this sort of life – they all do it they go rotten!' I just listened, hoping that I would do the right thing & not allow my anger & *fury* & disgust to burst forth. 'And – *you've* never understood me ... – you don't like marriage the way *I* like it, it's just the way you've been brought up! just narrow & stupid & priggish! You don't think its "nice" to talk about sexual matters, I always felt that you didn't like me to touch you!

'I've always been lonely, ever since I was a kid. My people were always thinking of themselves, & I had to read a book & keep out of the way. I had no brothers or sisters & no friends. I didn't like people then & I don't now. I *hate* them – everyone – I was never *allowed* to have friends in my home (if yer could *call* it a home!). Anyhow

I'm rotten through & through, & have been for years & now you know!'

Ming asked, if she tried 'to do all the things you say I *don't* do & you keep right away from this woman for always can we try once more to be happy?' He replied, in a muffled voice,

'I didn't know *this* sort of thing was ever forgiven.' (I hadn't *said* I'd forgive it, but hastened to do so, if he really would stay at home with his [family] and I'd even try to emulate a *prostitute* if that was what he wanted ... [)]

N. continued to blame me for all his misdeeds until I really felt that it *must* be my fault! tho how this could really be I don't know for we lived a perfectly normal married life until the last 3 years. I *wasn't* prudish, & he did as he liked & how & *when* he liked, & he *must know* this & really *does*, but is desperately looking for an excuse of course for his own behaviour.

He says I'm not to be 'tired' as his Mother was always 'tired' & he's sick of hearing the word. I'm not even to *mention* pictures, art, or beauty in any way at all & especially music (which he says is vile) I'm to keep the children out of sight & not do anything for them ... [they will break the lease on their house and move to another house at Lindfield] & he would try to work in the garden & take an interest in it – that he really *could* up there etc, so we both promise to start all over again & try to be happy once more.

1:45 am!!!! Heavens I'm sleepy. This is one of his late nights & the only chance I get to keep this diary! I think we *are* going to Lindfield.'

And so she concluded her account of their argument.

But having moved house, Ming continued to suspect Norman and confronted him one night. In the ensuing argument, in which Norman told Ming he was 'through' and was leaving, Ming threatened to 'turn the tables' on him and leave *him* with the children. 'If there is nothing to stop *you* going out of this house forever, there's nothing to stop *me* either,' she told him in a fury. Norman apologized 'frantically', and a few days after this altercation Ming sought the assistance of an evangelical Christian group in the hope of effecting Norman's moral reform.

It seems highly unlikely that Ming would have invited Mary to stay while in the throes of such domestic drama. She may well have wanted to re-establish her past with Mary, but surely not *this* unpleasant aspect of her emotional dependence on her. Perhaps she could not bear for

Mary to see her continuing to endure the marital problems she had all those years ago. And, as Mary's family was moved from Brungle to Erambie Mission at Cowra at around the same time as the Stracks moved to the new house at Lindfield, once again the women lost touch.[6]

* * *

Meanwhile, Ming had written to Del at Nortown, several months after she had left, to see how she was. Despite the bitterness of her departure, Del wrote back the day she got Ming's letter, telling Ming she 'was very pleased to hear from you and to know that you are all well'.

> Well Mrs Strack you ask me how I was treated at the place you left me at [the Salvation Army office] they were very kind to me all the day and there were lots of Girls to talk to and I felt quite happy onely I was thingking about you all the time. I landed home safely My Aunty, Sister and Cousen was at the station to meet me. the town looked so lovely after not seeing [it] for that long and when I got home I could not help laughfing there were little houses all over the flat it looked so funny ...[7]

She concluded her letter with the firm direction, 'don't you send me any money Mrs Strack'. Returning to a life of poverty, Del seemed uncomfortable with the economic disparities between Ming and herself, and determined as ever to make her own way in the world. Her next letter apologized for not sending Ming a gift, 'I would have sent some things to you only the money I had I had to see the Doctor with'. She added, 'I would love to come back to you onely I am getting married soon even if I wasent getting married I couldnt come back like I am I am as poor as every one hear.'[8]

When Del's first baby was almost two, and with another on the way, she would reluctantly be forced to ask Ming for assistance. But even then she couched her request carefully, after making the point that her husband 'will work when he can get it but there's no work for any'one'. 'Mrs Strack if you know of any'one that has any little Baby's cloths they want to give away I would be very thankful if you could get them for me.' Again, she apologized for not reciprocating, 'Well Mrs Strack I can't send you any thing for Xmas you understand how things are.' Ming sent one of her 'parcels' for Christmas (with gifts for the baby and her husband) and another later the next year, both of which Del thanked her for graciously. Del's discomfort at being in a position of need was made evident by the fact that when she finally got her wages from the Board, she felt she could visit Ming – although there is no evidence that she, like Mary, ever did. [9]

Ming had sought Del out late in 1937 to ask her whether or not she had got her trust money from the Board. At this time, the hope that Ming had expressed in March 1934, when she presented Del to the Feminist Club, was becoming a reality. Pressure from a combination of directions had led to a sympathetic NSW Labor member, Mark Davidson, successfully getting up the 1937 Parliamentary Select Committee Enquiry into the administration of the Board. An Aboriginal political organization, the recently emergent Aborigines Progressive Association led by Aboriginal activists Bill Ferguson and Pearl Gibbs, was calling for full citizenship rights for Aboriginal people and an enquiry into the Board's administration with a view to its abolition. Meanwhile, the powerful anthropologist, A. P. Elkin of Sydney University, was pressing for the reform of the administration to allow for his own appointment as an expert in Aboriginal culture – he rallied behind the cause of disaffected Board employees (a former manager and a former assistant matron) in calling for an enquiry. Various women's organizations were also taking a keen interest in the calls for reform, seeking the appointment of their own representative. The Feminist Club was one of these groups, and through her ongoing connection with it, Ming was preparing to give evidence to the enquiry of the abuse of Aboriginal girls in service and the Board's maladministration of the apprenticeship system. Almost certainly Ming wrote to Del for further evidence.

She learnt that Del had not had her record cleared or, more importantly, her trust monies reimbursed. In 1935, Del had told Ming that she was still unable to get more than a small portion of her trust monies, and although she was looking after her sister's two children while her sister was in hospital, the local police were pressuring her. 'I wanted to write for more money ...,' she told Ming, 'but Im two frighten the policeman said to me Mr Pettit not boss over you now I am and if you don't get some work I will send you back to the board.'[10]

The Board vindictively refused to remit her wages even after her marriage, on the spurious grounds that her pocket money book was not in order. Now, in 1937, in reply to Ming's letter, Del told her of her troubles:

> Well Mrs Strack the Policeman came to see me yesterday about money owing to me he said your name I couldn't catch what he said whether you rote him a letter or not. I told him the fault lies with the Board they should have seen to my Money Book at Smiths any how I said I didn't want anything to do with the Board they did a lot

of dirty things to me. and the less I have to do with them the Better. You know Mrs Strack I rote to old Pettit a long time ago about my money and he rote back and said you want to see Mrs Strack about that, when you turned of age I had nothing to do with you you were free and should have arranged with you for full pay I rote back and told him it didn't seem as though I was free when he sent the Police after me. and I said wy didn't you tell me when I was with Mrs Strack in[s]tead of saying it now I said its got nothing to do with Mrs Strack I said you paid me right as far as we knew it was Mrs Smith that you should have seen that my Money Book was altered. any way Mrs Strack I'm not letting money matters worry me ...[11]

Del did eventually get her money, writing to Ming around mid- to late 1938, 'I got all my money from the board as far as I know. I received 20 £ & he said thats how much I only had but that was four years ago.'[12] Why the Board decided to pay her is not explained, but it is probably not coincidental that the Board once again began pursuing Ming for the monies owing to Del's trust account in August 1938, having made no efforts to chase these up since January 1934.

The amount claimed had dropped substantially; Ming was now told she owed £3 11s 4d, a sum which accounted only for the period between Del's arrival in her service and her supposed eighteenth birthday. Ming denied liability. The matter was heard at a Board meeting in December 1938 and it was decided to allow her arrears to lapse.[13]

By this time, Ming had turned her back altogether on the 'milk & water' philanthropy of the APNR and was vigorously campaigning for the rights of the Aboriginal apprentices through the Committee for Aboriginal Citizenship. This relatively radical body acted in concert with the Aborigines Progressive Association to agitate for the abolition of the Protection Board. In the context of the times, the right of Aboriginal people to remain with their own communities entailed the attainment of citizenship rights, for these were seen as the only way Aboriginal people could be freed from the discriminatory and overbearing policies of the 'Persecution' Board. Ming's experiences with Del had shattered her complacency about the Board's apprenticeship scheme; her contact with Aboriginal activists since then had brought her to a more radical position. But everything else paled into insignificance compared with the news she had heard of Mary in January 1938.

* * *

Ming had probably sought out Mary at the time as she wrote to Del in late 1937, getting an update on how she was and more evidence to present to the enquiry. The answer Ming received from Mary's husband horrified her. William wrote:

> Dear Mrs Strack,
>   I received your letter today. It came from Cowra Mission. I am living in Yass with my sister-in-law Sarah Todd and also my six children. You will get such a shock when I tell you in my letter about my wife Mary, she is dead six month now and I gave all the children to her sister Sarah to care for them ... Times are very hard these days to live. It takes a lot to keep six children although Sarah, my wife's sister, is very good to them and trying to rear them all up. I will bring my letter to a close ...[14]

At 37 years of age, Mary had died of pneumonia, that chronic disease of poverty. Like her grandmother Hannah years earlier, she left behind her children, ranging from her eldest girl and namesake born in Sydney, Mary Hannah, now ten years old, to a six-month-old baby boy. 'My poor little faithful Mary died, neglected & starving & terribly ill, at the settlement at Cowra,' Ming wrote on the back of William's letter. '– a *scandal* indeed, for she had done so much for me, & I could not trace her'. It is easy to imagine the intense shock – and guilt – with which Ming would have registered the news of Mary's death.

In a furious letter to the editor of *The Sydney Morning Herald*, written as Ming joined an emerging movement for Aboriginal rights two months later, Ming went on the attack, calling the Protection Board 'a great poisonous fungus' and holding up Mary's experience as an example of the Board's 'ghastly treatment' of Aboriginal girls. 'They have cared for my children with a devotion which I hope I may fully repay', she wrote,

> and there are no native people in the world (or whites) whom I would rather have in my home; they are absolutely honest and trustworthy, and a white child would be very much safer in their care than in the hands of many white girls or men.
>   ... They have been exploited long enough, and in spite of the desperate efforts of some Politicians to hush the matter up, the facts are, that young Aboriginal girls *are* taken from their parents under any pretext whatever, and sent to so-called 'training' homes for a short period, where they are forbidden to keep in touch with their families (are taught in fact to despise them) and thence to Employers ...
>   One girl worked for ten years at service, and after many months of legal battling the board was *persuaded* to pay her the munificent sum

of £64 0s 0d! ... 6 months ago this faithful and devoted little soul died, starved and neglected at one of the Board's Stations, when she was seriously ill.

In all *our* illnesses this girl devoted herself, night & day to us, yet in *her* illness there was *not one* kindly *white* hand held out in sympathy or protection ...[15]

Increasingly, over the years, Ming had come to see the Board as the instrument of destruction of her relationship with Mary – the obstacle to her holding out her hand. She contrasted the love and protection she felt she offered to Mary to the callous treatment Mary received from the Board. This contrast had been heightened for Ming by the experiences she had after Mary left, with Alma and Del, but Mary's death was the most horrible evidence of this contrast. The inequality of race between the two women which had put Ming in a position to offer to care for Mary was made grotesque by the way Mary died, and from this time on Ming not only campaigned against the Board's apprenticeship policy, but also for the granting of full equality, through Aboriginal citizenship rights. Never a democrat, this was a difficult position for Ming to come to and one which depended on her enjoying an altogether different relationship with Aboriginal women.

Part IV
Pearl Gibbs

15
Just ordinary justice

Walking along a busy city street in Sydney one day in 1937, Mrs Pearl Gibbs, one of the leading forces of the recently established all-Aboriginal organization, the Aborigines Progressive Association, ran into two girls she knew. They were on their way to a tea-party, hosted by a white woman, a 'Mrs Strack'. Pearl had just returned from Brewarrina Aboriginal Station in western NSW, where she had been collecting evidence of the Board manager's son's sexual assaults on young women in the dormitory there. Intrigued by what the two girls told her, the older woman accompanied them to the gathering where she met Ming, and found, in some respects, a kindred spirit.

'The high, airy Victorian style room was papered in beige, edged by heavy dark chocolate skirting-boards and architraves, with enormous sash windows draped in long lace and net curtains,' wrote Bill Ferguson's biographer Jack Horner.

Pearl saw half a dozen girls spending the time quietly in chatter, passing plates of biscuits or teacake and sipping cups of tea. Then she saw emerging from the kitchen Mrs Strack, dressed and trained to be a lady, vivacious, mettlesome, younger than Pearl and greeting her with not a trace of condescension. Pearl waded into Mrs Strack's firm resonant conversation and found they had in common a personal hatred of the Protection Board policies.[1]

Pearl Gibbs told Jack Horner that she 'took a liking' to Ming. Recently arriving from the South Coast, she could have shared some harsh facts about the way the people at Wallaga Lake were being treated at that time had Ming raised her stories of her childhood there (which she undoubtedly did). They would have swapped stories about their respective struggles on behalf of Aboriginal apprentices to wrest wages from the Board. Pearl had escaped Board apprenticeship herself, but working as an independent domestic servant in Sydney in the 1920s, knew some that hadn't. She had supported some of her apprenticed friends in demanding their trust money from the Board, walking across the green swathe of the Domain behind the Board's city office with them to confront the Board officers with the same lack of success as Ming. Pearl had a passion and an outspokenness that easily matched Ming's hatred of the Board, describing her first experience of public speaking, in the Domain that year: 'I shook and I shivered and the ladder was rocking ... I was so fighting mad, I didn't know what to say first because there were so many things ... . They had to get me down on the ground and then I started.'[2] But of course Ming and Pearl Gibbs were positioned in fundamentally different ways *vis-à-vis* the state and the Aboriginal apprentices.

Ming's 'tea-party' idea – holding weekly gatherings for Aboriginal apprentices to share tea and biscuits – represented her attempt to provide a partial solution to what she saw as the cause of their loneliness and vulnerability, their isolation from their communities. As a method of genteel political action, it was virtually the only kind of respectable public activism available to women of Ming's class and time, and certainly the only way she could meet Aboriginal girls in a group.

Ming's tea-parties followed a well-worn and generally reactionary tradition of bourgeois women's philanthropy. During the First World War, girls' recreational clubs were considered an admirable means by which elite women could mould 'motherless' working-class girls into good wives and mothers for the nation's future. The Australian Women's Guild of Empire organized similar tea-parties where the ladies waited on the wives of unemployed men during the Depression, explicitly to combat working-class radicalism by exposing the wives to the ways of their social betters. Ming, who had been a member in the 1920s, may even have got her idea from the Guild. Her tea-party solution was consistent with a campaign of the United Associations of Women, the umbrella organization of conservative women's groups formed in 1932, including the Guild up to 1938. In 1937, Jessie Street, then the UAW leader, proposed forming social clubs in the suburbs for domestic servants: 'not only [would] this prevent the girls from being lonely but it was protection to them from making friends of undesirable strangers'. The UAW's aim was not to civilize workers as such, but to counter the shortage of reliable domestic servants that so vexed the elite women of these groups.[3]

Despite such conservative antecedents, Ming's weekly tea-parties, at which she served the girls 'refreshments' from April 1937, were inherently subversive and overtly challenging. Jack Horner recorded that 'she was keen to do this because by Board rules the girls were not supposed to meet'.[4] By arranging such gatherings in contravention of the Board's strictures against employers allowing the apprentices to socialize with each other, Ming was reacting defiantly to the prescriptions that had been placed on her as an employer by the Board. As she wrote in a 1938 letter to the *Sydney Morning Herald*, the Board issued 'definite instruction' to employers that apprentices were not 'to mix with other dark girls' and that their correspondence was to be censored.[5] So in many ways the tea-party was an extension of her campaign in Del's defence.

For getting Del back to her community had been a bitter-sweet victory. She had not achieved her aim of exposing the Board or even of getting Del's trust monies returned. Disgusted and enraged by the weakness of the APNR, Ming had begun to look seriously towards the women's movement to push for changes to the Board's policy and practice.

In January 1938 Ming would claim that over the previous three years she had 'not left a stone unturned' in trying to improve conditions for Aboriginal people, but unfortunately there is no evidence to support her claim. Her friend in the APNR, Bettune Bryce, had asked if she should nominate Ming for membership of the National Council of Women (NCW) back in September 1934. Then, just before Del left in October, Ming got in touch with the NCW leader, Linda Littlejohn, who agreed (as a Justice of the Peace) to be a witness to the affidavit Ming had constructed out of her diary. At the same time, Mrs Bryce asked Ming to help her form a sub-committee within the National Council of Women to 'deal with Aborigines & to help Dr Elkin', the anthropologist who was taking a keen interest in the possibilities of reforming Aboriginal administration in the state. Ming intended to do this on her return to Sydney from Blackheath – 'will try with all my might' – but the move to Davistown forestalled such activities. She may well have taken it up when they returned to Sydney in early 1935, though again, I could find no evidence to confirm this: the surviving papers for both the NCW and the Feminist Club do not cover the years in question, and the UAW papers for these years making no mention of any input from Ming.

Ming's diaries for those years focused not on Aboriginal issues, but on the Oxford Group, which she and Norman had joined in early 1936 in the hope of saving their marriage. Stressing personal and social reform by a return to Christian morality, and aimed at winning the allegiances of influential men, the Oxford Group was similar in values and to a certain extent political outlook to the New Guard. In her diaries there is no mention of any involvement with Aboriginal people or issues up until late 1937. It is intriguing, however, to find that a reader in the *Australian Women's Mirror* supplement of January 1935 gave Ming's name as a 'notable Australian woman' for her activities on behalf of Aborigines. A 1935 letter from a Mrs Anna Morgan, an Aboriginal woman who had been publicly campaigning in Melbourne against the NSW Board's apprenticeship policy, thanking Ming for her invitation to stay with her should she visit Sydney – 'if there were more like you, we might be treated better', she wrote – represents the only firm trace of Ming's interest in Aboriginal politics in the mid-1930s. [6]

A letter reveals that Ming was able to get the use of the Oxford Group rooms at 242 Pitt Street for her tea-parties by April 1937. It is a shame that no more documentation of Ming's earliest attempts to set up these servants' tea-parties survives, for to organize these meetings she must have had a measure of cooperation from sympathetic white employers, as well as contacts amongst the workers. For the girls themselves, isolated in their suburban prisons, word-of-mouth may not have been very effective. For those who could and did attend, such outings no doubt provided a welcome relief to the girls themselves, the chance not only to socialize with each other, but for one day a week, be waited on themselves. However, it was also an opportunity for the girls to air their grievances against the system, particularly the non-payment of the wages held in trust, giving Ming more fuel for her unflagging determination to expose the Board. Pearl Gibbs must have seen the potential here and also that in Ming the Aboriginal movement had a useful ally.

* * *

Ming wrote in her diary of attending the hearings of the 1937 Parliamentary Select Committee Enquiry into the administration of the Board, but her papers provide no insight into how she came to be there. She was *not* there through her connections with the United Associations of Women, the APNR or the anthropologists, but it might have been Pearl who initially persuaded Ming to appear as a witness. [7] The two women sat together during some of the hearings through November and December, and Pearl introduced Ming to a fellow APA activist Bill Ferguson (from Dubbo) and Burraga, or Joe Anderson, who gave Ming, to her delight, a handmade hatpin in the shape of a boomerang.

Ming intended to give evidence of the abuse of Aboriginal servants and the Board's maladministration of the apprenticeship system, but she did not get her chance, due to the lack of a quorum on the two occasions she was supposed to speak.[8] Her experience was entirely typical, and by January 1938 it was clear that, while much evidence was still to be presented and many witnesses to be called, lack of interest on the part of politicians was leading to the undignified collapse of the enquiry.

As the enquiry crumbled, Pearl Gibbs persuaded Ming to write to the NSW Premier, B. S. B. Stevens, to ask him to agree to an interview with Bill Ferguson and Pearl. The leader of the United Australia Party might have known Ming through her earlier political activities in the New Guard and her support for the UAP: she also claimed later that he was a member of the Oxford Group.[9] In this letter, Ming introduced herself not as an activist, but as a mistress. 'For generations my people have employed, have loved & understood the Aboriginals of N.S.W.,' she wrote. 'I myself have had them always in my home. I have known them in their own natural environment & I know their dire need of just ordinary justice.'

'The members of the Board are either members of Parliament [or] *ex*-policemen – *what a farce* – they neither understand nor *care* for the sufferings of the gentlest race in the world,' she continued. Suggesting that the Board needed both a church representative (a reflection of her involvement in the Oxford Group) and a woman – because '*all* the employees handled by the Bd. in Sydney, are girls, poor little human flotsam' – Ming then asserted that the present deplorable conditions on Aboriginal reserves were 'mainly because not *one* man on the so-called Protection Bd, had been trained in Anthropology'.[10] Ming had clearly been influenced by an aside made to her by Professor Elkin one day during the enquiry. 'All this misery could have been avoided if there had been *one* man or woman trained in Anthropology on that A.P. Board,' he had said to her.

But Ming had her own 'very special reason' for making this request, as she explained to Stevens. She knew 'that the Communist Party has offered to help them, even with money, & there is no reason in the world why they should not accept this help, except their own innate loyalty "to the Government" & their faith in you personally to see that they do get justice. If you could just realise what this means – there are 9000 Half C[astes] & 1000 full bloods in N.S.W.' The

Communist Party had indeed been involved in a recent appearance by APA leader Bill Ferguson before an audience of trade unionists and other labourites.[11] Pearl Gibbs did not trust the communist influence in the Aboriginal movement (she said as much later[12]) and possibly had had a word or two to this effect in Ming's ear. Already a staunch anti-communist on principle, Ming would have viewed this left-wing interest in the Aborigines' Progressive Association with suspicion and alarm.

Ironically, incongruously, Ming was about to find herself – at the behest of Pearl Gibbs – the secretary and treasurer of a political organization that was explicitly designed to enable the Aborigines Progressive Association to take advantage of the financial support offered by left-wing groups and labour organizations.

* * *

With the sudden and terrible news of Mary's death still reverberating, Ming accompanied Pearl Gibbs to a public protest meeting held at Adyar Hall, Sydney, in early March 1938. Organized by the theosophist, health food proprietor and former anarchist Mick Sawtell, and chaired by his friend Albert Thompson, a unionist and editor of the *Labour Daily*, speakers included the two APA leaders Jack Patten and Bill Ferguson, as well as Reverend Morley from the APNR, the writers Jean Devanny and Mary Gilmore, the feminist anthropologist Caroline Kelly, and two Labor Party politicians. The meeting deplored that nothing had resulted from the Select Committee, asked for an immediate 'reconstruction' of the Protection Board (to consist of 'public-spirited' white men and women, and Aborigines elected by Aborigines) and decided to appoint a committee of five 'to further the cause of the Aborigines' Progressive Association'.[13]

The inaugural meeting of this 'Aborigine Citizen Committee' was held on 15 March. Present were Mick Sawtell, Pearl Gibbs, Jean Devanny, Queenie Sutherland and Bill Danne – possibly representing the 'committee of five' proposed at the Adyar Hall meeting. Sawtell was elected as chair and the objective of the group was stated as being the achievement of 'full citizenship rights for the Aborigines'. Ming was not there, but she was certainly involved, for the meeting was held in the Oxford Group room on Pitt Street, presumably by arrangement between Ming and Pearl.[14]

Ming did not, in fact, attend a CAC meeting until the third meeting, held on 5 May 1938, when she was made secretary, Mick Sawtell president, the unionists Albert Thompson and John Steele vice-presidents, and Samuel Rosenberg of the Howard Prison Reform League, M. Lauder (another unionist, who would not stay long), Pearl Gibbs, Bill Ferguson and Queenie Sutherland (about whom I could find nothing other than she lived in north Sydney) committee members. The group was now formed constitutionally on a motion of the APA leader Bill Ferguson.

It was actually the second incarnation of the Committee for Aboriginal Citizenship, usurping the role of an original Citizenship Committee set up in 1937 and headed by the right-wing nationalist publisher P. R. ('Inky') Stephensen, who had published both the APA newsletter *Abo Call* and the APA's manifesto *Aborigines Claim Citizen Rights!* The emergence of this second white support group in the wake of the enquiry mirrored the rift between the APA leaders Jack Patten and Bill Ferguson. Ferguson was unhappy with Patten's association with Stephensen and his wealthy patron J. Miles, largely it appears because of the refusal of Stephensen and Miles to accept the funds offered by the labour movement and by public subscriptions. Sawtell, who had originally introduced Patten to Stephensen and Miles, and had been involved with the first CAC, now brought Ferguson into the labour movement fold through his connection with Albert Thompson. And so at the next meeting of the Citizenship Committee, Ferguson announced that he had registered *his* faction of the APA (now officially split from Patten and his supporters) as a public charity and wanted the CAC to do likewise, 'so that they could collect money to help his people'. Ming, appointed treasurer as well as secretary, was to 'do the deed'.

The Aboriginal activists of the 1930s were engaged in a delicate balancing act. An earlier group in the 1920s, taking an approach inspired by the black nationalist movement in the United States, though larger in its heyday than the APA, had been 'hounded' by the police acting for the Board and virtually erased by 1938. For Ferguson, it was an object lesson in the need 'to get the public on our side'.[15] The 1930s APA maintained the Aboriginal-only membership rule of the earlier Australian Aboriginal Progressive Association, but was geared strongly towards marshalling support, both ideological and financial, from the wider society. But with flamboyant political animals like Sawtell and Stephensen taking a prominent role, the Aboriginal activists were always in danger of being dominated. The result was a persistent tension between their request for acceptance in white Australian society and their demand that they be allowed to take control of their own destiny (although the two were not mutually exclusive). 'Well, what do you want us white people to do about it?' Stephensen had asked Patten in an early radio show publicizing the new group. 'We want to be regarded as normal, average, human beings, the same as yourselves,' Patten responded. 'We ask you to study the problem ... from the Aborigines' point of view,' they stated in their manifesto, *Aborigines Claim Citizen Rights!* Patten told his Aboriginal audience at the 'Day of Mourning' rally held on Australia Day, 26 January 1938, that 'Our purpose in meeting today is to bring home to the white people of Australia the frightful conditions in which the native Aborigines of this continent live':

> This land belonged to our forefathers 150 years ago, but today we are pushed further and further into the background. The Aborigines Progressive Association has been formed to put before the white people the fact that Aborigines throughout Australia are literally being starved to death. We refuse to be pushed into the background. We have decided to make ourselves heard. ... As regards the Aborigines Protection Board of New South Wales, white people in the cities do not realise the terrible conditions of slavery under which our people live in the outback districts ... . We are looking in vain to white people to help us by charity. We must do something ourselves to draw public attention to our plight ... . We have had 150 years of the white men looking after us, and the result is, our people are being exterminated. The reason this conference is called today is so that the Aborigines themselves may discuss their problems and try to bring before the notice of the public and of parliament what our grievance is, and how it may be remedied. We ask for ordinary citizen rights, and full equality with other Australians.

Ferguson continued in the same vein, 'We have been waiting and waiting all our lives for the white people of Australia to better our conditions, but we have waited in vain':

> Surely the time has come at last for us to do something for ourselves, and make ourselves heard. This is why the Aborigines Progressive Association has been formed ... . We now have a Committee who are bringing before the public the injustices which our people have suffered. Our revelations have astounded many white people, who did not realise that such conditions as we describe could possibly exist in a free country. Now let me explain that our object is to abolish the Aborigines Protection Board. [Applause] We are going to abolish that Board, no matter how long it may take. Everything points to the fact that, within a short while, many people will support us among the white citizens of Australia.[16]

It was an interesting experience for Ming to be involved in such political collaboration. I believe that she would not have become involved were it not for the encouragement of Pearl Gibbs, especially given the union background of most of the male members of the Committee. But Pearl, who attended virtually every meeting of the Citizenship Committee and appears to have been crucial to its instigation (Horner pointed out that it was her offence at Miles' arrogance that caused the final split), had high hopes that the activists could win the support of the white women's organizations. 'Those of my race who understand our economic conditions have not a great deal of faith in what the white man promises to do for us. We know that we must carry on the fight ourselves,' she wrote in an article published in *Woman Today* magazine a few months later. 'Ah! My white sisters, I am appealing to you on behalf of my people to raise your voices with ours and help us to a better deal in life.'[17] It was an appeal that Ming, with her own high hopes of the feminist movement, could not resist.

*   *   *

Ming's first action as honorary secretary of the CAC was to draw attention to 'the position of Abo. [sic] girls in Sydney – no meeting place whatsoever!' (Inexplicably, the Oxford Group rooms were apparently no longer available.) At the next meeting, held in the second week of May 1938, she reported that she had received the promise of a donation of 12s 6d a week as 'rent for a room to use as Club for 3 months or meeting place, also in which to sell their crafts'. As CAC secretary she sent a formal letter the next day to Albert Thompson, requesting that his paper, the *Labour Daily*, 'open a fund to enable the Aborigines to obtain Citizen Rights'. Such funds were to be used as follows: '1. To enable Mr. Ferguson to visit the "out back" [sic] and organise his people ... 2. To provide rent for a room in the city in which our Aboriginal people could meet together; and also help finance it by selling their own beautiful hand-work.'[18] And so, the *Labour Daily* announced in May 1938:

> Attempts to alleviate the plight of Australian [A]boriginal girls are being made by a newly-formed body of citizens known as the Committee for Aboriginal Citizenship.
>
> In outlining the ambitions of the committee yesterday, Mrs Kingsley Strack, secretary, declared that the members intended taking every step to focus public attention on what she described as 'a national scandal'.

The Citizenship Committee (CAC) was going to establish 'head-quarters' for Aboriginal girls in service to 'congregate' and to display and sell their handicrafts. The plans included, the article continued in bold typeface, the aim of 'set[ting] up a magisterial inquiry into the trust fund into which the girls' wages were paid by their employers'. 'The girls are entitled to their money whenever they want it, but we claim that they have to wage a long and sometimes losing fight to get what is their own property,' Ming was reported as saying.[19]

Ming had also suggested in notes planning the Club that while the young women attending would 'enjoy' and 'quickly learn' from talks and lectures, as Aboriginal girls they could teach '*us*' 'generosity, hospitality, truth, courage & courtesy & the love of the Great Spirit – for these things they have *always* known'. Her ambitious plans represented a refinement and an extension of her original tea-party conception. Since late 1934, from Blackheath, Ming had entertained hopes of leaving Norman and supporting herself by opening a 'sort of artistic coffee or tea room & make it unusual with a studio at one end'. She had also begun writing articles for *The Women's Weekly* on Aboriginal legends, customs and local sites, hoping (again unsuccessfully) to escape her financial dependence upon Norman. (For Ming, as a number of other white women before and since, repackaging 'authentic' Aboriginal culture for popular consumption represented a way of achieving public recognition *and* a small income.) Although neither pleasant dream ever came to fruition, they were the seeds of her plan to make the apprentices' tea-room self-supporting.

In her endeavour, she would for the first time discover the existence of a far-flung network of concerned white women from diverse backgrounds. Mary Bennett, the teacher at a United Aborigines Mission at Mt Margaret, Morgans, in Western Australia, had already proved herself a formidable adversary of the Western Australian Aboriginal administration when Ming wrote to her about her Club proposal in late May 1938. Implacably opposed to the 'inhuman' laws that enabled the removal of Aboriginal children and the 'dismemberment' of their families, Bennett encouraged Aboriginal women to sell hand-made items on her home mission as an alternative to domestic service, and supported moves elsewhere to establish 'depots' and exhibitions of Aboriginal handcrafts. She was very sympathetic to Ming's scheme for a Girls' Club. 'Your aims are the true ones,' Bennett congratulated her warmly in May 1938, sending her 'examples of the weaving, raffia etc done here to furnish the club'.[20]

Helen Baillie was a nursing sister in Melbourne, who had helped form the Victorian Aboriginal Fellowship Group in 1932 and was, with

A. Burdeu, one of the two non-Aboriginal people involved with the Australian Aborigines League in Victoria. Bennett put Ming in touch with her, promising Ming in her letter she would arrange for 'our wonderful Miss Baillie to order a Framlingham made chair for your girls' club'. Baillie suggested mainstream recreational groups such as the Girl Guides and the YWCA for Aboriginal girls in service. '[T]hey don't make friends easily as they are conscious of colour (tho' some of these girls were almost white), and so are lonely,' Baillie wrote as an argument for pressing them into these white girls' groups.[21] She was also opposed to the practice of withholding the girls' wages: 'Of course if the natives had to[o] much money they would only waste it but they should have a right to spend the money they earn. It should not be paid into an account they never see,' she protested in 1936.[22] An energetic if rather erratic person, Baillie kept up a long and rather tiresome correspondence with Ming through 1938 about a mix-up over where she had sent the folding chair made by Framlingham residents, and would at a later date organize Ming to open an exhibition of Aboriginal craftworks. (A 'very funny experience' wrote Ming, who had been virtually railroaded into it by Baillie.)

If Bennett and Baillie, respectively, represented the contemporary pro-Aboriginal white women on the frontier and in the city, Erica Wedge, who acted as Ming's hostess in Cootamundra on an Oxford Group visit in May 1938, was their counterpart for the small country towns that dotted rural Australia. She took Ming to see the Cootamundra Aboriginal Girls' Home in what was evidently an established gesture of womanly philanthropic interest, rather than a visit of investigation. Ming made a brief report in the CAC minutes that she had seen 'two white (apparently) children there, made some enquiries'. There was little real significance in such a visit, which being marked by special treatment of both the visitors and the visited (Ming and her friends were honoured with a musical performance) did not reflect the day-to-day experience of the inmates. (As one Cootamundra inmate later recalled, 'Most of the time we wished that someone would come like official or something, because we had a real Sunday dinner.'[23]) But Erica Wedge was inspired by Ming, writing a month later to tell her that she was going to set up a kind of Sunday school group for the Cootamundra girls. She had also arranged for an exapprentice who was now employed as an assistant in the Home – 'the sweet girl from the Home. The one in the kitchen, do you remember her[?]' – to visit a friend of hers in town. 'I thought she wouldn't be shy & strange at Amy's,' she wrote. '... we had such a happy afternoon & such lots of laughter, & little Margaret was laughing away & seemed so happy ...'[24] Describing Margaret, actually a woman of 32, as 'a sweet girl' is an indication of her approach. What all the white women Ming now met had in common, of course, was a maternalistic attitude towards Aboriginal women, which Ming, after her previous experiences, no doubt found heartening.

The response of Aboriginal people to Ming's Girls' Club proposal is unknown, and indeed there is no evidence that the Club ever functioned regularly, if at all. (Like the tea-parties, it required the cooperation of sympathetic employers as well as the participation of the Aboriginal girls.) It seems that Pearl Gibbs viewed what Ming called her pet scheme quite favourably, as some years later she brought Ming to a meeting at La Perouse, the Aboriginal settlement, to discuss forming a Club there.[25] Nothing came of this, and in 1942, Ming wrote in despair that she had tried for years to 'find even a *room*' where the Aboriginal girls in service could meet ('surely in their own land we could spare this much for their comfort, books to read & a cup of tea together would at least be a beginning') but without success.[26] But the Girls' Club idea had been quickly subsumed by other concerns preoccupying the Citizenship Committee. Ming's privileged position of class and race made her useful to the Aboriginal movement in other ways that were both more practical and more political.

16
The stone of anthropology

From the outset Ming and Pearl were brought together not as servant and mistress, not even as victim and defender, but as two concerned activists. Ming's telling of 'the story of wronged aboriginal woman to women' at public meetings was considered to be appropriate women's work by her white male colleagues; the Aboriginal men at the head of the movement similarly considered Pearl to be a more appropriate person than they to speak on women's issues.[1] As a two-woman team it was difficult for Ming to sustain the maternalistic approach she had customarily adopted to Aboriginal women, not least because Pearl was somewhat older. Pearl was intensely proud of her own mother, and as a token of her regard for Ming she gave her a studio postcard portrait of her, further deflating any presumption by Ming of a maternal role. The fact that Pearl herself was also a mother, with a son involved in the war that had so recently broken out, encouraged Ming's identification with her as an equal – Ming's son Peter was now an air force pilot. The two became close, personally and well as politically, as evidenced perhaps most profoundly by Pearl confiding in Ming about sensitive personal relationship matters.[2]

This relationship between the two women was particularly unusual for its time. Throughout Australian history at least until the Second World War the most common relationship between individual Aboriginal and white women was that of mistress and servant; the maternalism towards Aboriginal people so characteristic of the organized women's movement of the time actually mirrored the traditional idealized domestic service relationship. As these two passionate women shared a platform before these women's groups, they must have made something of an impact. I can imagine how optimistic they must have felt in those heady days of protest.

* * *

Figure 11   Ming in her garden at Lindfield, Sydney, 1938. Author's collection.

The Aborigines Progressive Association's main agenda was, at it stated, the attainment of full citizenship rights for Aborigines. By this they meant not only suffrage (while some Aboriginal people were, in theory, entitled to vote in state and Federal elections, most were unable to exercise this right, or did not know they could), but freedom from a range of discriminatory state laws and practices denying them civil rights enjoyed by other Australians. The Federal Constitution had not only denied Aboriginal people the universal right to vote, but also specifically denied the Commonwealth the power to make laws for Aboriginal people, the states jealously guarding their colonial prerogative to deal with 'their' Aboriginal populations as they saw fit. As the twentieth century wore on, in NSW the regime of the Protection Board became increasingly draconian, to the point that, after 1936, Aboriginal people could be forced onto Board managed stations by law, where they were obliged to endure all kinds of abuses, ranging from the petty to the debilitating. The Board could insist that the wages of any Aboriginal worker be paid into its own coffers, and the practice of removing Aboriginal children, now into a third decade of legislative sanction, was rampant.

Following the demise of the 1937 Select Committee, the NSW Deputy Premier and leader of the Country Party, M. F. Bruxner, had announced piously in March 1938 that the 'administration of [A]boriginal affairs affords little reason for satisfaction, and the Government has decided upon a reorganised system with a new deal for these remnants of the Stone Age' in the government's policy speech. Public interest in the issue of reforming the Board was at its height and it was in this atmosphere of promise that Gibbs and Ferguson set up the new Citizenship Committee. Their APA quickly tempered the original demand for the abolition of the state control altogether for Aboriginal representation on a reformed administration.[3] This may have been necessary to secure white support, for most white Australians had difficulty accepting that Aboriginal people might not need some form of non-Aboriginal guidance, even if it was not the bureaucratic model offered by the Board as it was currently constituted.

The APA activists could countenance calls for Board representation alongside Aboriginal from sympathetic groups like the labour unions, church groups or women's organizations. But they were resolutely and consistently opposed to the drive for an anthropological 'expert' to be appointed to the Board (a move led by Elkin). The surge of white interest in anthropology during the 1930s was a way in which white people enjoyed 'the pleasure of feeling superior', the APA manifesto declared.

Ferguson stated blankly: '[W]e resent any further treatment as scientific speccements [specimens].'[4]

Within a few weeks of the Stevens-Bruxner ministry's return to power in April 1938, Pearl publicly appealed to her 'white sisters' not to give her people 'the stone of anthropology'.[5] Soon afterwards the United Associations of Women (UAW) wrote to the Board proposing that Caroline Kelly (the anthropologist and social worker who had represented the UAW and the APNR, as well as Sydney University, before the 1937 Enquiry) be appointed to that Board as an anthropologist; they also wrote to the Premier nominating Kelly.[6] Kelly's credentials made her the ideal candidate from the perspective of the women's organizations. As UAW president Jessie Street would complain later, whenever the feminist groups 'make representations for women to be appointed to Boards, we are told that we have no-one qualified to suggest', but Mrs Kelly had 'better qualifications than the persons already appointed'.[7] Women, like Aborigines, had to justify their ability to exercise any kind of public role. But the women's groups' decision to turn to Kelly was viewed with alarm. Ferguson distrusted the 'scientists', Elkin particularly, and had made his hostility to Kelly clear in the course of the 1937 Enquiry. It seemed to the APA activists that the anthropologists intended to make out that the Aboriginal people were 'naturally backward', and so requiring their 'expert' protection and control.

Ming, and many other women like her, was an enthusiastic supporter of Elkin, admiring his efforts to rehabilitate the image of traditional Aboriginal culture. During the enquiry, she had written to Elkin expressing her desire to 'do what ever I can to help Mrs Kelly', and explaining at length how she had come to be interested in the cause of Aboriginal reform through her childhood contact with the Wallaga Lake Yuin. '[F]rom my earliest childhood the Aboriginals – men, women & children have been my close companions & teachers,' she told him, going on to describe how the elder Merriman took her around the area, 'hand-in-hand' teaching her his culture:

> Then one day, as the sun was setting … I sat with 'Merriman' & an old & silent woman of the Tribe, upon a huge granite rock on the Lakes edge. I too was silent as 'Merriman's' old brown hand held mine firmly, in case I slithered over the edge, & at last, as mists glittered & Merriman's eyes grew more & more sombre, he broke the silence, saying 'We were *better* dead – my people!' *My* heart almost stood still, as great tears splashed down upon the granite – poor 'Merriman', I dared not ask the reason, but I vowed that I would help his people what *ever* it was …

You see, I lived in a selfish world & I forgot my promise to these dear & utterly defenceless people, but now I *know* what I must do, & I shall never cease until they *do* receive justice. Many people have become broken-hearted & hopeless at the ever-lasting delay I almost gave up too, but I have found a new sense of power to help me this time ... [8]

While on the Citizenship Committee, in fact, Ming joined a throng of others to attend the popular evening classes run by the professor and another anthropologist, Camilla Wedgwood, at Sydney University. There is no doubt that the APA activists would have found Ming's admiration of Elkin difficult to accept. While Pearl privately told Ming that she had previously 'tried to avoid the Old Way' because of Board repression, but had more recently found out her 'totem' from some South Coast women elders,[9] she remained distrustful of the anthropologists' concern with the distinctiveness of Aboriginal culture. When Ming wrote to Elkin in March 1938 about her decision to enrol in his classes, declaring she admired him because he had 'devoted' his life 'to the study of these people, not only as an Anthropologist, but because you loved & understood them as human beings', we get a sense of the tone of an argument she may have had with Pearl.[10]

Pearl utilized Ming's connections with the various women's groups to provide communication between the APA and the women's movement, the two women speaking together before various women's clubs and other associations between 1938 and 1939. For Pearl Gibbs one of the most important roles Ming could play was to try to persuade those groups not to endorse Caroline Kelly as their chosen representative. In fact, Ming did become a vociferous opponent of the UAW's nominated representative, carrying through this aspect of the CAC platform with singular determination. It was an indication of the extent of Pearl's influence.

Helen Baillie had sent Ming an invitation to attend the annual meeting of the APNR in November 1938, thinking Ming might find Kelly, the APNR's secretary, 'very sympathetic & helpful regarding your Club & shop'. Ming did attend the meeting, which was held on the day the NSW government announced its intention to appoint a Superintendent of Aborigines Welfare, who would be chairman of a reconstructed Aborigines Welfare Board. Ming, who already despised the APNR, was unimpressed by the insipid resolution that arose, and singling out Kelly's speech in a letter she wrote about it later, launched her attack on Kelly.[11]

Then, in February 1939, Ming wrote to the *Sun* in response to a brief article citing Kelly. Disappointed by the return of 'half-caste girls ...

trained for domestic work in white households' to their reserves, Kelly had attributed this failure to raise their 'social status' to the racism endemic outside the reserves, as symbolized by segregated church congregations. It was a red rag to Ming, who angrily responded that this alleged racism was 'another of Mrs Kellies [sic] "Herrings"', aimed at diverting attention from the 'real truth, which is, not the church & not the white population which needs an awakening but the whole policy of the so called Protection Bd.'

'All this talk causes the Aborigines themselves a vast amount of amusement,' Ming continued, 'for the facts are well known to them & they have no patience with insincerity they have a keen perception & recognise the publicity agent at work immediately.' Reading this, I have no doubt that Pearl Gibbs was responsible for Ming's change of attitude towards Kelly. These facts, Ming continued, were the removal of the girls from their own reserves, their subsequent return to different reserves and the starvation conditions there. These deliberate government policy formulations were the cause of Aboriginal oppression, which she accused Kelly of obscuring for the sake of personal advancement: 'Perhaps when we are not looking for self help or jobs for ourselves we are in a better position to both see & speak the truth.'[12]

The day Ming wrote this letter, a new Superintendent of Aborigines Welfare, Alfred Lipscombe (ex-superintendent of Dr Barnado's Homes and author of a book on breeding livestock) was appointed to take the place of the Police Commissioner on the Board. Several days later, Ming drew up a new CAC public circular, which exhorted the appointment of 'an Aboriginal man *and* woman' representative, a women's organization representative, a labour representative, a church representative, and the granting of citizenship to all NSW Aborigines. The suggestion for a woman's representative specifically stated that such woman should be 'not a social Anthropologist, since the Government has already decided upon a man [Elkin] to fill this position'.[13]

Copies of this letter were sent out in March 1939 with a covering note requesting 'approval' to a range of individuals and organizations, including all the major women's organizations in NSW. Though the circular did get the support of some, including the ALP's Women's Advisory Council, there was not a very favourable response from the conservative women's groups – both the Housewives' Association and the Racial Hygiene Association politely declined to support their demands. The President of the UAW, Jessie Street, told Ming that 'as a result of your letter', the UAW had convened a sub-committee to consider the treatment of Aborigines. (She didn't mention that she had advised this sub-committee – headed by a Mrs Blanks, who had represented the UAW alongside Kelly during the enquiry – to lobby for the training of Aboriginal children to work on farms, 'as the shortage of domestic workers is so acute'.) Street enclosed a letter on the UAW letterhead for the Citizenship Committee to forward to the Chief Secretary if they wished, endorsing the appointment of a male and a female Aboriginal representative to the Board 'in some capacity', labour, women's and church representatives, and the granting of citizenship to NSW Aborigines. However, the UAW sent a separate letter to the Chief Secretary, recommending 'that Miss Camilla Wedgwood should be the woman appointed to the Board'.[14] As Wedgwood was also a social anthropologist, their recommendation was in direct contravention of the CAC's suggestion, which would explain their surreptiousness.

The Feminist Club sent their own four-point resolution of suggested appointments to the Chief Secretary in response to the CAC circular. No mention was made of citizenship rights, and in her covering letter to the CAC, the president (Ming's friend Preston-Stanley had been replaced by Norma Cameron) drew Ming's attention to their omission of this crucial fifth point, asking her for 'further details'. 'Does the suggestion of full citizen's rights include all natives whether on reserves, settlements or living as ordinary citizens?' she asked. Citizenship was a privilege and not a right for Aboriginal people, it seemed. The Feminist Club proposed that Aboriginal representatives should be appointed only to a 'sub-committee' to the Board 'with a view to studying the problem of educating the Aborigines for full citizenship'. Evidently, the Feminist Club did not consider Aboriginal people capable of administering themselves to any degree. The concern with the supposed 'problem of educating the Aborigines' was a clear allusion to the argument for the appointment of anthropologists. And indeed they explicitly endorsed Kelly as their preferred women's representative – 'as she has made a thorough study of the question of the Australian Aborigines both from the point of view of an Anthropologist and a Social Worker'.[15]

Some months later, the Protection Board itself resolved that a woman experienced in educational and welfare matters should be nominated, and suggested the Education Department's newly appointed female inspector of domestic science schools. Board member H. J. Bate had a letter from Ming around the same time. 'I am in receipt of your letter of the 27th August,' he had written, 'and in reply have to state that in no circumstances will the woman you refer to be appointed to the Board.

I think that if she were, everybody would immediately resign.[16]

As no copy of Ming's letter has been located, her nominee remains unknown, but Bate's surprising rancour raises speculation. Possibly Ming had suggested Pearl Gibbs.

Only a few weeks earlier Ming had privately expressed her consternation on hearing from Mick Sawtell, that the Police Commissioner and Board Chairman Mackay had promised him a position on the new Board. There was one condition: he would drop the current, but long-standing, campaign by the CAC for Aboriginal farmer Percy Moseley's rights to his land at Kempsey. (Sawtell agreed.) Ming was concerned that the offer was a tactic to disband the CAC.[17] What Pearl Gibbs thought of the offer is not known, but perhaps Sawtell's apparent duplicity motivated the pair to put up Pearl's nomination instead.

Together, Pearl and Ming attended the next annual conference of the APNR in October 1939. Caroline Kelly was also at the APNR meeting, as temporary secretary. Ming and she crossed swords, as Ming recorded in her diary:

> Was attacked by Mrs Kelly an *awful* woman, for, as *she* said 'Stirring up trouble on all the Stations in N.S.W.'! I said 'you flatter me I didn't know I had such powers'. I had a word quietly with Professor Elkin afterwards, & told Mrs Kelly she couldn't speak the truth ...

Ming responded to the implied slight that Aboriginal people were incapable of initiating their own political action by writing another letter to the paper, pointedly ridiculing Kelly. Having asserted that 'Half-caste & Aboriginal people in N.S.W. are entirely fit for Citizenship far more so than many of our politicians', Ming went on to state that Aboriginal people 'are mostly more intelligent in their Natural tribal States than some white people',

> and their marriage laws & Social Codes are so intricate that few white men & *no* white women have ever mastered them all ... not even the women who call themselves 'Tribal Sisters' (to the extreme mirth of the Aborigines) be it said who immediately conjure up pictures of somewhat portly female anthropologists prancing ecstatically to the strains of some Aboriginal dirge & attired in somewhat meagre belts of 'ochre', sparsely dotted with Emu feathers

At this point Ming took the opportunity to show that she herself, while also incapable of 'mastering' Aboriginal culture, had a personal rapport with Aboriginal women that no white anthropologist could claim.

'[O]ne Aboriginal woman said to me,' Ming wrote (was this Pearl?), 'I hope a *fan* was added.' 'I asked why & the reply was "to hide the blushes of our "Tribal Sister"!'

Ming concluded that Aboriginal people required civil rights and Board representation. 'This is the very *least* we can do,' she exhorted her white readers, to 'make amends for the past' and to 'shoulder our responsibilities even at this late hour'.[18]

For Ming, her relationship with Aboriginal people had acquired a much more practical dimension. In her work on the Committee, she represented Aboriginal women's concerns with two major issues, child endowment payments (which the Board typically withheld from Aboriginal mothers) and domestic employment. As an upper-class white woman, she could assist Aboriginal parents, being able to call on girls working in their employers' homes and mediate with employers, where they could not. Ming also went to the Parramatta Industrial School during her time on the Committee, to meet the girls there and, in at least one case, to intercede for them. (A mysterious note to Ming from 'Eileen', apparently an Aboriginal domestic worker, promising to make breakfast for the family, remains as solitary proof that during this period Ming gave shelter to at least one Aboriginal girl.) A number of letters among Ming's papers attest to the existence of Aboriginal networks, in which concerned families would actively seek out sympathetic whites to help them.

Having again become an employer herself early in 1939, when she successfully wrested Jane, an ex-apprentice, from her mother's household, Ming was increasingly aware of the complexities of the Aboriginal response to the Board policy and their opposition to the control of what Pearl Gibbs called 'the Persecution Board'. In August 1939, for instance, an Aboriginal woman living in inner-city Sydney Mrs Brown, wrote to Ming to ask her to help 'a little girl'. Lynda was a friend of Mrs Brown's daughter, the two girls having met in Cootamundra Home. She was 19 years old and had finished her four years' apprenticeship with her employer in Sydney, but 'still they hang on to her'. Mrs Brown enclosed Lynda's letter to her, and asked Ming if she could visit her at her employers as they had refused to allow her to see the girl. Lynda had written that her workload was heavy, and 'I wont to go home where I came from and Mrs English [who had replaced Miss Lowe as Homefinder in 1937] doing her best to keep me under them but the first train I can get home I am going home and they are not going to stop me I can tell you.' Writing to Ming shortly afterwards, Lynda then told her she could live with her grandfather in western NSW – 'he will take me any time untill I find work ... near him'. She had many relatives in the country, 'and I would very much like to go home to them all and if you can help me to get home I would be very greatful as soon as you can please Mrs Strack'. Ming replied and then received another, more anxious letter from Mrs Brown. Lynda had been in to see her:

> What has me worried is that she keep's on talking about running away, and going home, she says she has nearly got her Fare saved. I asked her last night to promis me she would do nothing till, I wrote to you, I was wandering if you would ring her up and make an appointment for her to see you one evening this week ...
>
> I don't like to trouble you dear Mrs Strack, but I would like you to see her and talk with her, it would be terrible for her to run away, Good-ness knows what would become of her ...[19]

The following year Mrs Brown's husband Edward, now living in central NSW, wrote to Ming in May 1940 to let her know that Lynda had been returned home. Now, he asked her, 'could you see to the return of my Daughter'. He had found out from the Board that her indenture would expire in March and was told to arrange a position for her at home, if he wanted her to come back home. Having found her a situation 'at 10/- a week' his daughter had still not been released. That 'means that my girl as lost £2-0-0 & perhaps lose a good job,' he wrote, 'The A.P.B. seems to have the girls as Slaves.' He wrote her a further letter enquiring about his daughter's trust money – 'as usual they try to do her out of it,' wrote Ming.[20] These letters highlight the importance for Aboriginal people at this time for the rights that might protect them and their children from exploitation. Likewise some friends of Bill Ferguson, from a large country town in NSW, hoped Ming might be able to find their daughter a domestic situation in Sydney, independently of the Board. They were not opposed to her working in domestic service far from home, only their inability to have any say in the matter.[21] Reading these letters, I can understand why Caroline Kelly's 'tribal sisterhood' struck Ming as being so ridiculous.

* * *

Such letters also highlight the role played by Aboriginal men as husbands and fathers, in the face of a policy which marginalized them, relegated them to the sidelines, and indeed denied their existence. While in the midst of putting together all these fragments of stories, I got a phone call from a man called Ron, on behalf of his wife, Brenda. They had my phone number from Peter Read, the historian who founded Link-Up NSW, an organization dedicated to reuniting removed Aboriginal people with their families. (Earlier, I had contacted both Peter and Link-Up to let them know what I was doing.) For some reason Peter Read thought I might have something on Brenda's father. To my amazement, I did. Guy Jones, an Aboriginal horse-breaker and boundary-rider from Warangesda, had gone to the Citizenship Committee in January 1939, his daughter Iris having mysteriously disappeared some two years earlier from her position as a servant to a married female teacher on one of the Board's stations. Iris, now 22, had been removed by the Board at six years of age and her father had been keeping an ear out for her ever since; but from the explosive details Sawtell reported, in his query to the Board, it appears that Iris's father had heard some unsettling rumours about the 'protection' his daughter had been receiving:

> The girl was apprenticed to the school master & relieving manager at Farwest reserve, named Shaw. Shaw used to take the girl for night drives in his car, & when his wife was away the girl used to sleep at his house. The girl became pregnant, & was sent away, but no body knows to where. Her father does not know. The aborigines ask our committee to seek the aid of the police, but I feel sure that we should consult your Board first.[22]

When Brenda (Iris's daughter) got in touch with me she already suspected that her father was a teacher and assistant manager on a Board station. Brenda had been able to access various records scattered through the state archives which included references to a dossier complied by the Board in 1939, and now missing, reporting on the manager's 'alleged paternity'. For Brenda that letter from Sawtell to the Board recording her grandfather's concern was crucial. She had grown up knowing she was Aboriginal – her mother continued to support her and see her throughout her life, although she lived with a white foster-mother – but other that had had no contact with her Aboriginal family.

The Board had replied to the CAC in February 1939 that inquiries were being made. By April they had a report together which they referred to the police department to see whether Shaw's 'alleged paternity' could be corroborated. This became the missing file, sent in May from the police to the Child Welfare Department, with a 'view to the institution of proceedings against Shaw for maintenance'. The Board then decided to advise the Education Department to dispense with Shaw's services as 'his conduct and indiscreet relations with the half-caste girl Iris Jones ... could not fail to have a subversive effect on the people of the Station and his position as Teacher'. His services were terminated at the end of June 1939. The evidence, however, was judged insufficient to institute maintenance proceedings.[23] Nor did the Board see any reason to inform the Citizenship Committee or Guy Jones of Iris's whereabouts. Ming wrote again to the Board in July demanding to know where she was. 'You will be aware of course (since the Bd is responsible for this girl's welfare) that she became pregnant while at Farwest Station, then disappeared!' A stiff reply of August told her that the Child Welfare Department and the Board were investigating the subject, and it was 'not in accordance with departmental practice to disclose information regarding such matters to outside bodies'. [24] There was no further correspondence from the Board on the matter.

In fact, in 1937 Iris's mistress Sarah, who was also pregnant – her baby born only two months after Iris's – had taken Iris to Sydney, asking her brother and his wife to look after her. After the birth, Iris and her baby were placed in a Girls Shelter, and a year later, Iris went to work at a Sydney Hospital. She placed baby Brenda with a foster-mother and she was able to see her regularly. In April 1940, Bill Ferguson, at Farwest Station on one of his APA organizing trips, wrote to Sawtell and asked him to tell Ming that Iris and her baby had been returned to Darlington Point. Ferguson's information was inaccurate. Iris had indeed been eventually allowed to take her baby on a *holiday* to visit Darlington Point and her father but in the end, to her great disappointment, her daughter remained with the foster-mother. Although Iris worked to pay for Brenda's upkeep throughout her life, she never received maintenance payments or any other assistance from Shaw. Shaw was protected from any obligations by the Board forcing Iris to sign an affidavit at North Sydney Police Station stating that she would never speak of the father of her child.[25] Just as Iris had been prevented from knowing her own Aboriginal father, so her child, Brenda, would be prevented from knowing her white father. The Board liked to depict itself as rescuing fatherless children – but it was creating them.

Brenda introduced me to her own daughter, Dana, and we ended up becoming close friends. Dana's youngest child is the same age as my eldest, and at the age of two and a half the two boys, with their green eyes and honey-gold skin, looked uncannily alike. Watching them play, I ponder on the circularity of history, and the way that this history has brought us together. It's strange to think that my great-grandmother knew Dana's great-grandfather all those years ago; of how interconnected our worlds are.

* * *

Although Pearl Gibbs would be the only Aboriginal member of the Citizenship Committee (Bill Ferguson rarely appearing), Mrs Brown was one of a number of Aboriginal people associated with the Aborigines Progressive Association who attended CAC meetings on a more or less regular basis, and she knew Ming personally. It must have been deeply satisfying for Ming to be so called on after her experiences with Del and the 'milk and water' politics of the APNR. With the Citizenship Committee behind her, she could personally see to it that Aboriginal girls were returned to their families, from the Board that had taken Mary from her, all those years earlier, her 'one bright spot' she would never see again. Now she was working hand-in-hand with Aboriginal activists, and with Aboriginal families, at their invitation and direction. She was now keenly aware of the privileges of race she held, and no longer proud of them. Kelly's claim to 'tribal sisterhood' was, Ming knew, an absurdity.

By the time of the 1939 APNR meeting Pearl herself had come to symbolize Aboriginal equality for Ming. As in the previous year, the resolution arising was remarkably vague and ineffectual, urging the introduction of the reconstructed Board as soon as possible, to carry out an 'enlightened policy'.[26] Ming wrote to the editor of the *Daily Telegraph* afterwards, complaining that, again, 'citizenship was not mentioned, yet … we all know that citizenship is the *only* thing which will lift these people from the depths of despair & remove them from the clutches of the so-called Protection Bd'.

'Beside me at this meeting', she went on,

> sat a lady, a half-caste & a friend of mine her Mother is a much loved Aborigine & well known on the South Coast of N.S.W. her father was an Englishman a seaman in the British navy, her husband was a seaman, also in the British navy, and her son, is at this moment, somewhere at sea, in the Australian navy! Yet she possesses *no* Citizen Rights of any kind, instead she or her children may be pounced upon at any time by the Protection Bd. & sent to some Reserve or Station, labelled 'Aborigines' & this can be done & *is* frequently because the Aboriginal 'Act' gives the Board complete control over any persons even *suspected* of having Aboriginal blood![27]

Ming's defining of Mrs Gibbs as her social equal, a 'friend' and a 'lady', rather than a 'girl', was significant. Her identification with Pearl sharpened the reality of the 1936 amendments to Aboriginal legislation, under which Pearl was as vulnerable as any apprentice to the Board. And, Ming continued, such racial discrimination was unjustified in *any* case, 'Full blood Aborigines' also needed and deserved citizenship rights – they too 'fought side by side with white Australians in the last war'.

But Pearl was on the verge of pulling out of the Citizenship Committee. At the next meeting of the Committee, a week later, she and Ming sat listening to the anecdotes of Sawtell and Thompson of their experiences with Aborigines in Northern Australia. 'My little Half-caste friend Mrs Gibbs listened intently,' Ming wrote in her diary,

> I was most interested – we all were. [T]hey remarked afterwards that, there was a strangely peaceful mood upon everyone, that it was something about the room, & how good of Mr McNeil [the Oxford Grouper who owned the rooms] to lend it to us. I told them that this room was a sort of sanctuary where tired & worried people came & rested with Mr McNeil's h[and] upon them.

If Pearl was smarting from the APNR meeting and Kelly's comments, she would not have appreciated Ming's diary entry. Certainly, this was the last CAC meeting she attended. According to Horner, Pearl left Sydney because she was 'impatient' with the 'complacency' of her audiences, as well as having argued with Ferguson.[28] By early November she had left for the South Coast. Pearl sent Ming a painted handkerchief from Nowra wishing her and her family the best for 1940.

Although Ming may have been successful in destroying Kelly's ambitions of Board representation (Kelly in fact disappeared from the scene altogether within a few years) she did not successfully persuade the women's movement to support Aboriginal citizenship. When the new Welfare Board came in, complete with its programme of 'assimilating the Aborigines' under Elkin's expert guidance and with no Aboriginal representation, the conservative women's groups would welcome it enthusiastically, even though there was no women, 'trained' or otherwise, on the Board. While Pearl Gibbs would eventually be appointed to the Board in the 1950s as an Aboriginal representative (her position as a lone Aboriginal woman was extremely difficult, as one might imagine) no representative of the women's groups would ever be appointed.

With Pearl gone, Ming too would find her sense of purpose in pursuing the cause of citizenship and Board reform dissipate. Struggling to construct a new kind of relationship with Jane, the young Aboriginal woman she now had working for her, Ming would revitalize her concern with 'protecting defenceless Aboriginal women', instead.

17
Miss Pink wants my help

At first, after Pearl left, Ming was still riding on a crest, enjoying that 'sense of power' she had first felt when speaking before the Feminist Club on Del's behalf. After several long, busy years involved in the Aboriginal political struggle, although little had been achieved, she had come into contact with major white activists and could count herself among them. Her correspondence with them and her diary entries reveal a growing confidence in her political experience and familiarity with the principal players.

Ming gave a talk by invitation at a Feminist Club luncheon in April 1940 on the subject of Aboriginal rights – 'bit of an ordeal ... . Press were very interested, all questioned me afterwards. People wept.' The proceedings of the 1937 Select Committee Enquiry had finally been published, together with the report of a secret Public Service Board enquiry of 1938, and the parliamentary debate on the Aborigines Protection Amendment Bill had begun.

Ming took a keen interest in all this. On 7 May 1940 she visited Parliament House to see Mark Davidson, the Labor member who had headed the original enquiry into the Board and now strenuously opposed the bill, pointing out that it still gave the Board power to 'kidnap the children' and continue the 'extermination of the race'.[1] '[W]ent through Abo Bill with him – made amendments,' Ming noted casually in her diary.

The following day she wrote to Charles Duguid, a prominent South Australian doctor and missionary. She could see the acute disappointment the proposed bill entailed for the Aboriginal activists. The Act, she wrote, was 'a ghastly affair',

> giving heaven only knows what powers & protection to the *Abo. Bd.* itself, but *none* to the Aboriginal people! I wonder that they dare

bring forward such a thing. Michael Sawtell & I have done our best
to prevent it going any further & many others are doing their utmost
to stop its passage through the House, but to our great surprise Dr
Elkin appears to approve of it & Mrs Kelly has been, as usual, pot-
tering about between the Abo. Bd. and the Aborigines, until no one
knows upon which side she really is.[2]

But Ming was herself succumbing to her inability to see Aboriginal
people as equals capable of sharing power, writing to Duguid of 'our
beloved old Darkies' and her efforts to try 'in a humble way to help
them & sometimes to fight their battles for them – they are so utterly
defenceless'. Ming would have been well aware by 1940 that the term
'darkies' was demeaning to Aboriginal people. Pearl Gibbs used the
term ironically to highlight the racism of the Board, and Ming herself
had used it years earlier in much the same way, to attack her parents'
attitude towards Aboriginal servants – 'Pretty bright for a darkie?' she
had written sarcastically in her letter to her father about her mother's
apprenticed worker Annie. The patronizing tone of her letter to Duguid
reflected her eroding faith in the movement for Aboriginal equality and
independence.

A fortnight later, on 22 May, the new Welfare Board legislation went
through. It would take effect from June. Ming wrote to Sawtell several
days later announcing that she no longer wanted to act as secretary
for the CAC, and indeed thought that the committee 'should go out
of existence for a time'. Michael Sawtell had written to the Board's
Chairman offering himself for a position on the new Board (he had not
got his promised appointment after all). Almost certainly, Ming's decision was influenced by Sawtell's latest overture to the Board, although
she seemed content to leave the citizenship movement. Sawtell, for his
part, happily concurred with her suggestion to disband the CAC.

* * *

I find among Ming's papers a letter card dating from that period in her
life. Norman had finally got his own advertising agency off the ground
in 1937, and it was humming along nicely when they moved once
again, in August 1938. Their new house, at Wahroonga along the
Pacific Highway, shortly before it turns out to Hornsby and the
north coast, is gone now. Where there is only a large, dark-grey slab of
apartments today, the cartoon image on their change-of-address
card (drawn by one of Norman's commercial artists) shows a sizeable
cottage surrounded by fir trees, with an Enid Blyton elfin halo around
it. Following a laden jalopy through the garden gate and clutching an

assortment of dogs and cats come the Stracks. There's my Gran, a slim, elegant young woman of 18, with her typewriter (I have learned, in the meantime, that Gran typed all Ming's CAC correspondence for her); Peter in his air force cap and goggles; Helen grinning on her grinning pony – they had a pony now, too. Norman with a large camera (he has developed a great interest in photography and will take numerous photographs of my father when he is born). And Ming – almost marching – a lipsticked smile and an Eton bob, a boomerang pin in her hat, a handful of spears and an Aboriginal shield under one arm, and under the other what at first appears to be a large black cat, but is in fact a little black tribesman, complete with spear, headband and beard.

The image is both touching and disturbing at the same time. Suddenly I see how Ming's friends and family viewed her activities in the movement for Aboriginal rights – not as a threat, or even as a challenge, but as an amusing eccentricity. It also gives me an odd insight into how Ming herself understood what she was doing. The implication underpinning the caricature is that 'the Aborigines' themselves are 'hers', their cause her pet project. Looking at the picture, I can feel Ming's self-importance, her vanity. I can see how her life had finally become close to what she wanted it to be: successful, happy, in a home surrounded by a loving family who supported her engagement in the public world. (Even Norman supported her activities, assisting the Citizenship Committee in their campaign to embarrass the Chief Secretary with his queries, as 'a citizen and a taxpayer', about the composition and function of the Board.) And it highlights for me the curious sensation I get when studying these period of Ming's life, that the Aboriginal people in her life have become flattened out, unreal, distant. It's all a kind of mild, faintly ludicrous fantasy, that time in her life when she raced from meeting to public talk to luncheon trying to raise support amongst the women of her social circles for Aboriginal rights, hobnobbing with radical activists, writing to politicians, circulating petitions.

* * *

'Miss Pink wants my help,' Ming recorded brightly in her diary in August 1940. She had just been to lunch with the outspoken anthropologist, who was in Sydney drumming up support for her campaign to establish a secular reserve for the Walpiri in central Australia and for her own appointment as a protector or administrator. Pink was up against firm opposition locally and was now estranged from Elkin. It appears that Olive Pink hoped Ming could help her get the backing of the Feminist Club.

At the end of June 1940, shortly after suggesting the CAC go 'out of existence', Ming had become an executive member of the Feminist Club. (She had been an ordinary member since early 1939, after delivering a talk on Aborigines and citizenship at a Club luncheon.) A month later, she received a letter from Olive Pink, curtly asking if only 'mixed blood' people were involved with the CAC. This implied criticism related to Pink's recent attack on the Citizenship Committee.

Pink had argued in the press that the CAC's civil rights aims failed 'to prevent the extermination of the race', whereas she campaigned for the creation of secular reserves confined to 'full bloods' as the only way the survival of the race could be ensured.[3] 'No one could possibly doubt your sincerity,' Ming now wrote back diplomatically,

> in wanting to segregate the genuine Full Blood and in Queensland & the West where Full Bloods are comparatively untouched by Whites, I think it would be advisable, but that is something that I personally am not an authority upon .... [B]ut I *do* know something on the problem of N.S.W. There are the same two – Half Cast[e]s & Full Blood here also, but with the exception of a few of the very old 'Aborigines' who do long for the old freedom & primitive life of their ancestors, they all ask & almost implore us to help them live as we do, to dress, to behave, to be like white people. They even despise their black brothers & sisters & for this we can thank the 'Policy' of the A.P. Board of N.S.W. which deliberately set about this method of weaning the young Abo girls away from their parents by telling them 'they didn't want to live in' a Blacks Camp & be laughed at etc.[4]

Ming's ambivalence about the APA's demand for citizenship was evident in her reply. Despite her insistence that NSW people retained their distinctive culture, and despite her apportioning the 'blame' for any loss of this culture to Board policy, Ming too considered the relatively 'uncontaminated' culture of the people of central Australia more attractively, 'genuinely', Aboriginal.

Ming and Olive Pink had met before, through the United Associations of Women. In June 1939 Ming had worked with her, a visiting Northern Territory journalist Jessie Litchfield (who wrote for Albert Thompson's *Daily News*) and Jessie Street, the four women drawing up a list of ten recommendations 'concerning the care of Aborigines in West Australia, Queensland and the Northern Territory'. Their recommendations included the rejection of the principle of male protectors of Aboriginal women in favour of women protectors 'experienced in Aboriginal custom and belief', and the abolition of 'Board' control for 'mixed bloods'.[5]

Pink was disappointed at the time by Street's failure to support wholeheartedly her push for secular reserves through the UAW. And she was offended by Street introducing her to Ming, a relative nobody, writing that when invited to a 'meeting' by Street, she expected to meet the UAW committee – 'instead I met "Mrs Stracker" and "Mrs Litchfield" only ... [both] non-members I presume'. She expressed her disagreement with Litchfield but did not venture an opinion of Ming.[6] She may well have been even more vexed to realize that Ming was secretary of the white group that supported the Aborigines Progressive Association. Pink had, just a month before first meeting Ming, denounced Pearl Gibbs and the other Aboriginal activists in NSW in a letter to Street as 'puppets of whites', complaining that they 'get a hearing while the true Aborigines cannot put their side'.[7] For Ming's part, this little exercise with the UAW president, apparently of no practical significance, had preceded her overture to the UAW to support citizenship rights in NSW.

The two women did have some things in common, however. Pink was deeply suspicious of other anthropologists' motives and expressed her distaste for the UAW's 'old school tie' endorsement of Camilla Wedgwood as a Board appointee at the time.[8] And Ming would have undoubtedly applauded Pink's outspokenness, especially on the subject of the sexual exploitation of Aboriginal women – even though Pink was unsympathetic to protests about the sexual abuse of Aboriginal girls living in towns, unable indeed to find any sympathy for 'mixed-race women, as Aborigines or as women. (Consequently, her position on the removal of fair-skinned children from their mothers was unclear; Mary Bennett wrote to her in some consternation in 1937 having been told by the WA Protector Neville that Pink supported such a 'segregationist' policy.[9])

Now, Olive Pink was asking Ming if she had ever spoken before the UAW, apparently seeing Ming as a useful contact with the women's movement. Following their lunch together, Ming and Pink met again several days later at the Feminist Club, and decided that Pink should appeal to Prime Minister Menzies' wife for support. The following day the anthropologist sent Mrs Menzies a letter outlining her proposal and informing her that 'If desired, one married woman and myself, a spinster, are already ready to go at very short notice (Had we the means we would even pay our own fares but we have not)'. The 'married woman' was Ming.[10]

Ming's sudden, rather startling decision to throw off a suburban lifestyle was possible now that her family obligations were decreasing.

Norman had been called up for full-time duty with the Military Intelligence Corps in February 1940 and was living in barracks, Peter (now in the air force) had married and left home a month earlier, and 16-year-old Helen could be looked after by Narrelle. Narrelle too had married in July of that year, and lived with her husband, Bruce, in her parents' home. (A university friend of Peter Strack, Bruce had boarded with the Stracks following his parents' death in late 1938 or 1939.) And Ming's Aboriginal servant, Jane, who had been working for Ming since 1938, was away working for somebody else. Thus Ming was, for the first time in her married life, free to follow her own whims.

As a distinctively female mission to protect Aboriginal girls and women from 'marauding white men',[11] the campaign for women protectors of Aborigines on the frontier had captured the imagination of women like Ming and was well known by the time Pink approached her. Daisy Bates, Ming's hero, had been the first to call for the appointment of a female Chief Protector, in 1920. Both Bettune Bryce and Helen Baillie had been campaigning for women protectors since the early 1930s.[12] In 1938 Ming had written enthusiastically to Elkin of 'an absolutely new world' of Aboriginal spirituality that he had shown her, 'something we had never dreamed of'. She had declared that she 'personally would give the world to see Central & Northern Australia and am quite determined that someday I shall'.[13] Now, in collaborating with Olive Pink, Ming saw her opportunity to live out her dreams.

With Ming's support, Pink gave a formal address to the Feminist Club. She was well received, and Ming, with the president, Mrs Cameron, and Miss Grace Scobie (who had represented the Feminist Club at the 1937 Enquiry, and as an executive member of the APNR who had attempted to form a 'League for the Protection of Native Women' within the APNR, provided a key link between the two groups[14]), formed a sub-committee to represent Pink's proposals to the Federal government. Requesting £5,000 from the Federal government to organize 'mobile patrols' and food depots, they emphasized that the work of the patrols be 'placed in the hands of white women (not men), who will go in an honorary capacity but whose travelling and keep will be a charge against the sum allotted'. Both Ming and Grace Scobie formally offered their services.[15]

Olive Pink left for central Australia alone in early October, but Ming continued to make plans with Scobie and Cameron to join her.[16] The mood of the sub-committee was positive; Cameron had been promised a supportive article by the sub-editor of the weekly magazine *Woman*, and an 'excellent article', in her view, appeared in the next week's issue.[17] Nevertheless, crucial support from the Federal government was not forthcoming, and in early November Ming and Cameron decided to write again to the Prime Minister. Then, following a 'long talk' with Scobie (who though present when Ming and Cameron discussed writing, seemed to have dropped out of official involvement), Ming decided to compose a letter and send it to the Prime Minister herself.[18] Stating that her letter was written in a 'private' capacity only, Ming asked Mr Menzies to clarify the government's position. Would they make living expenses and travel available to her? she asked. 'If it is not too late I am still ready to go.'

Despite her opening disclaimer, Ming was in disgrace with Cameron, who demanded she read a copy of her letter to the Club at the next meeting:

> your own reply [Ming had written to Menzies] stated that Missionaries and people from other parts were already at Alice Springs and doing patrol work. You also said that 'food supplies were under Military Guard'. The whole point is that women, not men, should be doing the work of caring for [A]boriginal women and secondly that it is unnecessary for food supplies to be under military guard, as far as [A]borigines are concerned. They are absolutely honest, but hunger and stark starvation will drive them to the camps with dire consequences.
>
> Will you please let me know what the position is. I do not ask permission to do this work as a favour but because I believe it is right and proper to protect the most defenceless race in the world.[19]

Ming was obliged to apologize 'for her indiscreet action and it was pointed out that Executive Members should not write to Government officials mentioning that they are members of the Feminist Club Executive on matters which are discussed in that Executive'.[20]

The secretary for the Minister of the Interior, J. Carrodus, to whom Ming's letter had been forwarded, replied on 24 December, saying that the proposals submitted by the Feminist Club had been considered and it was decided that such patrols were unnecessary. This response effectively ended the Club's campaign. The 'mobile road patrol' was not mentioned again after a May meeting the following year, when Mrs Cameron reported that the Federal Administrator of Native Affairs had 'thanked us for the campaign which was conducted through the right channels as it had kept the Politicians alert'.[21]

The state did not share the view that 'women, not men, should be doing the work of caring for [A]boriginal women'. Despite the demands of the 1930s women's movement, encouraged by the 1929 Bleakley Royal Commission recommendation for the appointment of paid, empowered women protectors,[22] in 1932 the Queensland government discreetly abolished the state position of Protector of Aboriginals (Female); in Victoria, Anne Bon, the only woman member of the Board there (appointed in 1904), was 98 and 'living as a recluse' by 1934, with little influence on Board policy.[23] In 1937, at the conference of state Aboriginal authorities, the principle was stated definitively that the appointment of female protectors was 'not considered practicable'. Carrodus personally held (in a letter to Elkin) that such protection was not a job that should be entrusted to women, but 'could be afforded more appropriately by conscientious male protectors'. Carrodus was opposed to Miss Pink specifically, as were the police authorities in central Australia, she being characterized as being of 'a class [of women] that we find arrogant in their demands whilst acting as generally meddlesome busybodies' soon after her return to the Northern Territory.[24] It was not an environment receptive to Ming's dreams.

* * *

On 25 January 1941, Ming attended a public meeting on Aboriginal Citizenship organized by the third CAC. Sawtell had revitalized the group, following the announcement of the new Welfare Board without any Aboriginal representative on it, let alone Sawtell's promised appointment. A new recruit, Bill Onus, an Aboriginal man from Cumeragunja living in Newtown, was now secretary.[25] Sawtell had sent an invitation to the Feminist Club, giving notice that the following resolution would be moved:

> this Public Meeting of good loyal Australian Citizens urges all other good Australians to support in their various ways, the granting of full citizenship rights and status to the Aborigines. We also urge all Australian Governments to do their duty in helping the Aborigines to fit themselves for citizenship, especially in the matter of education.[26]

Ming, disappointed that she had not been able to attend the APA conference held a few weeks earlier at Coonabarabran (where a vote of thanks to her was passed), was keen to attend. Despite her gaffe in the Pink campaign, the Feminist Club agreed that she should represent them as an 'observer'.[27]

Ming heard Sawtell, Ferguson and Pearl Gibbs (who had come up from the South Coast especially for the meeting) speak on a variety of issues. The conditions of the Aboriginal apprentices in service and the withholding of their trust monies were emphasized by all three speakers. Pearl protested at the frequency with which girls in service were impregnated by white men and the failure of the Board to 'take steps to summon the father and compel him to support his child'. 'The Aborigines held no hate for the white men,' she told the audience, 'but they were beginning to hold a hate for the Administration, a contempt for the lack of interest, and a contempt for the boast of White Australia.'[28]

On presenting her report of the meeting to the Feminist Club, Ming was dismayed – though not surprised – by the Club's refusal to endorse the citizenship rights resolution passed there. Ming persevered, inviting Bill Ferguson to the Club a few days later (after first taking him to meet with Elkin) to hear another speaker on an Aboriginal children's clinic. '[I]t fairly made the Club shake,' Ming wrote with satisfaction, but she did not attend another executive meeting after that of 4 February, where she got into a fierce argument with another Club member over the rights of Aboriginal people to vote.[29] Ming tendered her resignation of her Club membership the next month. She told the president she was 'too busy'. In her diary, she wrote that she regretted resigning but 'couldn't afford it, hated giving it up as it was useful in lots of ways'. [30]

Ming was indeed very busy at the time of her resignation. Jane, who had returned to work for her in October 1940, was suffering renewed harassment from a powerful white doctor who lived locally, in the context of a long-running battle between herself and this man. Jane was on the verge of confronting the full force of institutionalized and personal racism, but in her case, the adversary was not the Protection Board.

Part V
Jane

18
A free Australian citizen

There was a spell of a few months, my Gran recalls, once the children were grown up and Norman was away at barracks, when Ming took up the habit of an after-dinner cigarette. She would sit back in a comfortable chair and take it out, holding the cigarette carefully between her thumb and forefinger. Gran, who had started smoking secretly at the age of 15 and continued to be a heavy smoker until well into her sixties, was amused by Ming's carefully cultivated vice – Ming thought she was being 'very feminist' and 'modern', Gran told me with a mischievous smile. She gave me Ming's old ashtray when I first came up to the North Coast, an elegant brass bowl with engraved oriental peacocks decorating the rim. It pleases me to imagine Ming in her prime, sitting back and puffing on her solitary feminist cigarette, elegantly flicking the ash into her brass bowl, watching the blue curl and waft of the smoke. I imagine it was on one such leisurely evening in January 1940 when she opened up the new women's magazine of the day, a newspaper supplement, *The Australian Women's Mirror*, to see a bold and heartless headline. 'Try an Abo Apprentice!' Quoting a happy employer – 'X has become one of the family and we have become very fond of her' – the article went to exhort white housewives to avail themselves of Aboriginal servants supplied by the state. No mention was made of the forced removal of Aboriginal girls from their families; rather, they were described as 'orphaned and neglected'.[1]

Its appearance at this time can be seen as a tactic by the soon-to-be reformed Board to deflect further criticism of its apprenticeship policy. The prominence of the conservative women's organizations in criticizing the Board's administration had the potential to cause some disquiet, at least, among those elite white women whose participation in the system was vital. Constituting a public relations exercise, it was the Board's first public advertisement of its apprenticeship scheme.

Ming, who had joined the Feminist Club executive that very month, was outraged, making numerous transcripts to show others and writing sarcastic comments on her own copy – despite the fact Jane, an ex-apprentice, had been working for her for about a year. A tall, slender young woman with a strikingly pretty face and an impalpable air of reserve that dominates Narrelle's memory of her, Jane had herself become 'one of the family'. She had been with Ming's parents at Pymble for over seven years, as a Board apprentice for six of those years, before she came to work for Ming. Then again, Jane's move to Ming's household had caused a major row between Ming and her mother. Ming's opposition to the Board's control would always ultimately lead her into conflict not only with other women of her class, but with the women of her own family.

Ming and Isobel were arguing over Jane at the end of 1938. In early December, Ming received a letter from Isobel's friend A. J. Vogan (the journalist who put her in touch with the APNR) who wrote that Isobel was 'considerably distressed over your action in taking her native-girl away from her!' 'It is *no business of mine* of course,' Vogan wrote diplomatically, 'save that I have known, & liked you all *so* long; *but please* do not carry out this idea!! *You have* often interfered with *others*, whom you saw doing wrong, just as *I have* with my "Black Police" ... – so you will recognise my right to approach you *re* this matter.'[2] Ming was furious.

'I am *amazed* that you should listen to such unmitigated *lies* from my so-called Mother,' she fired back. Over the past weeks her mother had been complaining to her about Jane, saying she was 'terrified' of her, Ming told him. When she told Ming that Jane would be leaving her and she would get another 'girl' from Condobolin – presumably through Ming's sister Helen – Ming offered to take Jane until she found another situation, 'as I desperately needed help'. Then Jane rang Ming herself, to tell her that she was only going into hospital to have her tonsils removed and fully intended to return to Pymble. In fact, Ming advised Vogan, Jane had not left Isobel at all – 'I have just rung up to see if Jane really *has* gone, but she answered the phone herself! & was amazed when I told her of Mother's lies to you'. In fact, claimed Ming, it was she who 'managed to smooth things over' when Jane and her mother clashed, persuading Jane to return to the Commons household.[3]

Ming professed great sympathy for Jane – 'a most intelligent gentle & lonely little thing, and like most of her people, an outcast'. Ming believed she was a target of abuse by her mother and her sister (who was visiting at the time), because Ming's father liked her. Ming saw Jane as an ally of her father, making 'life bearable for him' against the combined force of her mother and sister, and it was perhaps for this reason she continued to persuade Jane to remain with her parents. Indeed, she saw Jane as her ally in her parents' household, defending her and reporting to her when they talked about her, in much the same way as she had seen Isobel's previous servant, Annie.[4]

In January 1939, however, according to Ming, Isobel had called the police and demanded they arrest Jane. The police, having no grounds to do so, had brought her to Ming, 'saying, "Will *you* care for her?"' (which Ming did) although the rest of the family apparently continued to believe that Ming had 'taken Jane away' from her mother, much to Ming's disgust.[5]

Ming's attitude towards the Aboriginal people was inseparably bound up with her unhappy relationship with her family, and she clung tenaciously to the idea that she had a special affinity and obligation to Aboriginal people. Her 'rescue' of Jane must be seen in this context, as well as in the context of Ming's involvement in the Aboriginal movement at the time. At the same time, Jane may have been relieved to be so 'rescued' – at any rate, she would have had few alternatives.

* * *

'Jane' is not her real name – but then neither is the name she went by at Ming's. The name she lived and died under was not the name she was given by her parents at birth – that name was taken from her when she was registered as a ward at the Cootamundra Home, because there was already 'too many' girls with her name there.

When Jane was almost three years old her father had been forced to take his wife and young children off Brungle reserve (Jane's brother only one, and her mother was either pregnant or had a newborn baby) because the Board had a policy of insisting that 'young half-cast[e]s' like him 'should be earning their living away from an Aborigines Station'. In 1922, two years later, the Board policy changed. Faced with what amounted to an exodus of Aboriginal parents leaving the reserves to prevent the removal of their children, the Board directed managers to try to *keep* families on the stations. Those who did leave were to be 'followed up', to ensure 'the younger children receive schooling, and the older ones are not allowed to live a life of idleness'.[6] Desperation may have driven Jane's parents back to the reserve in 1923, after the birth of their fourth child – certainly, considerable pressure would have been put on them to hand over their eldest girl, whether or not this was the price of their reinstatement. The Board records claim that they placed their six-year-old daughter in the Cootamundra Home themselves, but Jane's family today – who remember her parents well – are adamant that this is untrue.[7]

Jane was in the Cootamundra Home for eight years, her time overlapping at the end with the two years Del was there. Ming wrote that Jane had made 'several attempts to escape from the home to return to her people' but was not successful, and so, wrote Ming, she had to 'crush down the longing for her own people whom she loved'.[8] Fourteen when she was sent out to service in 1931, Jane was shunted between a succession of Sydney employers until being transferred to Ming's mother in September 1932.[9] Here, Jane's father finally found her. He told Jane that her mother had died and that he had 'slept out in the open paddock [near the Cootamundra Home] through an entire and freezing winter', waiting for an opportunity that never came to seize her. Jane gave him 'all her money'. 'It was the only time I ever saw her weep,' wrote Ming, who was visiting at Pymble at the time.[10]

* * *

If the question of returning to her newly found and destitute father ever occurred to Jane, Ming never seemed to have thought of it. It seems odd though, as Ming had been so determined to get Del back and was at the time trying to secure the return of other workers to their communities – she traced Guy Jones' daughter for him later that year.

And while Ming claimed that she 'desperately needed help' when she first offered to take Jane in, this was an exaggeration as the children were practically grown-up – even Helen, the baby of the family, was a teenager. With no word from Jane on the matter, perhaps Ming's retention of her can be explained by Ming's need for her to bear witness to her triumph over Isobel. Ming had made practically no mention of Jane during the 1930s, including the two years Del was with her, despite her concern that Del was lonely. (At one point she asked Narrelle to give Jane a message when she was with her parents; after Del left, Ming referred to Jane just once, calling her 'a quiet, gentle creature'.[11]) Perhaps the two young women simply did not take to each other, but one might speculate that the strained relationship between Ming and Isobel, reflected in Ming's earlier letter regarding Annie, prevented any closer relationship developing between Ming and Jane.

Ming now saw a fundamental distinction between employing Aboriginal women as *independent* servants and employing them under the Board. Indeed, Ming would not have been able simply to take Jane from her mother were it not for the fact that Jane was then technically an independent worker, having completed her indenture in 1936. Jane had continued to work for Isobel after her apprenticeship expired in 1936. She had successfully applied for the reimbursement of her trust fund money in August 1938, possibly on Ming's advice, who was of course in the midst of her activities on the Citizenship Committee. (Jane's request warranted the special attention of a Board meeting, too.[12])

So Jane entered Ming's employ on a fundamentally different basis from that of the previous three women. Despite the fact that Jane had been with Isobel since she was 15 and might have felt she had practically nowhere else to go, she was not legally bound to Ming. Unfortunately, there is no record of what wage Isobel or Ming paid Jane as an independent worker. Ming did not record it; and the Board recorded only that Ming's mother paid Jane the apprentices' rate of 3s 6d a week until early February 1934 (two years before her apprenticeship formally terminated). In terms of her personal relationship with Jane, however, Ming was determined to treat Jane as 'a free and independent Australian citizen', as she put it.

* * *

One evening in September 1939, Ming arrived home from shopping in town to find Jane 'nearly in tears'. Jane had called her GP, Dr Nott,[13] at his residential Gordon surgery, and his wife, answering the phone, had replied that she 'would not have an Aborigine hanging round her husband's surgery', told Jane she was 'a great nuisance', and hung up on her. Jane was both hurt and indignant. Ming herself rang Mrs Nott and was told that 'she would not have Jane in the surgery & the reason being that Jane had eaten an ice cream [in the waiting room] & unless I got rid of Jane, she would have her sent to gaol'. Jane then rang the doctor at his town surgery and asked him if he no longer wanted her to attend. Ming, listening in to their conversation, reported:

the Dr replied, 'I don't know anything about that Jane, *certainly* I want you to come. Come to me whenever you like!!' But soon after this the Dr behaved like a lunatic ...

The doctor rang the Stracks not long after to insist that they control Jane. Ming wrote to him a week later, saying that she was 'astonished to be drawn into a dispute of so trivial a nature which was no concern of mine'. 'I do not enquire into Jane's actions,' she continued, 'she is a free Australian citizen & entirely independent. I have known her for years & place complete trust in her, she is in fact an exceptionally fine type of girl – honest truthful & intelligent.'[14]

The situation escalated before Ming got around to posting this letter. In mid-October 1939 an official from the 'Phone department' called on the Stracks with a complaint from Mrs Nott that 'someone is ringing her up, and she vows it is Jane!' '[M]ight be anybody,' snorted Ming in her diary. Five days later there was an 'awful hullabuloo at front door – Dr Nott trying to come in!' They were visited again and again by an official from telephone department, who told them calls to the doctor had been traced to their house. In January 1940, he called again to interview Jane about the doctor's complaints. Noting that Jane, an Aboriginal 'girl', was strongly supported by Ming, 'Honorary Secretary of the Committee for Aboriginal Citizenship', he recommended against proceedings being taken, with 'regard to the support Miss King would receive from Mrs Strack, and in the absence of definite proof'. In her diary, Ming recorded that the telephone department had threatened to disconnect their phone, 'as Dr Nott complained that *we* ring him'. '[T]he fellow must be crazy,' she wrote. 'Wonder what he *did* to Jane that he is so afraid.'[15]

Indeed, over the next few months a series of incidents involving the doctor caused Ming to reassess her view of the 'trivial nature' of the dispute. At one time, the doctor ran 'at Jane in his car right up on to the footpath, [but] missed her and struck the fence'. The most bizarre incident took place in January 1940 when the doctor apparently behaved like the classic villain of an old-fashioned melodrama. He 'burst through the front door of my home,' according to Ming, 'flinging one of my children [Helen] against the wall and gripping Jane's shoulder at the same time demanding to see me and telling Jane that "she would be dead before morning"'.[16]

A fat dossier compiled by the Postmaster-General's department includes the Notts' complaints of nuisance calls from Jane, some abusive and some silent, and a counter-allegation filed by Norman, stating that the Stracks had been plagued by 'no voice' calls themselves, which, he believed, 'originate from a Dr. Nott'. Jane, too, wrote to complain of harassing treatment from the phone department, as well as of getting 'pesting' calls from the doctor. 'I am sick of being blamed for ringing thier telphone all the time when I did not do it. [T]here is four people in that house all on to one,' she complained.[17]

In early February 1940, Ming, apparently suffering from nervous strain, took a fortnight's holiday by herself at a boarding house in Manly. One can only wonder how Jane coped. 'Jane had dinner ready beautifully, poor little beggar,' Ming recorded in her diary on the night of her return. 'Wish she was not so lonely and that this confounded Dr. would leave her alone. This telephone business is getting on my nerves.' Ming's compassion for Jane was mingled with self-pity, and her concern for Jane's loneliness did not extend to inviting Jane to eat with the family. Her daughter Helen recalls quite clearly that Jane had to eat the meals she cooked alone in the kitchen.

At the same time, Ming was determined to register her non-exploitative relationship with Jane. From the time Dr Nott's harassment commenced, Ming had taken to recording in her diary the actual work Jane did (which she had never done with Mary, Alma or Del). 'Turned out the house between us – Jane & I,' she wrote in one entry, not long after Jane had written to the Postmaster-General to complain. 'Vacuum cleaner going full blast.' She also, at times, recognized her own tendency to take Jane for granted. One night when the rest of the family had gone to the cinema, Jane and Ming had the house to themselves:

> Jane sat on the floor & talked & played with Jock [the family dog], I forgot she was there, till she suddenly bobbed up & said 'will you be sitting up & painting much longer?['] Poor little thing had been simply sitting there to keep me company … . She's a faithful little beggar …

But Ming's complacency was about to be shaken. In a shortage of experienced and competent domestic servants, Jane's services were valuable; and as an independent worker, she could demand wages and conditions from Ming that her previous workers could not. Ming was forced to recognize Jane's right to work for someone else even if this did not suit her at all.

'Jane marched off & left me in the lurch,' Ming had recorded with annoyance in her diary in March 1940. 'Returned later & I gave her a good talking to.' A couple of weeks later Jane started working weekday mornings and Saturdays for another woman at Wahroonga, for £1 a week. Ming 'missed her help terribly'. In May, Jane told her that Mrs Green had offered her 'double wages' to come and live with them. 'Jane very upset, naturally feels she would like the money,'

Ming wrote. 'What a rotten woman, Mrs G. is, a gentlemanly agreement only works when *both* parties to it play the game.'[18]

Though Jane continued to work part-time for Ming, her 'comings and goings' were a 'constant source of worry':

> I have a feeling of insecurity all the time, never know whether she is here or not, & there is so much to do & to think of. I am at my wits' end, trying to use sock machine, sew for Narrelle, wash & iron, cook, work, entertain visitors, interview various officials, etc, etc.

At the end of the month, Jane 'simply walked out' and went to work for Mrs Green full-time.[19] Her new mistress sent Ming a note playing down both her role and Jane's autonomy in an attempt to conciliate Ming: 'Will treat her as a valued loan! She is really so fond of you and all your family & I think she has only acted with a child's impulsiveness.' '[A] lot of palava,' Ming wrote with aggravation.[20]

Mrs Green was no doubt delighted to have found Jane. Although the records don't show that she ever availed herself of the Aboriginal apprenticeship scheme, in 1937 she had headed a deputation of 'ladies' to the NSW Premier to push for the training of girls for domestic employment to overcome the servant shortage. Premier Stevens had refused to see them, however, saying that change in the existing system was not 'desirable', due to 'relatively little unemployment amongst young women'.[21] Ming was not so pleased: her withdrawal from the Citizenship Committee in May coincided with Jane's abrupt departure. Perhaps Ming's chagrin at Jane's independence further deflated her enthusiasm for citizenship rights; certainly, without Jane's help in the home, she was less free to engage in outside activities. Ming did, however, become an executive member of the Feminist Club the following month while Jane was still away, but her new interest in protecting 'defenceless women' in the outback may have been at least partly related to her disappointment with Jane.

Jane returned, unexpectedly, in early October 1940. Ming somewhat gleefully recorded that Jane told her that the Greens had been 'entertaining Huns'. Within a month, a telephone department official visited the Stracks with a complaint about Jane allegedly using the phone to make harassing calls (calls had also been traced to the Greens' line while Jane was with them).[22] Less than a week later,

> 23rd [November 1940] Jane attacked by Dr. Police waiting to tell us – terribly battered ... Jane looks very ill. Can hardly move[,] stiff & bruised.[23]

Figure 12   Jane outside the courthouse during Dr Nott's trial for alleged assault, 1940. Sydney *Truth*.

The doctor had assaulted Jane on the street outside his Gordon house. Jane brought a civil suit against him at North Sydney police court the following month.[24] Remarkably, criminal charges of assault were not laid against him, though Jane had several witnesses who were prepared to testify, including the police, who had been called to the scene by a bystander. 'The doctor was right on top of me,' Jane testified in court, 'and when the police arrived they dragged him off.'

Dr Nott admitted the assault but defended his actions on the grounds that he had been subjected to a series of threatening phone calls and letters from Jane, and that she had thrown stones at the roof of his house that night and the night before. The magistrate found the assault proven, but dismissed the charges because he found the doctor had been 'subjected to continued annoyances'.

The doctor had claimed in court that Jane had made an extraordinarily number of abusive phone calls to him. 'You're a dirty, low-down dog, a murderer who operates when he is drunk, and killed a woman in hospital; you will get shot, you had better keep your children inside,' she is alleged to have said. An official of the Postmaster-General's department supported his testimony, giving evidence that he had personally 'rushed by motor car to telephone booths at Warrawee railway station and Wahroonga post office ... to find the girl King standing there'. While Jane denied altogether making the phone calls, she did admit that a 'friend' (rather incredibly, an Indian maharajah living on the North Shore) 'had written hundreds of letters on her behalf, to the doctor'. Without corroboration of this person's existence, it cannot be known whether Jane really did have the support of an eminent friend or whether she invented him as an alias. Ming herself was exasperated by Jane's 'untruths' regarding the identity of the letter-writer, believing this to have cost Jane the case.[25]

Ming had been very active in helping Jane to take legal action against the doctor for assault, arranging both the magistrate and a lawyer who agreed to defend Jane free of charge. She organized the serving of the subpoenas on the three police who had been called to the scene, and paid their witness fees herself. Evidently optimistic about the outcome of the case, she was bitterly disappointed when the magistrate dismissed the charge. This 'thoughtful, gentle' judge who had agreed to hear the civil case at Ming's request did not even award Jane court costs.[26]

The hearing of the suit against the doctor in effect became a trial of both Jane's and Ming's credibility, given the doctor's defence that Jane had provoked him. The magistrate found that that Jane was 'a person upon whose testimony little reliance can be placed'[27] – and by implication this applied to Ming also. In fact, the Postmaster-General's department, in compiling evidence in Jane's suit against Nott, had concluded that while they could not 'suggest any definite basis for the antagonism between these parties ... Miss King is greatly influenced by Mrs Strack'.[28]

Extraordinarily, the doctor's defence lawyer seemed to have had access to Board records, or police files, or the APNR records, dating back six years to the time Del was with Ming. At the outset he appeared to suggest that Ming could not possibly not know what Jane was doing, asking her incredulously if Jane was able to leave the house without her knowing, to which Ming replied, twice, 'Aborigines over 21 have a perfect right to come and go as they please'. Then, the doctor's lawyer referred to the incident of Del's assault in the park – which had never even come to court – to infer that Ming was negligent in her control of Aboriginal servants. 'Do you remember a girl being found in a park with a lot of men?' she was asked.

The lawyer went on to the subject of her 'lengthy correspondence' with the Chief Secretary's Department and with the Protection Board, and to her having had 'considerable trouble with various organisations in connection with [A]borigines', to which Ming replied that she had been 'trying to get justice in connection with their money that was not paid to them'. So it was established that Ming, being actively supportive of Aboriginal servants through the citizenship movement, was a troublemaker.[29]

On 15 December 1940, *Truth* newspaper published a sensational account of the case and Ming decided that she 'must' write something for the paper to 'get rid of stigma about these girls'.[30] She wrote a lengthy article indicting the treatment of Aboriginal people in Australia. Her original letter was toned down somewhat and published under the headline: 'Bitter Lot of Aborigines: Robbed of Children, Shamed, Assaulted'. The following is an excerpt from her original letter (content deleted from the published version is in italics):

> *...a defenceless woman and an [A]boriginal to boot – she can't hit back and has no friends.* This has been the history of the [A]boriginal people ever since the white man came to these *[our]* shores. A history of battery and assault, of shooting, poisoning and lies – after all, they are only [A]borigines!
>
> It may not generally be known that their babies and small girls are taken from their parents (this racket has gone on for thirty or more years) by the so-called Aborigines Protection Board which has the power to take an [A]borigine child or adult – at any time – anywhere. The children are the only thing in the world which the [A]borigines really love ... – all else has been broken and ruined by the white man, yet these children are taken away under any pretext whatever.

Ming went on to explain how the girls were taken to Cootamundra Home until required for domestic service, without consulting them or their parents. The published article included her statement that 'large sums of money [were] owed to the girls by the Board', but cut out a large chunk of her criticism:

> *They have been kept entirely out of touch with their people and are taught to scorn the [A]boriginal customs and camp life and become almost ashamed to admit that they are [A]boriginal or half caste, hence the inferiority complex – deliberately fostered by the Protection Board. They are lonely to the point of desperation in the homes of white people. They are not wanted, there is nowhere for them to go – nothing to do except work. Correspondence with their families is forbidden though desperate efforts are made at times by the parents to make contact with their daughters. This usually ends in some foolish act for which the girl is condemned and punished. I have a number of letters from parents and relatives in New South Wales asking me to try and find their daughters who they have not heard of in some cases for years ...*
>
> Aboriginals only want freedom and encouragement to develop in their own way. They would soon fit themselves into our way of life and in fact have already done so ...

Ming concluded by alluding to the colonial British promise, in the form of painted picture-signs, to dispense justice equally to black and white. Her reference to the final caption, depicting the hanging of a white man, was omitted from the published version.[31]

Ming's article represented the most articulate, coherent statement she ever made against the Aborigines Protection Board and its apprenticeship policy. In her hope that with it she might overturn the 'stigma' against Aboriginal women, she seemed still unaware that she was now classified as deviant by the authorities. Perhaps she was particularly unwise in her decision to resign her membership of the Feminist Club just at the point that the doctor lodged yet another complaint about the telephone (as she confided to Grace Scobie).[32] The real battle was just beginning, and it would culminate in a gruesome display of the utter powerlessness of an Aboriginal woman within white Australia; as it destroyed Jane herself, it destroyed Ming's hitherto indefatigable hopes of effecting change.

19
The bitter disappointment of trying to help

In mid-January 1942, Ming wryly compared herself to Lewis Carroll's 'looking-glass duchess [*sic*]' who cried 'off with her head!' with futile imperiousness at every opportunity. '[A]t the moment could cheerfully behead Jane also,' she continued with rising anger in her diary,

> have had to walk about half a mile in the heat every time I want to ring up, we are always short of pennies & the phone box is like a furnace, & the bitter disappointment of trying to help & really succeeding in rescuing these darkies, one after another, at terrific cost to myself in mental & physical strength, to say nothing of the nervous strain of not knowing what is going to happen next, & the money that I have had to spend, *and* the upsets & continual worry for the whole family. I feel utterly humiliated to think that after all this effort, Jane herself could let me down, & undo all I have tried to do for *all* her people ...[1]

Nearly two years after writing to Charles Duguid about the impending Welfare Board legislation and her resignation from the Citizenship Committee, Ming's use of the term 'darkies' was not softened in any way; now, her tone expressed anything but affection or respect. Completely isolated in her attempt to 'help' and 'rescue' Jane, Ming's agonized realization of her complete powerlessness and her wasted years of effort for Aboriginal rights coalesced into a sense of personal betrayal. Sadly, that was focused sharply on the one individual woman whom Ming had wanted so desperately not merely to 'save', but to hold up as proof to herself that Aboriginal women could exist as 'free Australian citizens' in this country.

The Stracks' telephone line had been under observation since two days after Jane's suit failed against Dr Nott in mid-December 1941, when Mrs Nott had complained Jane had made more annoying calls. (Mrs Nott also complained she had had a call from a local funeral parlour, 'in reference to a call they had received to the effect that funeral arrangements would be necessary'.) In January 1942, Ming had received a registered letter from the Postmaster-General's department stating that as 'this service is again being used repeatedly for the purpose of making calls of an annoying nature to another subscriber', her telephone would be disconnected in three days' time. Ming, who had taken the precaution of having a lock installed on their telephone in November 1940, was incensed: 'It is a deliberate lie as *I have the key* & *always* have it' (she wore it on a ribbon around her neck).[2]

But the telephone was disconnected, much to Ming's annoyance. They were, in fact, in the midst of moving, as the owners of their Wahroonga place were returning to live there in February. When Ming, Jane, Helen and Narrelle (now married to Bruce and with a baby on the way) moved to the new house at Neutral Bay, Ming found she was unable to get the telephone connected here also. In a furious letter to the Deputy Postmaster-General, Ming demanded that her telephone be connected or she would instigate legal proceedings: 'I feel this insult has gone quite far enough. ... The whole thing is a scandalous attempt or *conspiracy* to force me 1. to part with this girl 2. to damage my reputation 3. to have Jane labelled as a criminal ...' Ming having sought help from a Federal MP, within a fortnight the Deputy Postmaster-General saw 'no reason why your telephone should not now be reconnected'. But in the following month he wrote to her again telling her that she had to send a letter 'intimating that upon the telephone service being again made available to you, you will do your utmost to protect the interests of the Postmaster-General's department as well as that of other subscribers by preventing the [A]boriginal girl, Jane, from having access to the telephone or interfering, as she allegedly has done, previously, with subscribers to the telephone.'[3]

According to Ming, Jane herself had gone into the Postmaster-General's department and had been told that the telephone would be reconnected 'if she [Jane] would sign a document stating that she *had* made these calls! and would not do it again!! She did not sign of course.' Ming believed that the whole disconnection was a deliberate attempt to 'pin blame for any trouble with this Doctor's telephone upon myself or Jane'.[4] Nevertheless, in May 1941, she had to, because Narrelle, now heavily pregnant, fell ill with a serious kidney infection.

Ming carefully pointed out that this was not to be regarded as an admission 'that the girl has ever had access to my telephone or has interfered with subscribers to the telephone'. A telephone service was installed within a few days of receiving Ming's 'guarantee', though too late for Narrelle, whose baby – my father – was born the day after Ming sent it, following a particularly harrowing attempted home labour, which ended up in hospital.[5]

Jane wrote to the Postmaster-General's department again after the child was born, stating: 'If anything would have happened to [Mrs Strack's] Daughter' they would have been 'the ones to blame'. If the department had the proof it claimed that the Stracks' telephone had been used 'in an irregular Manner ... why dont the Department take it to court and be finished with it all[?]' 'Mrs Strack has no control over me what ever,' she asserted defiantly.[6]

Throughout June, in response to complaints by Dr Nott that he was still receiving threatening calls, the department placed both his line and the Stracks', now at Neutral Bay, under observation again. Though they recorded a number of 'no voice' calls to the Notts, 'nil irregular calls' were made from the Stracks' house. According to an official, however, Jane apparently rang the Postmaster-General's department herself, impersonating Mrs Nott with a high-pitched voice – so the official said – and saying, 'Why don't you do something to stop that black girl from causing so much annoyance, when are you going to take police action?'[7] But as far as Ming was concerned, life continued fairly quietly for some months thereafter.

Then, in early September 1941, Jane went to visit Ming's old friend Millicent Preston-Stanley (now Mrs Crawford Vaughan), who was living at Gordon. She returned home later that evening with the news that she had broken Ming's good umbrella on Gordon station, presenting Ming with the handle.[8] Three days later, a police sergeant arrived with a summons for Jane 'for damage to the Notts' property at Gordon', and advised Jane to get a lawyer. 'Dumbfounded', Ming demanded an explanation from Jane. Jane was agitated. 'She would not tell me anything about it, just kept on saying – '"*I'll* manage by myself, don't you do anything or get mixed up in it",' Ming wrote in her diary. Eventually Ming extracted the story from her:

'There is not *any* damage to property at all' [Jane said]. 'The Dr walked passed me on the other side of the line from his house (I was coming back to the station from Mrs Vaughan's house) and then suddenly turned and faced me and would not let me pass him. He peered into my face and said "I'll *murder* you." I asked him not to do that again and he hit me very hard across the stomach with his walking stick. I hit at him on the shoulder, with my – at least *your* umbrella – and he grabbed it from me. I held onto the handle and it came off in my hand. He ran to the top of the ramp and threw it down onto the railway line and I picked up a whole brick and threw it at him. It did not touch him but broke in half on the ground. I went down and looked in the long grass and couldn't find it. Then I heard a train coming and ran onto the overbridge and found that I had lost my little purse with my ticket in it, so I tore over to the pathway where the Dr had taken the umbrella and looked up and down, then I went to the Porter in the ticket office and asked him if he could lend me a torch to try and find it, but he hadn't one. So I went back and had another look and that time I found it and another train was just coming in and I ran and managed to catch it.

'I did *not* go onto the Dr's side of the line at all that night,' Jane concluded.

'Are you quite *absolutely sure* Jane, you were not anywhere *near* his house at all?' Ming asked.

'I am *quite* sure.'[9]

Despite Jane's plea that Ming should not get involved, the next morning Ming engaged a barrister for Jane, using her contact with Labor member Mark Davidson. Mr Healy, the barrister she found with Davidson's help, was a 'friend' of the Attorney-General, Mr Martin. Healy decided he would 'be a Christian' and represent Jane at the hearing for a 'fraction of the cost'.[10]

The court hearing was held a couple of days later. Again, Ming was initially optimistic, especially when the magistrate dismissed the doctor's claim that Jane had attacked him. He accepted, however, evidence given by a builder that every glass pane in his window had to be removed after Jane had allegedly broken two of them, at the cost of £20. Healy advised Jane to say that she wished the matter to go before the High Court: 'this she did in a perfectly clear voice, & in the midst of a series of very smug & self-satisfied grins from the Notts their Lawyer & witnesses ... . One face after another fell & fell till their mouths were wide open.' However, Ming's own face fell when 'that old devil of a Magistrate' declared he found the evidence proven and was sending Jane to trial at Quarter Sessions, setting Jane's bail '(with a vindictive glance down at me)' wrote Ming, at £40 – a substantial amount and double the alleged cost of the damage.[11]

Ming was horrified at the thought of finding that kind of money. The
court sergeant suggested she get together some receipts for her furniture. She 'tore' home:

> The house was empty. Narelle and Helen had gone for a walk with
> baby. It felt very lonely without Jane's voice or funny little grin. I
> went to the phone & rang Adela [a friend who knew the history of
> Jane's conflict with the doctor] – couldn't help me at all, said she
> didn't know of *any* one who could or would do that sort of thing
> [lend money for bail] ...

Ming searched the house for receipts without success, then rang the
court. The sergeant advised her to return and ask the magistrate if he
would accept an affidavit stating that her household possessions would
take the place of Jane's bail. With no time to make it back into town by
train and no money for a taxi, Ming was 'still sitting at the telephone'
when her daughters returned. Narrelle drove Ming into town: 'we
arrived at the Court door as they closed & *locked* it!' Ming managed to
get in and saw the Chamber magistrate, who agreed to accept her
household possessions in place of bail, '& so ... we brought poor Jane
home with us – we all felt as tho we had been through a mangle!'[12]
   Having Healy as a barrister may have seemed a coup, but the defence
his solicitor, Mr Faulkingham, put together consisted of nothing more
than evidence from a different glass company that it was not necessary
to replace an entire window when only two bricks (panes) were broken.
Though Healy told Ming that he would suggest to the Attorney-General
that the case be dismissed altogether, because the evidence offered at
the hearing by the doctor and by his wife was contradictory,[13] nothing
came of this. Despite Jane's own denial to Ming that she had even been
near the doctor's house, it seems her own defence was prepared to
accept that she had.
   Certainly, Jane did not help her own case. Three days after the incident she had sent off a ferocious-sounding letter to the Postmaster-
General's department, trying to scare off the telephone officials:

> Doctor Nott got a good bashing with a stick across the arms and face
> and allso a whole brick thrown at him and he got his arm broken.
> [A]nd I saw his surgery window smashed in two places.
>   Doctor rang the Police and told them what I had done and the
> police said he would have to take the action himself This all hap-
> pened on Thursday night.

He cannot prove that I did smash his window.
Very bad luck that we both meet each other at the Gordon Station
and then the fight started in the Gordon Park.
The Nott's were the first to start it.
(And I will end it all.)[14]

A few days before Jane's trial date was confirmed (the date reset on
2 January for 12 January 1942, having been inexplicably postponed
indefinitely from its original setting in October) another registered letter from the Postmaster-General's department arrived. As the Stracks'
'telephone service has again been used for the purpose of annoying
another subscriber, the Department has no option but to cancel the
service and recover the telephone'. 'I'm furious,' Ming wrote in her
diary, *'can't* believe Jane would dare to be such a fool when I've tried so
hard to help her.'[15]

On 12 January, Jane and Ming set out, 'only to find on arrival that
Mr Healy was too ill to attend Court ... must adjourn case'.
Faulkingham spoke with them outside the court. The tension between
the two women was evident when Ming again raised the issue of the
telephone department's allegations – she wanted the solicitor's advice
about lodging a complaint. '[I] was simply *thunder* struck,' Ming recorded, 'when Jane turned on me like a wild cat, saying "don't start bringing the phone into it – I wont have it talked about! It's got nothing to
do with *you!*" & glaring at Mr F. & me!!' Ming was outraged. Haughtily
telling Jane, 'We have finished with you for the present', Ming left her
to make her own way home from town, to 'cool off & get rid of the
superiority complex'. Ming's temper was not improved to find on her
return that the telephone had already been disconnected, and this time
the handset removed from the house.[16]

Ming went to the local phone box and called Norman at the barracks,
asking him to find out what was going on. The Postmaster-General's
department told Norman they could have the phone reconnected 'the
very moment' they informed that department that Jane was no longer
living with them.

Jane wrote to the Deputy-Director of the Department herself, probably the day that the phone was removed, in what may have been an
effort to reassure Ming of her good faith as much as to express her own
anger against her persecutors:

I am very shocked at your dreadfull behaver to Mrs Strack in doing
what you have done I think it would be better to have the matter settled in the High Court when my case comes on Mrs Strack private

Telephone has never be[en] used my [by] me at any time. Mr Giddey [an official in the Postmaster-General's department] has no rights to call me a lair [liar] and the men have no rights to asault me in the Public telephone They are getting a bit rought like there friend the Doctor.[17]

Jane had not wanted Ming to get involved in the first place, but now she had to deal with Ming's growing resentment and distrust. Not only was Ming deeply offended by the insult of having her telephone cut off, she was also frustrated by the fact that her furniture was tied up in Jane's bond. They were due to move, once again, to a flat in Cremorne in February, and she could neither store nor sell her furniture. It was at this time that she made her aggrieved entry about Jane letting her down.

Ming's resolute support of Jane and her refusal to countenance the allegations against her had been a source of stupefaction to the Postmaster-General's department[18] and no doubt to the Notts as well, but her commitment was being sorely tested. She was harried and humiliated, and then there was the difficult question of what was to become of Jane *after* the case. Ming had already decided that she could not afford to continue employing her; furthermore, there was no room for her at the new flat. So the question of whether or not Jane 'deserved' her support in purely personal terms became of crucial significance. If Jane did not 'deserve' such support, Ming could wash her hands of her with a clear conscience; yet if she did, Ming was obliged to stand by her.

The hope, indeed expectation, that Aboriginal people should be grateful for her benevolent interest in their troubles had always been entangled with Ming's political commitment to fighting injustice on their behalf. In the pages of her diary Ming wrestled with the contradictions of her stance, now unbearably apparent as she was left to battle unappreciated and alone, without support from any of her old friends and contacts nor, it seemed to Ming, from Jane herself:

I dont think that there *could* be any dispair like this.

... After all these years I have simply devoted myself to these poor silly people.

It's the worst disappointment I have ever had, if Jane *has* done this to me. She is working ceaselessly in the house never seems to stop[.] If she *is* innocent of these charges I would be the lowest thing on earth to send her away & if she *is* guilty of these charges I am crazy to keep her for a single *day*. If only *only* I could know the truth. It's a heaven sent opportunity to wash my hands of the whole beastly business ... But it's terribly hard to climb down & swallow my pride & let them get away with this injustice, & there *is* a principle involved too.

Ming was unable to comprehend Jane's impatience with her inter-ference; she was blind to the fact that it had been her decision in the first place to 'rescue' Jane, against Jane's express wishes, and Ming now quite unfairly blamed Jane herself for the predicament she, Ming, was now in. But in her diary Ming gathered herself again:

> But I don't want to go on for ever fighting a battle for justice ... you can't put anything right by going about it halfheartedly. It *must* be all or nothing, & few people are prepared to give their *all* they stop at the line of 'respectability' or of adverse public opinion or criti-cism, & with bated breath whisper – 'we cannot offend officialdom'.
>
> I think we can & *must* offend officialdom – stir it up, root it out, anger it till you *find* a vulnerable spot & let them *then* have a broad side – you will probably receive several yourself, but if you are absolutely right you can take it all, unperturbed.[19]

Unfortunately, the power Ming felt she possessed to influence what actually happened to Jane or any other Aboriginal woman was limited, however much in the 'right' she may have been, and it was difficult to 'take it all, unperturbed' when her own ego was so bound up in Jane's salvation.

In fact, Ming had become so involved that she really did not have any alternative but to continue to support her. She had put more than her reputation on the line. As she herself realized, she was 'hamstrung' by the fact that she stood to lose all her possessions if she cast Jane aside and Jane disappeared. Once again, she had become the reluctant gaoler of an Aboriginal woman whose rights of autonomy she was defending. Jane reacted to this additional emotional pressure placed on her with strenuous housecleaning – she 'had worked very hard & cleaned silver, & scrubbed bathrooms etc.' right up until the day before the case was heard.[20] There are echoes here of Del's 'ceaseless' work in the Blue Mountains as she awaited the verdict from the Board and the APNR – and Jane too, like Del, had really little choice but to stay.

* * *

Whatever the 'truth' behind the long-running dispute between Jane and her doctor, Jane obviously had a serious grievance against him that went further than the affront of his wife's rudeness. Dr Nott was no run-of-the-mill GP: he was a leading surgeon among Sydney's foremost doctors in Macquarie Street. Going through old copies of Australia's leading medical journal I discovered he published articles on his research and surgery and gave regular demonstrations of his work at meetings of the NSW branch of the prestigious British Medical Association. At one such demonstration in January 1940 he described two 'unorthodox' operations he had performed (only one of which was a 'success').[21]

So what was he doing with Jane? Jane had been seeing him regularly since March 1937. In a letter to her solicitor during the course of her trial in 1941, Jane explained that the doctor had been treating her for 'Tonsills Reumatism Leucorrhea [and] Period Pains', and that the doctor had given her 'twelve Injections in both the Arms up on the shoulders'. Jane also told Faulkingham that she paid the local chemist 15 shillings for each prescription for 'drugs' from the doctor, which the chemist purchased on Jane's behalf from a city chemist.[22] As Ming overheard in Jane's telephone conversation with the doctor, he still had two more injections to give her at the time her treatment was abruptly curtailed.

As far as Ming was aware, apart from the tonsillectomy and an attack of the measles, Jane 'was never ill nor in need of attention' yet

> [she] was receiving some kind of injections from the Doctor who charged her substantial sums each time and who saw her sometimes twice a week … . These injections had a peculiar effect on Jane and I believe they were a drug – for her chemist seemed very dubious about selling them to her and several times enquired why the Doctor was giving them to her.[23]

The doctor administered the injections at his residential surgery, making Jane's appointments, so Ming said, for 'the hour *after* dinner at night'. Jane herself was somewhat secretive about the course of injections she had received, writing to her solicitor that they were only to be referred to if the doctor himself 'does say anything in court about it'.[24]

Unfortunately there is no way of knowing what this expensive medication actually was. The 'leuccorhea' and 'period pains' Jane mentioned refer to two common female conditions, rather than illnesses requiring medical treatment as such. (The only surviving prescription for Jane is an order for a mild sedative tonic commonly prescribed for women's 'nerves' at the time, and was probably for her menstrual pain.) The fact that the doctor himself administered the drugs, in his residential surgery after hours, leads me to the suspicion he may have been sexually involved with Jane (especially coupled with the intimate nature of Jane's other complaints). However, it also suggests that the injections may have been deep intra-muscular injections, which would have been difficult for Jane to administer herself. The fact that the doctor exercised such close supervision over this, and also that he arranged for Jane to attend at night, lends itself to the suspicion that he may have been experimenting on Jane. As the local chemist did not keep supplies, the 'drugs' used were probably relatively unorthodox and perhaps quite new.

Presumably, they were related to her treatment for 'rheumatism' rather than the 'women's' complaints, as indeed may have been the tonsillectomy. My guess is that by rheumatism Jane meant the disease of rheumatoid arthritis – typically called simply rheumatism – a disease afflicting younger people and attracting increasing attention from the medical community at the time, particularly for 'the possible discovery of some means for its prevention'. Rarely fatal and more often attacking females, the disease was nevertheless a source of anxiety to the authorities. Treatment required lengthy stays in hospital when public beds were in short supply, but if not completely cured the disease tended to leave 'an invalid entirely dependent on the State'.[25]

Tonsillectomy and/or removal of the teeth, combined with bed rest and massage, was the traditional, although not overly effective, treatment. The use of injections of gold salts to treat the disease originated in 1929 in France, and its apparently miraculous curative effect was followed with great interest in Australia, as in the rest of the Western world. In Sydney in 1936, however, the near-death of a female patient treated with gold therapy alarmed the Australian medical community, leading to calls for extreme caution in its use and the admonition to doctors that the 'possible risks should be clearly outlined to the patient before the treatment commences'.[26] The following year medical researchers published a study of the 70 recorded cases of gold therapy treatment in Australia, finding that the extreme toxicity of the gold treatment, resulting particularly in haemorrhage and even death in female patients, made it 'imperative either to find some new compound which is less toxic or to minimize reactions in some other way'.[27] After 1940, various studies of experimental treatments for rheumatoid arthritis were published. These included research into a treatment involving the deep intramuscular injections of sodium aurothiomalate, a chemical compound made up 44.5–46 percent gold content, of increasing amounts first on a weekly basis, then fortnightly, then every six weeks. Researchers warned that this 'therapy should only be undertaken where facilities are available to carry out the tests specified under Precautions.'[28]

Was it possible that the doctor was conducting his own private treatment of Jane's rheumatism with the idea of finding a way of minimizing the toxic reactions? Could he have been testing a preventative treatment? (There are no signs that Jane ever, at any stage in her life, showed any symptoms of rheumatoid arthritis.) Jane's vulnerability, perhaps her willingness to please him, may have tempted him to use her to find the solution to a problem greatly vexing to the physicians at the time. Although I could find nothing in the doctor's published work to suggest he was interested in this field of research, if Dr Nott *was* involved in such research, it would fit Jane's circumstances.

As it turned out, the issue of her treatment never was raised publicly. However, following press coverage of Jane's original suit against Dr Nott, Ming was contacted by 'numbers of women' who had been his patients. 'They even thanked me for standing by Jane and one woman stated that he was a fiend and she feared he would kill someone'; another 'vows she will make him pay for ruining *her* life'.[29] Whatever her grievance, Jane was not the doctor's only enemy.

Whether or not there was any sexual misconduct on the part of the doctor cannot be known, although his wife's sudden hostility to Jane suggests that *she* suspected this. What *is* clear is that Dr Nott suddenly and unexpectedly terminated his treatment of Jane in September 1939, apparently to placate his wife. If he then found Jane not so easy to discard, the doctor had become worried, perhaps, about the impact not only on his marriage, but on his professional reputation.

The threat was only enhanced by Jane's connection with her voluble and outspoken employer – and the girl had already humiliated him by dragging him into a civil court and splashing his name across the papers.

By the end of 1942 the doctor did not have to worry about Jane any more, at all.

20
Then we must all be insane

After weeks of uncertainty, Ming learned that the case had been finally set for a date several days after their planned move. As Ming needed to be able to sell her furniture prior to moving, she managed to persuade the barrister to arrange for the case to be brought forward to the following day. Stressed but somewhat triumphant, she returned home to give Jane the news.

But Jane was 'suddenly most hostile'. Ming did not cope well with Jane's unexpected reaction: 'I feel this is one thing I *cannot* stand.'

Jane went out later and when she returned Ming, who suspected she had rung Healy herself, ordered her not to ring him. 'She flounced off saying he had *told* her to ring up.' Ming's demand that Jane not speak with her own lawyer, like her earlier aggravation with Jane for admonishing her in front of the solicitor, shows how determined Ming was to control the whole business herself. Oblivious to her irrationality, Ming recorded in her diary that lately Jane had been 'most strange and standing about in dark passages, listening to our conversation ... . She even opened and read one of my letters.' Obviously, Jane was feeling – and being – disempowered by the whole process.

The household was tense that night. At one point Jane broke the silence. 'I don't think the lawyers *want* to help me,' she glowered. 'I'll just have to do it all myself, why don't they tell me what to do!' Ming could not understand 'what has come over her'. 'I think the strain has really been too much for her ...,' she wrote, 'but for Jane, who should be everlastingly grateful that she has been saved from gaol, to become impertinent is the last straw'.[1]

Jane's 'impertinence', however, continued the next day, the day of the trial. Much to Ming's dismay they argued first thing in the morning and Jane simply disappeared:

up early for this wretched case. Jane will not hurry, finally said 'I'm not going!' I almost *fainted* I said 'you will dress at once the Case is at 10 o'clock, & you *must* be there, remember we have the Bond to settle.['] She replied 'Mr Healy told *me* 20 *past* ten!' I didn't believe her & repeated, 'dress at *once* Jane & if you misbehave yourself now, you will lose this case & be sent to gaol'. She again said I'm not *going*, & you'll *get* yer £40-0-0. I said if you are not ready in ten minutes I shall ring the Police & they will *take* you to Court. Jane flew off saying 'they *wouldnt* they are not that type!!['].

... I felt quite sick, no sign of Jane so I left alone.

Ming went straight to Healy's rooms, where she leant that Jane had just rung his secretary to tell him 'that she was *very* annoyed with Mr Healy & that he could just *wait* for her, & that he should have consulted *Jane* & not *me*!!' 'The impudence of her,' fumed Ming, waiting there for Jane, as Healy went on to the court. 'She has obviously grown too big for her boots.' Eventually, Ming gave up and went to the court herself, where she found the case had already started, and there was Jane, 'sitting in the wired-in dock, looking very pleased with herself, & self-confident'.

In the courtroom, Healy 'spoke splendidly', according to Ming, and 'suggested there might be something behind it all':

then the Crown Prosecutor got up & said Mr H was trying to ruin & blacken the Dr's character & this was a *low* thing to do & unworthy of Mr Healy etc. Then the Judge summed up & stressed all the points in Dr N's favour & looked disdainfully at Mr H. ... I waited while the Jury went out to decide the case ... presently the Jury filed in. Then 'guilty' was announced.

Ming told the judge she had tried for two years to protect Jane from the doctor, who had assaulted her the year before, and would no longer take responsibility for her protection, that Jane 'would only be safe from him in the country'. The Judge said that he 'would not be hard on Jane' and that he would send her for one week to Long Bay gaol for medical observation, prior to sentencing. 'This seemed strange to me,' wrote Ming, 'as she was not ill & no question of sanity had arisen.'

It was an awful blow, poor Jane, she looked so terrified standing in that beastly wire cage arrangement. I couldn't look at her, they would not allow me to see her before she left the court. I was there till 4 o'clock & then came wearily home to a house, half packed up for removal on Friday ... I can't bear to look at poor old Jane's room, & don't know what to do with her things, must pack them up ...

But her anger with Jane was still evident in the way she wrote up their earlier argument in her diary that night. 'Poor silly little thing,' Ming wrote. 'I have been treating her as tho she was white & forgetting that after all, they are still primitive people & liable to have a sort of vacuum where their brains aught to be.'[2] Ming's faith in Aboriginal equality had evaporated.

Three days later, Ming wrote to the judge, outlining the 'facts' behind Jane's story. 'This Aboriginal girl was one of the unfortunate children whom the Aborigines Bd. removed from her perfectly happy family circle at a very early age.' She went on to describe how 'utterly desolate & lonely' the girls were in Sydney:

to be suddenly alone in a strange home & amongst all white people terrifies them, they are not permitted to correspond with their own people, nor to meet other dark girls, & gradually they become like little haunted shadows, moving about silently & escaping when they can, out into the darkness, for this is the only time that they are unmolested. Sometimes a white man befriends them as the Dr evidently did in Jane's case, & in return he would receive the most unswerving & unfailing loyalty & genuine affection ... & this friendship had gone too far for [it] to be broken off without an explanation of any kind ...

But even as Ming went on to assert the 'intelligence' of Aboriginal people and the detrimental effects of government policies of removal, she concluded: 'There is a thousand years' difference between their social life & ours & they cannot be expected to bridge this is one leap, we must be patient & gradually the primitive thoughts & acts which rush suddenly to the surface will be kept under control.' A commonplace of her time and reminiscent of her explanation of Del's apparently inexplicable behaviour years earlier, it showed how completely Ming had retreated from her commitment to Aboriginal rights. She could not provide that protection, Ming told the judge – her new flat was too small to keep Jane – and Jane should be found a situation in the country.[3]

Ming returned to court a few days later to hear what sentence the Judge was going to impose. Again, the case was adjourned, because Jane did not appear – 'they said she was too ill to come'. Her case came up again the next week; again Jane was absent, but this time, a report declared that Jane had been 'certified insane'.

Ming was staggered. She asked Healy what he thought of this 'unbelievable' outcome.

'I suppose she has been stubborn and refused to speak to them, and been very much on her dignity and so they have had to certify her insane. But,' he added reassuringly, 'it will only be for a week or two, for as soon as she says I'll speak to you now or be a good girl they will let her go and she will be all right.'

Ming told Healy that she wanted to see Jane. The barrister advised her to get a permit immediately as Jane would be sent very soon from Long Bay gaol to Callan Park asylum.[4] Ming got the permit that same day.

* * *

At Long Bay gaol Ming was led to a padded cell, 'and behind the bars was Jane, lying flat down on a mattre[ss] on the floor':

Her hair was tangled and unbrushed and there was a dull and hopeless expression in her eyes ...

I said 'can't we go in or Jane sit up or come out here to us? this is dreadful, is she ill?['] 'oh no,' the Matron said, 'she would attack you and is violent.' I said 'this is scandalous, she is as sane as we are, some awful thing has been done to her, why?'

Matron said 'she has broken a window and climbed on her bed, flown at the wardresses like a wild cat. We took her bed away and put her in a padded cell.'

I said 'Jane was quite calm when she came in here'. We [it is not clear who was with Ming, possibly Healy or Norman] then talked with her, she said she was afraid of them. She had a lump on her head above the temple and it was very sore, we saw it for ourselves.

Jane said 'Please get me out of here, *could* you do something, I just want to come home.' In an exceedingly weak voice. She continued 'I hate these Dr's. because they say I'm mad, they *want* me to be mad, but I just can't *be* mad.[']

Then she asked about each one of my family and said she would love to see my daughter's baby of whom she was very fond. She sent little affectionate messages to them – and all this in a perfectly sane and normal voice and manner, tho she was obviously very weak.

Then she said (and showed a natural indignation) – 'I don't like the wardresses, they *will* keep on saying that I am married and that

I have lived with a chinaman. You know that I have never done that, don't you?' With a most appealing look in her eyes.

Of course I knew that it was untrue, and realized *why* she had flown at them all. I asked her what she would like me to send her in the way of clothes – and she said 'I'd like my brush and comb and toothbrush and dressing gown, but it would be useless to send the rest as I could not wear them.' I asked her if she felt ill and she replied 'I just feel very cold.'

If *this* is the conversation of a certified insane person then we must all be insane. I feel that this is a terrible injustice, and told the Matron so.

The matron 'explained' to Ming that insanity could come on 'very suddenly', giving as an instance another inmate 'who had recently killed her own baby in a fit of madness'. She told Ming that Jane 'had stolen a dress from one of her other so-called mental patients, and that things had disappeared, and Jane had been accused of taking them'.

Such an accusation as this would certainly make Jane fly at them like a wild cat. Jane has always been trustworthy and scrupulously honest. Such an insult added to everything else was enough to break her spirit ...

'Is this how we treat *white* first offenders? when they are found guilty of breaking 2 glass bricks?' Ming remarked, but even then she fell back into the very stereotypes of primitiveness that trapped Jane:

I said [to the Matron] you wont *break* this type of girl, you will only *kill* her – I said 'she should never have been sent to gaol at all, this place above [all] would depress & terrify her, *no* Aborigine can stand being confined in a small space & they have a horror of walls, they are lonely & afraid & they will make some primitive [illegible] attempt to escape whatever the cost, they become desperate & at last their self control bursts its bounds, & they smash something. Result instantly certified insane['] ... . And now through our great 'justice' a lone Aboriginal girl, frail & nerve wracked, lies on the floor of the cells, at Long Bay Gaol, driven to desperation by taunts, branded as a lunatic ... .

In a matter of days they will send her to Callan Park where I cannot see her for one month. Yet this girl was perfectly sane & able to speak to the jury herself on the day she entered Long Bay gaol.

I wonder how many of the jury have ever studied Abo. problems, or even *seen* an Aboriginal girl ...[5]

* * *

Ming was about to find out just how isolated and marginalized she really was. Her first action following Jane's committal was to write to the popular and well-respected Dr Duguid of South Australia, whom she knew through her work on the Citizenship Committee – he had told her then that her views were 'practically 100%' in accordance with his.[6] Now Duguid advised her to go to the APNR – 'Ask them to investigate the case to its depths. If the finding is that Jane has been hounded to desperation an appeal for justice will be made and the facts given publicity by every body interested in [A]borigines'.[7]

Two days later, Ruth Swann, the secretary of the APNR, told the APNR president – the anthropologist and now Welfare Board member Professor Elkin – that Ming had rung her with 'a long story without beginning or end'. She had asked Ming to send her a 'written report of the affair', which she enclosed for his perusal. Ming was a 'biased person whose mind is not open to reason,' said Swann, and she did 'not want to have any dealings with her, beyond being sufficiently polite to prevent her from saying nasty things in public about me and the A.P.N.R.'.[8]

Swann knew Ming, having been present at APNR meetings throughout Del's case. And as she had replaced Caroline Kelly as APNR secretary in 1940 she would have been well aware of the effect of the 'nasty things' Ming had said in public about her predecessor.[9] Ironically, Ming may have successfully ousted Kelly from the public sphere, but now it rebounded against her.

'Sufficient politeness' was the extent of the APNR's assistance. At the next meeting (April 1942), a sub-committee consisting of Colonel Howard, Mr Rofe and Swann was appointed to 'investigate representations made by Mrs Strack on behalf of a half-caste girl who is at present a patient in the Parramatta Mental Hospital'. This sub-committee was certainly unlikely to be sympathetic, especially as Ming's old friends the Bryces were being marginalized,[10] and in fact nothing more of Jane or Ming was ever mentioned in the APNR records. Duguid wrote again to Ming in June, asking for the 'latest', but of course there was no news.[11]

Elkin was no help at all. Back in November 1941, while waiting for Jane's trial date to be set, Ming had hoped he might use his not inconsiderable influence in some way. Elkin, however, could 'not quite see how I can do anything in the papers about it ... I suppose the Board's officers should really be watching the her [*sic*] interests, but as you do not desire that, I shall not do anything officially.'[12] The professor's eagerness to distance himself from Jane's case at this earlier stage would have had much to do with the APNR's later reluctance to help.

Nor was Ming able to get support for Jane from her contacts in the Feminist Club, as she had done in Del's case. Her outspoken advocacy of full citizenship rights had alienated her from the organized women's groups. By now the Feminist Club had firmly endorsed the new Board, while the UAW was anxious to negotiate with the government in the hope that they might get a female representative on the Board.[13] Swann said that both Grace Scobie and Mrs Thorne (wife of the former superintendent of the 'Half-Caste Home' at Jay Creek, Central Australia, whom Ming had met through Helen Baillie and Mary Bennett) had 'warned her to beware of the other lady'. But it appears that Ming did not even attempt to approach the Feminist Club or any other women's body on the issue.[14]

Ming did not look for support from the CAC either. The third CAC now campaigned almost purely to get an elected representative of the Aborigines on the Board, and as Sawtell cautioned Ferguson in April that year, 'friendly relations at all times, with all people' were required in order to secure representation on the Board.[15] In such a conciliatory atmosphere, it seems no group was anxious to get involved in a complicated scandal over an Aboriginal servant.

Ming's energy for mobilizing support for Jane was also seriously undermined by a sudden and unexpected downturn in her marriage. On Friday, 13 March (a 'bad luck day' Ming wrote in her diary), Norman rang from the barracks to say that he was coming to see her. Ming hoped that he would be staying the night, but he wanted a divorce. Two days later, '[I] might join Jane in the mental home,' Ming wrote, continuing wearily that she was trying to get the Howard Prison Reform League (to which she had connections from the CAC) and the APNR to help get Jane released, but could do 'nothing more'. The remainder of the entry was devoted to her worries about the marriage. 'Oh if *only* I could talk to someone about this awful behaviour of N's,' she wrote. 'I can't bear to because he *might* come back as he did before, & I have always been thankful afterwards that I did not discuss it at all with anyone ...' This time, however, Norman was serious. On 20 March, Ming received a registered letter from him insisting on a divorce; she told Peter when he returned to Sydney on leave seven days later, and wrote to Narrelle at Armidale (where she and her baby had gone for the duration of the war) two days later.

Ming and Helen went to stay with Narrelle in April.[16] By coincidence, Narrelle and her baby were billeted with a local doctor, Ellen Kent-Hughes, who was interested in the local Aboriginal people and one of Elkin's keenest correspondents. After Ming's return to Sydney in early May, Dr Kent-Hughes wrote to Ming telling her that if she could get Jane released, she could find Jane work locally. [17] But Ming's energies were consumed throughout the remainder of the year by the impending divorce, as well as by the hospitalization of her beloved father in September and then his death in October. The pain of her loss was made worse by the fact that he had died after falling ill whilst visiting his *other* daughter at Condobolin. Caught up in her own worries, Ming stopped thinking about Jane, and in fact there was no mention of her at all in Ming's 1942 diary after March.

* * *

In March 1943, a year after Jane had been admitted, a woman telephoned Ming, wanting to tell her about the treatment Jane had received at Long Bay. 'I was amazed & asked her to meet me tomorrow ...,' Ming wrote. 'It does seem strange after one year.'[18] Meeting her the next day, Ming discovered that she was a white woman who had been in the Long Bay gaol herself at the time Jane was committed, and that Jane had given her Ming's address. As this address had been for Ming's old place at Neutral Bay, Mrs Connor could not find Ming, until she came across a brief article by her published in the *Daily Mirror* that month, which had included her address in the by-line. (The subject of Ming's piece was 'an Aboriginal legend' from Wallaga Lake, concerning Aboriginal *weejas*, or spirit guides.[19])

Mrs Connor now told Ming that the warders 'deliberately *drove* Jane till she was frantic & threatened to throw a stool at them'. Another inmate, according to Mrs Connor, tormented Jane 'till the girl was beside herself with indignation then they [k]nocked her about & put her in a padded cell'. Mrs Connor told her 'how much she had loved Jane & had tried to help her & keep with her as much as possible ... when they tried to make out that she [Jane] was mad'.

'Some of the things she told me made me ill,' wrote Ming with distress in her diary that night, 'the *bashing* & the injustice were *scandalous*. What *can* I do now to help Jane? ... *Surely* such fiends must *pay* for the things they do to innocent people.' Some days or weeks later, 'I have been thinking of poor Jane & that matters could not be *worse* for me or for her what *ever* I do & I will not let Jane down – or the care of these poor despised Aborigines for the devil himself. So I went up to Parramatta this afternoon to the Mental Hospital ... . I eventually saw Jane':

> She has had her hair cut but other wise unchanged. She bounded away from the Wardress to me & said, 'When can I go home? I just want to get home to you. I am quite alright, but I suppose I have to stay here like the rest of them!'
> I said, 'There's a lovely garden for you to walk in Jane.'
> She said, 'Yes, there's a lovely garden but *I* haven't *seen* it – they won't let me walk in it.'!!
> I said, 'Do you stay in bed?'
> Jane said, 'No I just sit here and do nothing. *Couldn't* you get me away from here, they say I've lost my memory. I haven't but I don't tell *them!*'
> I asked did a Dr see her and she said, 'Yes, a brain specialist – he said he was – he told me he could see into my mind and read my thoughts – do you think they can?' She said, 'I can't tell you anything because they are always watching, look at them now.' (Three wardresses watching Jane, from the door.) She said, 'It's awful, they watch you all night too. You can't sleep.'
> When I was leaving she walked to the door, but to my astonishment the wardress said to another, 'Grab her arm, she might run away.' So this was probably what she *had* tried to do, poor little wild thing, to be kept shut up week after week would drive them mad. I came away feeling depressed ...[20]

In reality there was absolutely nothing that Ming could do.

* * *

Ming had been attempting the impossible in her relationship with Jane. She was trying to employ Jane as an 'equal' who might 'come and go as she pleases' in a society structured on inequality. Indeed, her employment of Jane was predicated on the very mechanics of racial, class and gender oppression; Jane's services would not have been available had she not been removed and indentured in the first place. But for Ming Jane was a test case of her society's commitment to allowing Aboriginal women to 'fit themselves into our way of life'.

It was not such an unrealistic expectation, at least not from Ming's perspective. By 1942 Jane had absorbed the values drummed into her by white society: as Ming observed, she was hardworking (to the point of obsession), frugal with money, had no discernible sexual life, and before she was out of her childhood had 'crushed down the longing for own people'.[21] What Jane demanded – when confronted by the drastic rejection of her doctor 'friend' – was simply respect, and it was this that was ultimately denied her.

Albert Memmi, a polemicist of the 1960s, wrote of the 'dramatic moment' when the colonized realises that 'his [sic] liberation [must] be accomplished through systematic self-denial'. 'Nonetheless,' continued Memmi,

> the major impossibility is not negating one's existence, for he soon discovers that, even if he agrees to everything, he would not be saved. In order to be assimilated, it is not enough to leave one's group, but one must enter another; now he meets with the colonizer's rejection ... . Everything is mobilized so that the colonized cannot cross the doorstep, so that he understands and admits that this path is dead and assimilation is impossible.

But once the colonized realize the futility of pursuing assimilation, elaborates Memmi, 'self-denial' is replaced by 'a recovery of the self and of autonomous dignity'.[22] As Jane's lawyer Healy surmised, the problem was probably that Jane 'had been very much on her dignity'. In the eyes of the court and the medical profession, as an Aboriginal woman, Jane's dignity was itself a threat.

The state did not commit Jane to an institution because she was insane. We tend to forget today how radical the earlier movement for Aboriginal citizenship, for Aboriginal equality, was in its time, just as we forget how inherently challenging was the maternalist feminist concern with protecting 'defenceless' Aboriginal women, though we can recognize its weaknesses today. We are also mistaken if we read Jane's committal, and indeed the high rates of incarceration of Aboriginal people generally, as just the therapeutic state sweeping up the broken remnants of political policies. For taking her part, Ming was marginalized and ostracized, and Jane herself was left to rot in a mental asylum. The evidence showed that Jane was not prepared to accept and submit to the intolerable price of her presence in mainstream Australia – to be a 'little haunted shadow' – but rather that she was prepared even to pit herself even against a man who represented a pinnacle of white male authority. If Jane had been white, and if she had then had the temerity to challenge the doctor, she may well also have been put away. But being black, her destiny was assured.

And so Jane's committal marked the end of Ming's active involvement in Aboriginal politics altogether. She had come to feel that she was fighting an unwinnable battle, while her personal difficulties with Jane had highlighted the implausibility of her favoured scenario of kindly white mistress single-handedly rescuing a grateful black servant. It appeared that Ming's intervention, if anything, had undermined Jane's already slim chances of escaping incarceration. Ming's consummate failure to save Jane from this fate left Ming in a position where both personally and politically she appeared profoundly inadequate, powerless, even ridiculous – a foolish, meddling, hysterical woman. Like Memmi's sketch of the 'colonizer who protests', everything confirmed Ming's powerlessness, her inability to converse with the colonizer, her solitude, bewilderment and ineffectiveness: 'He will slowly realize,' concludes Memmi somberly, 'that the only thing for him to do is to remain silent.'[23]

* * *

Ming had lived half a century when Jane's committal finally crushed her enthusiasm for the fight. Three months after their last meeting, Ming finally took the step she had long been dreading and divorced Norman on the grounds of adultery, in a spectacularly messy public divorce.[24] Narrelle then left *her* husband Bruce and moved to Ming's flat with her baby son. On top of all this upheaval, Ming's son Peter, soon to be 28 and with a four-month-old son of his own, was killed in a freak aircraft accident in 1945. These traumatic events, coming within the space of a few years, put an end to Ming's old life. She bundled away her voluminous papers and diaries documenting the political activities of this life and barely spoke of them to anyone again. She did continue to collect political clippings throughout the years and sent a letter to the papers for the 'Yes' vote on the 1967 referendum on Aboriginal citizenship, but her activities were turned towards cultural rather than political pursuits – meeting Albert Namatjira at an exhibition, following the making of *Jedda* with interest. Finally compelled to be self-supporting at 51 years of age, Ming took up what had been a hobby, china painting, in earnest, becoming somewhat renowned for her Aboriginal portraits on plates.[25] Her masterpiece was a large china fruit bowl with a portrait of Merriman surrounded by the detail of the 'Legend of Creation', which she never sold. Having been effectively silenced, Ming retreated into her nostalgic childhood memories of a more innocent colonialism.

Lives are lived forward, but the past is only understood in retrospect. 'We know the end before we consider the beginning and we can never wholly recapture what it was to know the beginning only.'[26] My Gran gave me Ming's precious Merriman plate, and as I look at this unspeaking image that Ming painted at the end of her story, its encoded representation of Ming's own 'origins' legend, I think about the process of forgetting that has gone on not only in my own family, but in Australian history generally.

When I began my own journey, the Aboriginal assertion and demand that 'White Australia has a Black History' had a powerful reverberation for me. Having previously had no inkling that such a history was embedded in my own family, I could not understand how such an important history could have been so comprehensively forgotten. I began piecing together Ming's story from this knowledge. Intrigued by what had set her, such an unlikely Aboriginal activist, on such an unusual path, it wasn't long before I worked out where the story had ended for Ming. Failure to redeem herself on such a dramatic and personal level compounded the political failure of the 1930s Aboriginal citizenship movement, and Ming stopped speaking. Memories fade without reiteration, and leached of their potent stories, the material traces of her history that remained visible in my family – the Merriman plate, the hand-tinted photograph of Mary – become signs not of resistance, but of complicity and complacency – signs of a history that indeed might be left to fade.

By the time I came to the end of my journey, the relationships between Ming and her domestic servants had become part of a much larger history, of the generations of young Aboriginal people stolen from their families and communities. A controversial history, generating questions about missing monies, exploitation – financial as well as sexual – genocide and atonement, all attended upon by phalanges of neo-conservatives. Ming may have wanted to forget what was for her a story that ended in failure, such abjection. Yet her story tells us that at the very height of these policies of Aboriginal child removal, both black and white people, disgusted by the dishonesty, the cruelty, the callousness of the system, opposed them at no little cost to themselves. That there could be and was sustained and outspoken protest from one who directly benefited from the system and knew it intimately.

At the end, I hear Ming's silence as an awareness, not only of her own powerlessness, but also of the unspeakably painful truth of her unwilling but inescapable complicity. But were she to see today the equivocations, the nitpicking, the outright denial of this history, I know that Ming would speak out now, and as passionately as ever. The 'Stolen Generations' history is not a figment of a fervent late twentieth-century imagination. It is historical reality, and its brave and bitter stories are woven together throughout the generations of our shared history.

Epilogue

21
She learnt her lessons well

As Ming's story approached its devastating conclusion, Mary's widowed husband arrived on Ming's doorstep at Wahroonga, with Mary's first-born daughter, Mary Hannah, in tow. He asked Ming if she would take her in and look after her, but – as my Gran recalls – Ming felt unable to do so. Whether this was before or just after Jane's committal, and whatever her reason, we might speculate that Ming felt very guilty about turning her back on Mary's child. Nevertheless she did so, and another of the ties to her past was severed. In the end, the one and only link with Ming's past that did endure, despite a hiatus of 20 years, was her connection with Jane. And so it was Jane, and not Mary, who saw out Ming's waning years, as a direct result of government policy.

* * *

When I first met Ally, Jane's niece, she told me of how her mother, Jane's younger sister, had always told her and her brothers and sisters about their missing aunt, the eldest girl who had been taken away and never seen again. The other three, also taken at some point, had all made their way back home, but not Jane. Ally told me about how, when the Link-Up people finally found Jane, an old lady living in Sydney, they had told her that she might be better off not going to see her. Jane didn't really want to know Aboriginal people, they told Ally. 'I just can't understand why she would have been like that,' Ally said sadly.

At the end of her life, Jane had become one of the first cases handled by Link-Up NSW, an organization established to reunite Aboriginal children who had been stolen from their communities with their families. The eventual meeting in 1981 between Jane and her nephew was deeply depressing. One of the Link-Up workers, Coral Edwards, described how Jane dressed in her best, then went down on her knees to sweep up the alley behind her boarding house, before they took a photograph of her. A removed child herself, Edwards concluded with obvious pain:

> This woman is just a shell now, doing the only thing she knows. Cleaning. She should have been an Aboriginal grandmother by now, surrounded by her family, and all the warmth and love that goes with it. Instead she says, 'I don't mix with Aboriginals, you know.'

If the Aborigines Welfare Board still existed today, its members might be very pleased with Jane. She learnt her lessons well.[1]

* * *

The removal and apprenticeship policy carried out by the NSW Aborigines Protection Board was riven with contradictions, grotesque in its manifestation. Aiming to control the Aboriginal population overall by containing and controlling the bodies of young Aboriginal women, the state placed them in an impossible and untenable position. The doorsteps of their employers' households were thresholds not on to a hopeful future, but into oblivion and despair. Taken from their own communities, they were to be held captive in a society that disdained and despised them. While Ming saw all her efforts as wasted and futile, Jane's entire incarcerated life epitomizes the tragic waste of the Stolen Generations.

Taken from her family at six years of age, Jane had spent all her childhood in the Cootamundra Home and all her youth in domestic service. At 26 years of age, she was confined in a mental asylum where she remained an incredible 20 years. In 1961, she was finally discharged – against her will – into the care of a Catholic hostel. Jane had protested that she was indeed 'mentally ill' and 'should not be anywhere but a Mental Hospital'.[2] Her reluctance to leave is not surprising: she was 46 years old and had no family, friends, home or money, and extremely little prospect of finding work.

In the 1960s the state government began a drive to move inmates of psychiatric institutions out of state care and back to the care of their families. Jane was allotted a caseworker, who contacted the Aborigines Welfare Board and found, predictably, there was no information about Jane's family's whereabouts, even though Jane herself supplied her real name and the names of her father and siblings. Apparently in desperation, the caseworker got in touch with Ming in April 1961, though there had been no contact between the two women since Ming's visit in 1943.[3]

Jane sent her first letter to Ming from the hospital the same day. She was disappointed that 'you could not come up on the Wednesday some time ago' and offered to visit Ming at the weekend. She told Ming that most of the other patients went 'home' for the weekends now.[4] Ming wrote to Jane's caseworker in September, having spoken with Jane. She reported that Jane seemed 'frightened' that she was to be returned to Cootamundra Home if she could not find a job. Emphatically stating that it would be a 'fatal mistake' to send Jane to work or live anywhere in the vicinity of the doctor's home (he was still in residence at nearby Gordon), Ming told the caseworker that she was not able to provide for Jane herself, but that she was making enquiries at a local hospital to see if there was any work available. Evidently Ming's enquiries were unsuccessful, as Jane was discharged to the care of a Catholic hostel a few months later.[5]

Here Jane earned her board and theoretically a small income by selling raffle tickets for the charity that ran her hostel, a source of much aggravation to her. Forced to ask Ming for a loan of £8 when the charity failed to pay her at the end of the year, and took her pension for board, Jane wrote angrily to Ming she 'never knew anything so disgracefull' and she planned to leave the hostel as soon as she could find a cheaper place to live. '[I]t is Disgracefull we have to pay all our Money and have nothing left for ourselfs. Just fancie Old Ladies putting up with all that Mental Worry.'[6]

Jane was herself the only remaining contact, outside of Ming's family, who had been with Ming throughout her 'political' years. In 1966, when Ming was approached by Horner to be interviewed on her recollections of Bill Ferguson and the Aboriginal movement, Ming made sure that Jane participated in this interview.[7] While the two women had little in common, they did have a shared past of sorts, and it was undoubtedly this that kept them together.

In 1968 Jane wrote to tell Ming that she was now living in a much cheaper boarding house at Lewisham, the pensioners having all been replaced with 'Social Workers'. 'We are all pleased to have our freedom after long years of living there,' she wrote. In 1973, after several more moves between boarding houses, she wrote that she would soon be finding her own flat: the 'Housing Commission has put me on their Waiting List at last. I turned 54 on the 2nd of March 1973'. As Jane herself attained a certain venerability, the social distance between her and Ming (now 81 years of age) was closing. 'Life creeps on faster than ever,' she continued, as one elderly lady to another. 'The Days are very Hot allways are at Easter Time. The [Easter] Show I might go too I dont know yet. Well Joan there is not much more to tell you. Only myself very pleased about going away forever.' [8]

Jane never did get her own flat. She moved to another boarding house in Stanmore, and from there down the road to another (close by a massive inner-city terrace I shared with five others during my student days), where she spent her remaining years. In 1977 she wrote a long letter to Ming – 'I have been thinking of you alot... There is nothen like a real good Friend in Need. what do you think[?]'[9] Her next, and last surviving, letter to Ming provides a haunting image of what was possibly their final meeting. Jane had gone to visit Ming, who was living with her married daughter, Helen, and afterwards Ming had given Jane some money for the taxi fare home:

> I left s2.10s on your table and keep s2 for myself. The Taxi never turned up so I came back and called and 3 times but no answer so I closed your Door and Left The gentleman [Ming's son-in-law] was in his yard but he never spoke to me. I hope you keep well and happy for allways[10]

Ming slipped into senility from this point on (1978), and the letters and cards from Jane ceased. Five years later, Ming went to live with Narrelle, near Coffs Harbour. She died soon after, in a private hospital, aged 91. Her boxes of memories, mementos and papers, including the letters from Mary, Del, Alma and Jane, and the carved ivory handle of a broken umbrella, were stacked in my aunt's garage and quickly forgotten.

Jane died, seven years later, alone in her boarding house room.

A Note on Sources

Ming's extraordinary papers, now lodged with the National Library of Australia in Canberra as the Joan Kingsley-Strack papers, provide the basis for my reconstruction of her story. They include her personal diaries and correspondences, as well as the papers of the Committee for Aboriginal Citizenship. I have generally cited her sources only where they refer to letters or to the CAC records, rather than citing her personal diary entries exhaustively. I have supplemented her papers with a wide range of contemporary records and other sources held in Australian libraries and archives. These include the papers of individuals, organizations and government bodies, including the official records of the NSW Aborigines Protection Board. I further relied on a range of published contemporary sources, such as the NSW Parliamentary Debates (published annually and held at the State Library of NSW), government reports and newspaper articles. Books and journal articles I have drawn on – that is, published secondary sources – are cited in the notes and publication details follow in the Bibliography. For those readers who are interested to trace the archival references and sources that make up the bulk of my research, I suggest they see my unpublished history thesis, 'My One Bright Spot', which is lodged with the History Department at the University of Sydney. Readers who wish to contact me for further details or to add information, can write to me care of the History Department, Flinders University, GPO Box 2100, Adelaide SA 5001.

Abbreviations and locations of archival sources referred to in the notes

AA	Australian Archives, Canberra
AE	A. P. Elkin Papers, Fisher Archives, University of Sydney, Sydney
AFG	Australian Fellowship Group Papers, Australian Archives, Canberra
AIATSIS	Australian Institute of Aboriginal and Torres Strait Islander Studies, Canberra
APB	Aborigines Protection Board (NSW) records, Archives Office of NSW, Sydney.
APBR	Aborigines Protection Board (NSW) annual reports, State Library of NSW, Sydney
APBSR	Aborigines Protection Board Salary Registers, Archives Office of NSW, Sydney.
APBWR	Aborigines Protection Board Ward Registers, Archives Office of NSW, Sydney.
APNR	Association for the Protection of Native Races: Minutes held in Elkin Papers, Fisher Archives, University of Sydney, Sydney.
AT	Albert Thompson Papers, Mitchell Library, Sydney.
AWB	Aborigines Welfare Board (NSW) records, Archives Office of NSW, Sydney.

AWBCF   Aborigines Welfare Board correspondence files, Archives Office of NSW, Sydney.

BPA AAV   Board for the Protection of Aborigines (Victoria), records, Australian Archives, Melbourne.

BPA PRV   Board for the Protection of the Aborigines (Victoria) records, Public Records of Victoria, Laverton.

CD   Charles Duguid Papers, National Library of Australia, Canberra

EDU   Education Department Files, Archives Office of NSW, Sydney.

FC   Feminist Club Papers, Mitchell Library, Sydney

JKS   Papers of Joan Kingsley-Strack, National Library of Australia, Canberra

NSWPD   New South Wales Parliamentary Debates, State Library of NSW, Sydney

OP   Olive Pink Papers, Australian Institute of Aboriginal and Torres Strait Islander Studies, Canberra

PDCF   Premier's Department Correspondence Files, NSW, Archives Office of NSW, Sydney.

PITSG   Parramatta Industrial Training School for Girls records, Archives Office of NSW, Sydney.

PMGD   Postmaster General's department records, National Archives of Australia, Sydney.

RP   Sir Robert Archdale Parkhill Papers, National Library of Australia, Canberra

UAW   United Associations of Women Papers, Mitchell Library, Sydney.

Notes

Chapter 1

1 See Carolyn G. Heilbrun, *Writing a Woman's Life* (New York: Ballantine Books, 1998), 39, 68.
2 M. E. McGuire, 'The Legend of the Good Fella Missus', *Aboriginal History*, vol. 14, no. 2 (1990), 124–51; M. Tonkinson, 'Sisterhood or Aboriginal Servitude? Black Women and White Women on the Australian Frontier', *Aboriginal History* vol. 12, no. 1 (1988), 27–39; L. Riddett, '"Watching the White Women Fade": Aboriginal and White Women in the Northern Territory 1870–1940', *Hecate*, vol. 19, no. 1 (1991), 73–92.
3 Jackie Huggins, Jo Willmot, Isabel Tarrago, Kathy Willetts, Liz Bond, Lillian Holt, Eleanor Bourke, Maryann Bin-Salik, Pat Fowell, Joann Schmider, Valerie Craigie and Linda McBride-Levi, 'Letter to the Editors', *Women's Studies International Forum*, vol. 1, no. 5 (1991), 505–13, 506.
4 J. K. S. to Elkin, 19 January [1938]: AE. Notes on Wallaga Lake, n.d.: JKS NLA MS 9551.
5 S. Gilbert and S. Gubar, quoted in Heilbrun, *Writing a Woman's Life* (1988), 33.

Chapter 2

1 Notes, written *c*. early 1920s and dated '1918': JKS.
2 Notes, n.d.; Diary entry (recollections), 12 December 1936: JKS.
3 Diary entry, 1 May 1934 (retrospective); J. K. S. to solicitor, 17 May 1943: JKS.
4 Dengue fever – an infectious tropical viral disease, causing fever and acute joint pain.
5 Mary to J. K. S., n.d., *c*. early 1920s, addressed from East Kew, Melbourne: JKS.
6 Judith Rollins, *Between Women: Domestics and Their Employers* (Philadelphia: Temple University Press, 1985), 157.
7 J. Stobo to M. Stobo, 19 December 1924: JKS.
8 J. K. S. to Morley, 31[March 1934]: AE.
9 APB Minutes, 14 May 1926: APB.
10 *Sydney Morning Herald*, 29 October 1924, 12; 9 January 1925, 8; 10 January 1925, 16; 11 February 1925, 16. APB Minutes, 13 May 1927, 8 July 1927: APB.
11 Raymond Evans, 'A Gun in the Oven: Masculinism and Gendered Violence', in Kay Saunders and Raymond Evans, eds. *Gender Relations in Australia: Domination and Negotiation* (Sydney: Harcourt Brace Jovanovich, 1992), 203.
12 J. K. S. to an unnamed recipient (possibly never sent), 16 October 1926: JKS.
13 J. K. S. to Morley, 31[March 1934]: AE.
14 Jean Magill to J. K. S., 21 October 1926: JKS.

Chapter 3

1 Over 70 per cent of the removed children listed on the Protection Board's registers were female. Furthermore, 73 per cent of those girls were placed in indentures as compared to only a quarter of the boys who were removed. See Heather Goodall, '"Assimilation begins in the home": the state and Aboriginal women's work as mothers in New South Wales, 1900 to 1960s', Ann McGrath and Kay Saunders eds. *Labour History: Aboriginal Workers*, No. 69 (Sydney: Australian Society for the Study of Labour History, 1995), 81–4. Heather Goodall, '"Saving the Children": Gender and the Colonization of Aboriginal Children in NSW, 1788 to 1990', *Aboriginal Law Bulletin*, vol. 2, no. 44 (June 1990), 6. Victoria Haskins '"A Better Chance"? Sexual Abuse and the Apprenticeship of Aboriginal Girls under the NSW Aborigines Protection Board', *Aboriginal History*, vol. 28 (2004), 43.

2 *The Sydney Morning Herald*, 20 December 1876, p. 3; cited Susan Lindsay Johnston, 'The New South Wales Government Policy towards Aborigines, 1880 to 1909', MA thesis, University of Sydney (1970), 28.

3 Anthony Trollope, *Australia and New Zealand*, vol. II (Leipzig, 1873), 151, 256; cited William J. Lines, *Taming the Great South Land: A History of the Conquest of Nature in Australia* (North Sydney: Allen & Unwin, 1991), 115.

4 See Ann Curthoys, 'Good Christians and Useful Workers: Aborigines, Church and State in NSW 1870–1883', Sydney Labour History Group, *What Rough Beast? The State and Social Order in Australian History* (Sydney: George Allen & Unwin, 1982), 50–1.

5 Henry Reynolds, *The Law of the Land* (Ringwood: Penguin, 1987), 32–4.

6 *NSWPD*, 24 November 1914, 1353–5.

7 *NSWPD*, 15 December 1909, 4550.

8 *APBR* 1911.

9 *NSWPD*, 27 January 1915, 1951, 1967.

10 *NSWPD*, 24 November 1914, 1353.

11 APB minutes, 18 April 1912: APB.

12 Heather Radi, entry on G. E. Ardill, in Bede Nairn and Geoffrey Serle, eds. *Australian Dictionary of Biography, vol. 7, 1891–1939* (Melbourne: Melbourne University Press, 1979), 90, 91.

13 Jim Fletcher, 'Transcript of an interview with Mr A C Pettitt in June 1977, re Aboriginal education', AIATSIS PMS 5380, 8.

14 APB minutes, 15 March 1915.

15 Copy letter, Pettitt to Hon. Secretaries, Local Committees, 28 March 1914; Circulars Nos. 5 (6 April 1914); 18 (7 August 1914); 35 (10 November 1914); APB Copies of Letters Sent 1914–1927: APB.

16 APB minutes, 6 April 1916; see also 15 March 1915: APB.

17 *NSWPD* 24 November 1914, 1354.

18 APB minutes, 6 April 1916, 26 April 1917, 6 December 1917: APB.

19 Merri Gill, *Weilmoringle: A Unique Bi-cultural Community* (Dubbo: Development and Advisory Publications of Australia, 1996), 40, 41, citing George Magill to Donald Mackay, 27 December 1913.

20 Jean Magill to J. K. S., 2 April 1926: JKS.

21 APB minutes, 22 March 1900, 26 April 1900, 31 May 1900: APB.

22 APB minutes, 7 July 1898, 6 October 1898, 19 June 1906, 3 July 1906, 11 May 1911: APB.

23 APB minutes, 21 April 1892, 19 May 1892, 16 August 1900, 27 September 1900, 4 October 1900, 29 November 1900, 3 January 1901, 31 January 1901: APB. Tilba Tilba Progress Committee Minutes, 31 March 1892, 7 April 1892, 5 May 1892 (supplied by Laurelle Pacey, personal communication 1995).

24 Jennifer Sabbioni, 'Aboriginal Women's Narratives: Reconstructing Identities', *Australian Historical Studies*, vol. 27, no. 106 (April 1996), 76.

25 Phillip Pepper and Tess de Araugo, *What Did Happen to the Aborigines of Victoria, vol. 1: The Kurnai of Gippsland* (Melbourne: Hyland House, 1985), 145; Phillip Pepper and Tess De Araugo, *You Are What You Make Yourself To Be: The Story of a Victorian Aboriginal Family 1842–1980* (Melbourne: Hyland House, 1989), 73.

26 C. H. Grove, in *The Gap* magazine, 1925: quoted in P. D. Gardner, *Gippsland Massacres: The Destruction of the Kurnai Tribes 1800–1860* (Victoria: Ngarak Press, 1993), 83.

27 Bain Attwood, 'Charles Hammond: Aboriginal Battler', *Gippsland Heritage Journal*, vol. 3, no. 2 (1988), 16.

28 '*My Heart is Breaking*', *A Joint Guide to Records about Aboriginal People in the Public Records Office of Victoria and the Australian Archives, Victorian Regional Office*, Canberra: Australian Government Printing Office, 1993, 112 M. F. Christie, *Aborigines in Colonial Victorian 1835–86* (Sydney: Sydney University Press, 1979), 201. Diane Barwick, 'Coranderrk and Cumeroongunga: Pioneers and Policy', T. Scarlett Epstein and David H. Penney eds. *Opportunities and Response: Case Studies in Economic Development* (London: C Hurst & Co, 1972), 35–6.

29 Tess de Araugo, personal communication, 24 June 1996. I am indebted to Tess de Araugo of Victoria for her generosity in sharing her previous detailed research compiled on Cecily's life. Unless otherwise stated, further information on Mary's grandparents' comes from Tess de Araugo's research into the Victorian Board for the Protection of Aborigines records.

30 A similar case in 1879 is described in '*My Heart is Breaking*', 79. For more information about the regulation of inter-racial marriages during this period, see Katterine Ellinghaus, 'Regulating Koori Marriages: The 1886 Victorian Aborigines Protection Act', *Journal of Australian studies* no. 67 (2001).

31 APB minutes, 29 October 1914, 5 November 1914, 24 September 1914: APB.

Chapter 4

1 K. Reiger, *The Disenchantment of the Home: Modernizing the Australian Family 1880–1940* (Melbourne: Oxford University Press, 1985), 96.

2 Mary to J. K. S., 9 January 1927: JKS.

3 Mary to J. K. S., n. d., c. 11 January 1927: JKS.

4 Mary to J. K. S., 19 January 1927: JKS.

5 Mary to J. K. S., 30 January [1927], postmarked 3 February–5 February 1927: JKS.

6   Mary to J. K. S., 13 February 1927, postmarked 8 March–12 March 1927: JKS
    Papers 9:12.
7   Manuscript diary entry, 8 June 1933 (recollection): JKS.
8   J. K. S. to Morley, 31 [March 1934]: AE.
9   Manuscript diary entry, 8 June 1933 (recollection): JKS.
10 Lake Tyers Register of Correspondence, no. 148, 20 July 1927: BPA PRV.
11 APBSR. Lake Tyers Manager's Reports, for week ending 3 August 1928. Lake
    Tyers Register of Correspondence, no. 195, 7 September 1928: BPA PRV.
12 Mary to J. K. S., 27 October 1927: JKS.
13 Burns to J. K. S., n.d., attached to J. K. S. to Mary, 13 February 1930 [returned
    'Not Known at this Address']: JKS.
14 *APBR 1926.*
15 In Ellen J. Sicles, ed., *The Letters of Elizabeth Kendall Bate* (Surry Hills:
    privately printed, 1967), 75.
16 APB minutes, 14 July 1910: APB. *APBR 1910.*
17 Horner–Adams correspondence: AIATSIS PMS 4179.
18 *NSWPD*, 24 November 1914, 1353.
19 M. E. McGuire, 'The Legend of the Good Fella Missus', *Aboriginal History*,
    vol. 14, no. 2 (1990), 124–51.
20 George Taylor, 'The Quest for the Australian Girl: Part II, Her Humorous
    Sister', *All About Australians*, 1 April 1907, 229–35, cited in Sharyn Pearce,
    '"The Best Career is Matrimony": First-Wave Journalism and the "Australian
    Girl"', *Hecate*, vol. 18, no. 2 (1992), 72.

Chapter 5

1   Diary entry, 12 December 1936 (recollections); Doctor to Norman Kingsley-
    Strack, 10 April 1930: JKS.
2   Diary entry, 12 December 1936 (recollections): JKS.
3   APBWR.
4   J. K. S. to the Matron, Bomaderry Home [draft], 15 June 1933: JKS.
5   Diary entry, 9 November [1939]: JKS.
6   Notes, undated, *c*.March 1932, on a New Guard letterhead: JKS.
7   J. K. S. to the Matron, Bomaderry Home, 15 June 1933: JKS. J. K. S. to Morley,
    31 [March 1934]: AE.
8   J. K. S. to the Matron, Bomaderry Home, 15 June 1933: JKS.
9   APBWR.
10 JKS to Donald Commons, 28 September 1932 [draft]: JKS.
11 APBWR.
12 J. K. S. to Morley, 31[March 1934]: AE.
13 J. K. S. to the Matron, Bomaderry Home, 15 June 1933: JKS.
14 Alma to J. K. S., n.d., stamped from Urunga Station 25 October 1932, post-
    marked 28 October 1932; Alma to J. K. S., n.d., postmarked 21 December
    1932: JKS.
15 Herb Simms, personal communication, 1998.
16 James Miller, *Koori: A Will to Win* (London: Angus & Robertson, 1985), 159,
    162, 166, quoting Jean Begg (1983).

Chapter 6

1 Report of a conference of Victorian mission managers to consider the Victorian Board for Protection of the Aborigines' resolutions of 2 August 1882, Melbourne, 18 August 1882: BPA AAV. *NSWPD*, 27 January 1915, 1952, 1958; Joy Damousi, *Depraved and Disorderly: Female Convicts, Sexuality and Gender in Colonial Australia* (Cambridge: Cambridge University Press, 1997), 69.

2 Tara Geldard, 'The Industrial School for Girls at Parramatta: Context, Continuity and Change 1887–1920', BA (Hons) thesis, University of Sydney (1993), 55, 93.

3 *APBR 1910*.

4 APBR 1910.

5 *NSWPD*, 24 November 1914, 1353.

6 'Aborigines; Race Dying out: Fate of Girls', *Sydney Morning Herald*, 29 October 1924, 12 (citing a Board official).

7 Memo, Acting Secretary APB to Manager, Aboriginal Station, Terry Hie Hie, 13 May 1918, APB correspondence file: Copy reproduced in Carla Hankins, '"The Missing Links": Cultural Genocide through the Abduction of Female Aboriginal Children from their Families and their Training for Domestic Service, 1883–1969', BA Hons thesis, Sociology, University of New South Wales, Sydney, 1982, Appendix C, 6.1.10. *Select Committee on Administration of Aborigines Protection Board, appointed during the session of 1937–38 – Proceedings of the Committee, Minutes of Evidence and Exhibits* NSW Legislative Assembly, Sydney, 1938, in *Joint Volumes of papers presented to the Legislative Council and Legislative Assembly ...*, vol. VIII (Sydney: NSW Parliament, 1940), 49.

8 See Inara Walden, '"That was slavery days": Aboriginal Domestic Servants in New South Wales in the Twentieth Century', *Aboriginal Workers: Labour History* no. 69, eds A. McGrath and K. Saunders (Sydney: Australian Society for the Study of Labour History, 1995), 200; Inara Walden, 'Aboriginal Women in Domestic Service in New South Wales, 1850 to 1969', BA (Hons) thesis, University of NSW (1991), 70, 91. 'Aborigines; Race Dying out; Fate of Girls', *Sydney Morning Herald*, 29 October 1924, 12; Regulation 41 (d), *Government Gazette* no. 48, 2 April 1913; *Select Committee on the Administration of the Aborigines Protection Board, Minutes of Evidence*, 130; AWB minutes, 21 January 1941, 25 February 1941: AWB.

9 APB minutes, 15 March 1915.

10 APB minutes, 25 June 1919; 30 October 1918; 14 May 1919.

11 Letter accompanying policy statement, dated 3 April 1916; APB minutes, 6 April 1916.

12 APB minutes, 8 February 1917; 3 April 1918.

13 Heather Goodall, *Invasion to Embassy: Land in Aboriginal Politics in New South Wales, 1770–1972* (Sydney: Allen & Unwin, 1996) 142.

14 James Miller, *Koori: A Will to Win* (London: Angus & Robertson, 1985), 166, citing recollections, Jean Begg.

15 'Aborigines; Race Dying out: Fate of Girls' (citing a Board official).

16 APBSR.

17   F. Maynard to an Aboriginal girl, 14 October 1927: PDCF A 27/915.
18   E. B. Harkness, Memo to the Premier, 'Matters Relating to the Aborigines of New South Wales': PDCF.
19   Eileen Morgan, *The Calling of the Spirits* (Canberra: Aboriginal Studies Press, 1994), 64.
20   Quoted in Heather Goodall, 'A History of Aboriginal Communities in NSW, 1909–1939', PhD thesis, University of Sydney (1982), 150.
21   Mrs C. Morgan quoted *Labor Call*, 20 September 1934, quoted in Goodall, *Invasion to Embassy*: 187.
22   Russell McGregor, '"Breed out the colour" or the Importance of Being White', *Australian Historical Studies*, vol. 33, no. 120 (October 2002); Barbara Cummings, *Take This Child ... From Kahlin Compound to the Retta Dixon Children's Home* (Canberra: Aboriginal Studies Press, 1990): Pat Jacobs, *Mister Neville* (Fremantle: Fremantle Arts Centre Press, 1990).
23   Megregar '"Breed out the colour"', 288–9.
24   See Fiona Paisley 'No Back Streets in the Bush: 1920s and 1930s Pro-Aboriginal White Women's Activism and The Trans-Australia Railway; *Australian Feminist Studies*, vol. 12, no. 25 (1997); Fiona Paisley, *Loving Protection? Australian Feminism and Aboriginal Women's Rights 1919–1939* (Melbourne: Melbourne University Press, 2000); Marilyn Lake, 'Frontier Feminism and The Marauding White Man', *Journal of Australian Studies: Australian Frontiers*, no. 49 (1996).
25   *Australian Women's Weekly*, 8 September 1934, quoted in Rosemary Campbell, *Heroes & Lovers: A Question of National Identity* (Sydney: Allen & Unwin, 1989), 32.
26   *Aboriginal Welfare–Initial Conference of Commonwealth and State Aboriginal Authorities, held at Canberra, 21st to 23rd April, 1937* (Canberra: Commonwealth Government Printer, 1937), 12, 14, 16.
27   Figures calculated from APBWR. See Victoria Haskins, '"A Better Chance"?: Sexual Abuse and the Apprenticeship of Aboriginal Girls under the NSW Aborigines Protection Board', *Aboriginal History*, vol. 28 (2004).
28   Walden, 'Aboriginal Women in Domestic Service', 119–20.
29   Margaret Barbalet, *Far from a Low Gutter Girl: The Forgotten World of State Wards: South Australia 1887–1940* (Melbourne: Oxford University Press, 1983), 92, 94, 239.
30   Human Rights and Equal Opportunity Commission, *Bringing Them Home: A Guide to the Findings and Recommendations of the National Inquiry into the Separation of Aboriginal and Torres Strait Islander Children from their Families* (Canberra: Human Rights and Equal Opportunity Commission (with AIATSIS), 1997), 194.
31   Heather Radi, 'G. E. Ardill', in Bede Nairn and Geoffrey Serle, eds, *Australian Dictionary of Biography, vol. 7, 1891–1939* (Melbourne: Melbourne University Press, 1979), 91; letter accompanying policy statement, A. C. Pettitt to Chief Secretary, 3 April 1916, enclosed in APB minutes, 6 April 1916: APB.
32   APB minutes, 11 May 1916: APB.
33   See John Maynard, '" Light in the Darkness": Elizabeth McKenzie Hatton' in Anna Cole, Victoria Haskins and Fiona Paisley, eds, *Uncommon Ground: White Women in Aboriginal History* (Canberra: Aboriginal Studies Press, 2005).

34 APB minutes, 6 August 1914, 3 September 1914, 29 March 1917: APB. Carolyn Harwood, 'A History of Aboriginal Women in New South Wales 1930–1950', BA (Hons) thesis, University of Sydney (1984), 50.
35 *APBR 1916.*
36 APB minutes, 16 September 1915, 16 November 1915, 23 September 1915, 6 April 1916: APB.
37 Gungil Jindibah Centre, *Learning from the Past: Aboriginal Perspectives on the Effects and Implications of Welfare Policies and Practices on Aboriginal Families in New South Wales* (Lismore: NSW Department of Community Services, 1994), 41.
38 Horner–Adams correspondence: AIATSIS.
39 *NSWPD*, 27 January 1915, 1958, 1951. *NSWPD*, 24 November 1914, 1354, 1353.
40 APB minutes, 3 April 1918: APB.
41 APB minutes, 22 March 1900, 28 June 1900: APB.

Chapter 7

1 J. K. S. to Morley, 31[March 1934]: AE; J. K. S. to Matron, Bomaderry Home, 15 June 1933: JKS.
2 Introduction, Manuscript diary, n.d., *c.*June 1933: JKS. All unreferenced quotations pertaining to Del's case hereafter are sourced from this diary.
3 Personal and place names are fictitous – other than the places where Del lived with the Stracks – to protect the identity of Del's descendants.
4 Cited in Vron Ware, *Beyond the Pale: White Women, Racism and History* (London: Verso, 1992), 55.
5 Transcript of conversation, J. K. S. with Del, 16 March 1933; Del's aunt to J. K. S., 13 September 1934: JKS. Inquiry Report, 16 July 1927; Mrs E— to Drummond, 30 April 1928, 28 May 1928, 30 May 1928, 4 June 1928: Nortown School EDU.
6 Transcript of conversation, J. K. S. with Del, 16 March 1933; J. K. S. to Beckett, 23 October 1934; Del's aunt to J. K. S., 13 September 1934: JKS.
7 APBWR.
8 Register of Warrants Received: PITSG.
9 Daily Admission and Discharge Registers: PITSG. APB Minutes 23 December 1927, 8 July 1927: APB.
10 APB minutes, 15 March 1915, 26 April 1917, 6 December 1917: APB.
11 APB minutes, 13 May 1927, 8 July 1927: APB.
12 Heather Goodall, 'A History of Aboriginal Communities in New South Wales, 1909–1939', PhD thesis, University of Sydney, Sydney (1982), 237–8.

Chapter 8

1 Again, as in the preceding chapter, all references to Del unless otherwise stated are drawn from Ming's manuscript diary: JKS.
2 'MY BABY: Homeless Girl's Cry in Court', article unreferenced, n.d. (*c.*1934) in Ming's scrapbook: JKS.

3 Jim Fletcher, 'Transcript of an interview with Mr A. C. Pettitt in June 1977, re Aboriginal education', 3: AIATSIS.
4 Transcript of conversation, J. K. S. with Del, 16 March 1933: JKS.
5 Parkhill Report: RP.
6 J. K. S. to Mrs Mitchell, 4 January 1934 [draft]: JKS.
7 Pettitt to J. K. S., 31 July 1933.
8 APBSR.
9 J. K. S. to the Matron, Bomaderry Home [draft], 15 June 1933: JKS.
10 Del to Pettitt, n.d., *c.*June–July 1933 [copy, handwritten by J. K. S.]: JKS.
11 Pettitt to J. K. S., 2 August 1933: JKS.
12 Pettitt to J. K. S., 3 October 1933, enclosing reminder notice dated 30 September 1933; Pettitt to J. K. S., 4 October 1933, enclosing agreement form, dated 13 January 1933: JKS.
13 J. K. S. to Pettitt, 4 November 1933 [draft]: JKS.
14 Pettitt to J. K. S., 15 December 1933: JKS.
15 J. K. S. Manuscript diary entries, 5 July 1933, 6 July 1933, 13 July 1933, 31 July 1933: missing excerpt held in Elkin Papers (AE).
16 Vogan to Elkin, 13 October 1933; APNR Minutes, 10 October 1933: AE.
17 Notes on Katie: AE. APBWR. APBSR.
18 APB minutes, 20 February 1930: APB.

Chapter 9

1 Notes, dated 1 September 1939: AE.
2 Transcript of conversation, J. K. S. with Del, undated, *c.*1933–4: JKS.
3 Del to J. K. S., 29 December 1936; Del to J. K. S., n.d., *c.* early 1935: JKS.
4 Horner–Adams correspondence: AIATSIS.
5 Judith Rollins, *Between Women: Domestics and Their Employers* (Philadelphia: Temple University Press, 1985), 210.
6 Transcript of conversation, J. K. S. with Del, 23 April 1934; Transcript of conversation, J. K. S. with Del, n.d., *c.*1933–4: JKS.
7 Transcript of conversation, J. K. S. with Del, 23 April 1934; Transcript of conversation, J. K. S. with Del, 16 March 1933: JKS.
8 Transcript of conversation, J. K. S. with Del, 16 March 1933: JKS.
9 Ibid.
10 APB minutes, 18 May, 27 July, 31 August 1928: APB.
11 Transcript of conversation, J. K. S. with Del, 20 April 1934: JKS.
12 Transcript of conversation, J. K. S. with Del, 2 August 1934: JKS.
13 Del to J. K. S., n.d., *c.*July 1934: JKS.
14 Pettitt to J. K. S., 15 December 1933; Pettitt to J. K. S., 8 January 1934, enclosing reminder notice dated 8 January 1934: JKS.

Chapter 10

1 Norman Strack to Detective-Sergeant Todd, 26 February 1934 [copy]: AE.
2 Again, as in the previous chapters, all details following including quotations, unless otherwise referenced, are sourced from the manuscript diary: JKS.
3 APB minutes, 1 December 1933, 11 January 1934: APB.

4 Keith Amos, *The New Guard Movement 1931–1935* (Melbourne: Melbourne University Press, 1976), 75, 76.
5 Eric Campbell, *The Rallying Point: My Story of the New Guard* (London: Melbourne University Press, 1965), 113, 116.

Chapter 11

1 'Are Abos Getting a Fair Deal? Scathing Attack on Officials', *Smith's Weekly*, *c.*October 1934 (citing earlier speech), undated clipping in scrapbook: JKS.
2 Adela Pankhurst Walsh to J. K. S., 7 June 1933: JKS.
3 Handwritten draft notes, undated, *c.*1934: JKS.
4 J. K. S. to Morley, 8 April 1934: AE.
5 Ibid.
6 Manuscript diary entry, 27 March 1934: JKS. As the Feminist Club records for this year are not available, Ming's record cannot be corroborated.
7 J. K. S. to Morley, 31[March 1934]: AE.
8 Morley to J. K. S., 4 April 1934: JKS.
9 Diary entry, dated 'Middle of April 1934': JKS.
10 'Are Abos Getting a Fair Deal?'
11 Memo of charges and costs re Aborigines Protection Board, Campbell to J. K. S., 14 March 1939: JKS.
12 Beckett to J. K. S., 30 April 1934: JKS. Beckett to T. E. Roth, 30 April 1934: AE.
13 Elkin to T. E. Rofe, 5 October 1937 [copy]: AE.
14 Diary entry, 16 May 1934: JKS.
15 Coughlan to Wallace, 27 April 1934 [copy]; Bryce to J. K. S., 12 July 1934: JKS.
16 Coughlan to Howard, 9 October 1934: AE.
17 Young to Morley, 3 April 1934: AE.
18 Ibid.
19 APBWR. The admission records (including birthdates) are typed and dated 31 May 1928 for both Del and her cousin May (whose was recorded as being a year younger than Del); the records for their 'disposal' (1930 for both) are in Miss Lowe's handwriting.
20 Quoted Stuart Rintoul, *The Wailing: A National Black Oral History* (Port Melbourne: William Heinemann Australia, 1993), 24–5. APBWR.
21 APBWR.
22 Transcript of conversation, J. K. S. with Del, n.d., *c.*1933–4: JKS. There are no Board records of either Del or Alice absconding.
23 Del's aunt to J. K. S., 13 September 1934: JKS.

Chapter 12

1 Diary entry, 3 May 1934: JKS.
2 Ibid.
3 Diary entries, 2 May, 5 May, 7 May, 8 May, 9 May, 11 May 1934: JKS.
4 Diary entry 5 May 34: JKS PPS.
5 Diary entry, 1 May 34: JKS PPS.

6   Manuscript diary entry, 8 June 1933: JKS.
7   Daisy Bates' husband's name was Jack, not 'Dick'.
8   Diary entry, 3 May 1934: JKS.
9   Diary entry, 27 May 1934: JKS.
10 Diary entry, 22 May 1934: JKS.
11 Letter, J. K. S. to Rofe, 6 June 1934: ELKIN PPS 69:1/12/153.
12 Letter, Beckett to J. K. S., 22 June 1934: JKS PPS 9:15.
13 APNR minutes, 19 June 1934.
14 Letter, J. K. S. to Rofe, 6 June 1934: AE.
15 Diary entry, 19 [June 1934]: JKS.
16 Draft letter, J. K. S. to Morley, 4 November 1934: JKS.
17 Diary entry, 16 July 1934: JKS.
18 Letter, Del to Helen Strack, n.d. [dated by J. K. S. July 1934]; Letter, Del to J. K. S., n.d. [c.July 1934]: JKS.
19 Drawing by Del, in letter, Del to Helen Strack, n.d. [dated by J. K. S. July 1934]; drawing by Del, n.d. [c.July 1934]: JKS PPS 9:15.
20 Diary entry, 19 June 1934: JKS.
21 Letter, Narrelle to J. K. S., n.d. [c.July 1934]: JKS PPS 9:15.
22 Ibid.
23 Notation by J. K. S. at foot of letter, Del to J. K. S., n.d. [c.July 1934]: JKS.
24 Letter, Del to J. K. S., n.d. [c.July 1934]: JKS; these letters have not survived.
25 Letter, Bettune Bryce to J. K. S., 22 August 1934: JKS PPS 9:15.
26 Copy, letter, J. K. S. to J. Jackson, n.d., c. mid-August 1934: JKS PPS: 9:15.
27 Ibid.
28 Letter, Jackson to J. K. S., 30 August 1934: JKS PPS 9:15.
29 Letter, Del's aunt to Del, dated 29 August 1934: JKS PPS 9:15.
30 Note, Del to Narrelle, dated Friday, August [1934]: JKS PPS 9:15.
31 Notes, loose in 1934 diary, undated c.August 1934: JKS PPS 2:10. The first page is missing.
32 Diary entry, 24 December 1934: JKS PPS 2:10.
33 Letter, Del's aunt to J. K. S., 13 September 1934: JKS PPS 9:15.

Chapter 13

1   Pettitt to Jackson, 4 September 1934; J. K. S. to Morley, 23 October 1934 [draft]; Howard to J. K. S., 4 October 1934; Aboriginal concession order for rail ticket, Blackheath to Sydney: JKS. Morley to Howard, 26 September 1934; APNR minutes, 19 September 1934: AE. Bryce to J. K. S., 19 September 1934: JKS.
2   Morley to Howard, 26 September 1934; Coughlan to Howard, 9 October 1934: AE. Howard to J. K. S., 4 October 1934: JKS.
3   J. K. S. to Morley, 23 October 1934 [draft]: JKS.
4   J. K. S. to Morley, 23 October 1934 [draft]; J. K. S. to Morley, 4 November 1934 [draft]: JKS.
5   Del to [unknown], transcribed by J. K. S., headed 'Letter written by Del' (original not seen), n.d.: JKS.
6   J. K. S. to Morley, 4 November 1934 [draft]: JKS.
7   Diary entry, 22 October 1934: JKS.

8 J. K. S. to Morley, 23 October 1934 [draft]: JKS. This letter, which was first addressed to Beckett, was possibly never sent.
9 J. K. S. to Walker, 18 November 1934 [draft]: JKS.
10 Morley, 'Memorandum of questions to be asked', n.d., c.September 1934 [copy]: AE.
11 APNR minutes, 16 October 1934: AE.
12 Coughlan to Howard, 9 October 1934; Howard to Morley, 12 October 1934: AE.
13 Clipping, unreferenced, n.d., c.1932, in scrapbook: JKS.
14 J. K. S. to Morley, 23 October 1934 [draft]: JKS.
15 Manuscript diary entry, 9 March 1933: JKS.
16 J. K. S. to Walker, 18 November 1934 [draft]: JKS.

Chapter 14

1 Mary to Helen Strack, 2 January 1935; Mary to Narrelle Strack, 2 January 1935: JKS.
2 Judith Rollins, *Between Women: Domestics and Their Employers* (Philadelphia: Temple University Press, 1985), 189–91.
3 Mary to Helen Strack, 2 January 1935; Mary to Narrelle Strack, 2 January 1935; Mary to J. K. S., 18 June [1935?]: JKS.
4 Mary to Narrelle Strack, 2 January 1935: JKS.
5 Mary to J. K. S., 18 June [1935?]: JKS.
6 Envelope addressed to J. K. S. c/o her mother from Mary, postmarked from Cowra, 13 May 1936: JKS.
7 Del to J. K. S., n.d., c. early 1935: JKS.
8 Del to J. K. S., n.d., c.1935: JKS.
9 Del to J. K. S., 1 November [1937] (dated by J. K. S.); Del to J. K. S., 29 December 1937 (dated by J. K. S.; envelope stamped and addressed by J. K. S., postmarked 30 December 1937); Del to J. K. S., n.d., c. mid-1938: JKS.
10 Del to J. K. S., n.d., c. early 1935: JKS.
11 Del to J. K. S., 29 December 1937: JKS.
12 Del to J. K. S., n.d., c. mid-1938: JKS.
13 Crown Solicitor to Campbell, 22 August 1938; Reminder notice to J. K. S., 30 September 1938; Campbell to J. K. S., 11 October 1938; Memo of charges and costs re Aborigines Protection Board, Campbell to JKS, 14 March 1939: JKS. APB Minutes, 7 December 1938: APB.
14 William to J. K. S., 13 January 1938; envelope postmarked 21 January 1938: JKS.
15 J. K. S. to the editor, 9 March 1938 (draft, fragment): JKS. Horner, personal communication 10 September 1993 (enclosed copy).

Chapter 15

1 Jack Horner, *Bill Ferguson: Fighter for Aboriginal Freedom* (Canberra: J. Horner, 1994), 106–7.
2 Quoted in Stephanie Gilbert, '"Never forgotten", Pearl Gibbs (Gambarni)', Anna Cole, Victoria Haskins and Fiona Paisley eds, *Uncommon Ground*:

White Women in Aboriginal History (Canberra: Aboriginal Studies Press, 2005), 106.

3 Jessie Street and Ruth Emerson Curtis, 'Australia's Helpless Housewives', script of radio broadcast play, 15 April 1937: UAW.

4 Horner, *Bill Ferguson*, 106.

5 J. K. S. to the editor, 9 March 1938 [draft, fragment]: JKS. J. Horner, personal communication, 10 September 1993 (enclosed copy).

6 Clipping, *The Australian Woman's Mirror*, 1 January 1935, 10, in scrapbook; A. E. Morgan to J. K. S., 18 February 1935: JKS.

7 See Horner, *Bill Ferguson*, 107.

8 J. K. S. to the editor, n.d., *c.*1938 (draft): JKS.

9 J. K. S. to the editor, *Truth*, 28 March 1944 (draft): JKS.

10 J. K. S. to Premier, n.d., *c.*January 1938 (draft): JKS.

11 Horner, *Bill Ferguson*, 1994, 63. See Memo, anonymous, n.d. (*c.*October–end 1937), 'Aborigines' Campaign': PDCF 12/8749B.

12 Faith Bandler, 'Birth of the Fellowship', in Faith Bandler and Len Fox, eds, *The Time was Ripe: A History of the Aboriginal-Australian Fellowship (1956–69)* (Chippendale: Alternative Publishing Co-operative, 1983), 3.

13 'Rights Demanded for Natives' *The Telegraph*, 4 March 1938: AT.

14 CAC Minutes, 15 March 1938: JKS.

15 Quoted in Horner, *Bill Ferguson*, 27.

16 Extracts reproduced in Bain Attwood and Andrew Markus, *The Struggle for Aboriginal Rights: A Documentary History* (St Leonards: Allen & Unwin, 1999), 81, 83, 87–8.

17 Ibid., 92.

18 J. K. S. to the editor, *Labour Daily*, 6 May 1938: JKS.

19 'Relieve Plight of Abo Girls', *Labour Daily*, 10 May 1938, clipping: JKS.

20 M. M. Bennett, *Human Rights for Australian Aborigines: How Can They Learn without a Teacher?* (Brisbane: 1951), 34–51; idem, *The Australian Aboriginal as a Human Being* (London: Aiston Rivers Ltd, 1930), 121–2; Bennett to J. K. S., 29 May 1938: JKS.

21 Baillie to Elkin, n.d.: AE.

22 Baillie to Morley, 25 February [1936]: AE.

23 Quoted in Carla Hankins, 'The Missing Links: Cultural Genocide through the Abduction of Female Aboriginal Children from their Families and their Training for Domestic Service, 1883–1969', unpublished BA (Hons) thesis, UNSW (1982), 4.3.10.

24 Wedge to J. K. S., 3 June [1938].

25 Gibbs to J. K. S., 19 November 1941; Diary entry, 16 [December 1941].

26 J. K. S. to Mr Cox, 20 February [1942] (draft): JKS.

Chapter 16

1 Burdeu to J. K. S., 18 April 1941: JKS. Heather Goodall, 'Pearl Gibbs: Some Memories', *Aboriginal History*, vol. 7, no. 1 (1983), pp. 20–2, 21.

2 Gibbs to J. K. S., 5 July 1938: JKS.

3 APB minutes, 18 March 1938: APB. Ferguson to Premier Stevens, 14 February 1938; Gollan to Premier, memo, 1 March 1938: PDCF. 'Blacks

Seek Abolition of Protection Board', *Daily Telegraph*, 16 October 1937, clipping: FC. J. W. Ferguson (Acting Under-Secretary) to Gibbs, 8 July 1938: PDCF.

4 J. T. Patten and W. Ferguson, *Aborigines Claim Citizen Rights!* (Sydney: The Publicist, 1938), 6. Ferguson to Premier (Stevens), 1 February 1939: PDCF.

5 Pearl Gibbs, letter to *Woman Today*, April 1938, 3; quoted in Megan McMurchy, Margot Oliver and Jeni Thornley, *For Love or Money: A Pictorial History of Women and Work in Australia* (Ringwood: Penguin, 1985), 106.

6 UAW minutes, 2 June 1938: UAW. UAW Secretary (K. Chase) to Premier Stevens, 6 June 1938: PDCF.

7 Street to Premier Mair, 6 July 1940: PDCF.

8 J. K. S. to Elkin, 19 January [1938]: AE.

9 Horner, personal communication, 10 September 1993 (notes from an interview with J. K. S., 3 March 1966).

10 J. K. S. to Elkin, 2 March [1938]: AE.

11 J. K. S. to Ferrier, 3 November 1938 (copy): JKS.

12 J. K. S. to editor, *Sun* [*c*.8 February 1939] (draft): JKS.

13 CAC resolution, *c*.27 February 1939 (draft): JKS.

14 Street to Chief Secretary, 6 June 1939 (copy by J.K.S): JKS. UAW minutes, 18 May 1939, 9 March 1939: UAW.

15 Cameron (President Feminist Club) to Gollan, 4 May 1939 (copy enclosed with Cameron to J. K. S., 4 May 1939): JKS.

16 Bate to J. K. S., 6 September 1939: JKS.

17 J. K. S. to Thompson, 3 August [1939] (draft): JKS.

18 J. K. S. to the editor, n.d., *c*. late 1939 (draft): JKS.

19 Mrs Brown to J. K. S., 1 August 1939, enclosing Lynda to Brown, 12 [*c*.July] 1939; Lynda to JKS, n.d., *c*.August 1939; Mrs Brown to J. K. S., n.d. [*c*. August–September 1939]: JKS.

20 Edward Brown to J. K. S., 1 May 1940. Diary entry, 31 July 1940: JKS.

21 Ferguson to J. K. S., 9 June 1941: JKS.

22 Sawtell to Pettitt, 20 January 1939 (copy): JKS

23 CAC Minutes, 1 February 1939: JKS. APB Minutes, 5 April 1939, 10 May 1939, 14 June 1939: JKS. Memo, Under-Secretary, Education Department, 26 June 1939: EDU.

24 J. K. S. to Pettitt, 17 July [1939] (copy); Pettitt to JKS, 1 August 1939: JKS.

25 Brenda, personal communication, 1998.

26 Kelly to the Premier (Mair, UAP–Country), 25 October 1939: PDCF.

27 J. K. S. to the editor, 10 October 1939 (draft): JKS.

28 Jack Horner, *Bill Ferguson: Fighter for Aboriginal Freedom* (Canberra: J. Horner, 1994), 85.

Chapter 17

1 *NSWPD*, 2 May 1940, 8293.

2 J. K. S. to Duguid, 8 May 1940: CD.

3 Pink, 'Full text of an article published in *Daily News*, 1/5/40'; Pink to editor, *Daily News*, 7 May 1940 (copy): OP; Clipping, 'Justice to Aborigines', *Daily News*, 8 May 1940: AT.

4   J. K. S. to Pink, n.d., *c*.July 1940: JKS.

5   'Proposals concerning the care of Aborigines in West Australia, Queensland and the Northern Territory': OP.

6   Pink to Street, 24 June 1939 (copy): OP.

7   Pink to Street, 28 May 1939 (copy): OP.

8   Pink to Street, 25 April 1939 (copy): OP.

9   Pink to Street, 28 May 1939 (copy); Pink to Litchfield, 16 August 1940 (copy); Bennett to Pink, 12 September 1937; Pink to Bennett, 18 December 1937: OP.

10   Pink to Mrs Menzies, 28 August 1940; Memo, Carrodus to Prime Minister's Secretary, 20 December 1940: Aborigines, Protection of – North South Road Construction Review, AA.

11   Marilyn Lake, 'Frontier Feminism and the Marauding White Man', *Journal of Australian Studies: Australian Frontiers*, no. 49 (1996), 12–20.

12   'Mrs Daisy Bates: Proposed Enquiry re. Aboriginal Affairs', AA. APNR Deputations, Notes of a Deputation, 29 May 1933: AA. Minister for the Interior (Perkins) to Baillie, 19 October 1932; Baillie, 'The Great Need for Trained Women Protectors for the Aboriginal and Half-caste Women and Children of Australia', paper delivered at the Conference of the British Commonwealth League, London, 1937: AFG.

13   J. K. S. to Elkin, n.d. [1938]: AE.

14   John Harris, *One Blood: 200 Years of Aboriginal Encounter with Christianity: A Story of Hope* (Sutherland: Albatross Books, 1990), 627. FC Minutes, 3 October 1939: FC. APNR Minutes, 15 March, 10 May, 21 June 1938, 21 March 1939, 24 September 1940: APNR.

15   FC minutes, 3 September 1940: FC. Cameron to Prime Minister (Menzies), 6 September 1940; Memo, Carrodus to Prime Minister's Secretary, 20 December 1940: Aborigines, Protection of – North South Road Construction Review, AA. Diary entry, 6 September 1940: JKS. FC minutes, 10 September 1940, 17 September 1940: FC.

16   Diary entry, 15 October 1940: JKS.

17   FC minutes, 15 September 1940, 29 October 1940: FC.

18   FC minutes, 5 November 1940: FC. Diary entry, 5 November 1940: JKS.

19   J. K. S. to Prime Minister, 21 November 1940: Aborigines, Protection of–North South Road Construction Review, AA. FC Minutes, 26 November 1940: FC. Diary entry, 26 November 1940: JKS.

20   FC Minutes, 3 December 1940: FC.

21   Carrodus to J. K. S., 24 December 1940: Aborigines, Protection of – North South Road Construction Review, AA. FC minutes, 6 May 1941: FC.

22   F. Paisley, 'Ideas Have Wings: White Women Challenge Aboriginal Policy 1920–1937', unpublished PhD thesis, History, La Trobe University (1995), 198–9.

23   *Records Guide, Volume 1: A Guide to Queensland Government Records Relating to Aboriginal and Torres Strait Islander Peoples* (Queensland: Queensland State Archives and the Department of Family Services and Aboriginal and Islander Affairs, 1994), 5. *'My Heart is Breaking': A Joint Guide to Records about Aboriginal People in the Public Record Office of Victoria and the Australian Archives, Victorian Regional Office* (Canberra: AGPS, 1993), 54, 132. Bon was not apparently replaced by another woman.

24   *1937 Commonwealth of Australia, Aboriginal Welfare, Initial Conference of Commonwealth and State Aboriginal Authorities*, Canberra, 21–23 April 1937, 4:

PDCF. Carrodus to Elkin, 20 September 1940 (copy). Memo, Carrodus to Strahan, 16 September 1940: Aborigines, Protection of – North South Road Construction Review, AA. Julie Marcus, 'The Beauty, Simplicity and Honour of Truth: Olive Pink in the 1940s', Julie Marcus, ed., *First in their Field: Women and Australian Anthropology* (Melbourne: Melbourne University Press, 1993), 117.

25 Jack Horner, *Bill Ferguson, Bill Ferguson: Fighter for Aboriginal Freedom* (Canberra: J Horner, 1994), 85, 112.

26 FC minutes, 21 January 1941: FC. Invitation to Aboriginal Citizenship Meeting: JKS.

27 Diary entry, 2 January, 4 January 1941: JKS. 'Report of the APA Conference at Coonabarabran', *Northwestern Watchman*, 2 January 1941, copy supplied by Jack Horner, personal communication, 10 September 1993. FC Minutes, 21 January 1941: FC.

28 Report of Meeting called by the Committee for Aboriginal Citizenship ... 25th. January 1941, 1–3: JKS.

29 FC minutes 21 January, 28 January 1941: FC. Notes, dated 25 January 1941, on Report of Meeting called by the Committee for Aboriginal Citizenship ... 25th. January 1941: JKS. Diary entries, 28 January [1941], 4 February 1941: JKS.

30 FC minutes, 11 March, 25 March, 22 April 1941: FC. J. K. S. to President (Cameron), 9 March [1941] (draft); Diary entry, 11 March 1934: JKS.

Chapter 18

1 'Aboriginal Domestics; Try an Abo Apprentice!', *Australian Women's Mirror*, 30 January 1940 (typed copy): JKS.

2 Vogan to J. K. S., 4 December 1938: JKS.

3 J. K. S. to Vogan, December 1938 (draft); Notes on back of letter, Vogan to J. K. S., 4 December 1938; J. K. S. to Finlay, 12 January 1939 (draft): JKS.

4 J. K. S. to Finlay, 12 January 1939 (draft): JKS.

5 J. K. S. to Mills, 18 September [1961]; J. K. S. to Finlay, 12 January 1939 (draft): JKS.

6 APB minutes, 21 January 1920, 13 September 1922: APB.

7 Her three-year-old sister, and her two younger brothers, aged four and six months, were taken at the same time, according to her niece, who was told this by Jane's sister, her mother: personal communication, 31 December 1993. There is no record of the other children's removal in the Board's files.

8 J. K. S. to Cox, 20 February [1942] (draft): JKS.

9 APBSR, APBWR.

10 J. K. S. to Judge [Clancy], 7 January 1942 (draft): JKS.

11 Diary entries, 9 May 1934, 29 December 1934: JKS.

12 APB minutes, 3 August 1938; Salary Registers: APB.

13 Not his real name.

14 Diary entry, 7 September 1939; J. K. S. to Cox, 20 February [1942]; JKS to Dr Nott, 13 September 1939 (draft and original, not sent): JKS.

15 Chief Investigation Officer, reports, 26 September 1939, 12 January 1940: PMGD. Diary entries, 24 October 1939, 29 [October 1939], 18 January 1940: JKS.

16 J. K. S. to the editor [*Truth*], 15 December 1940 (draft): JKS. Ming would later testify during the doctor's trial that the doctor had made this threat: 'North

Shore Doctor and a Girl Who Threw Stones', *Truth*, 15 December 1940, 18.
Helen corroborated Ming's account in her recollections, August 1994.
17 Jane to PMGD, 12 October 1939: PMGD.
18 Diary entries, 15 [March], 1 April, 20 [April], 12 May 1940: JKS.
19 Diary entries, 13 May [1940], 23 [May 1940]: JKS.
20 Letter, Mrs Green to J. K. S., 22 May 1940; Diary entry 20 May 1940: JKS. It appears that Ming wrote her entry under the wrong date (this diary being a pocket-book diary).
21 Premier Stevens to Mr H. B. Turner MLA, 30 December 1937: UAW.
22 Diary entries, 8 October 1940, 14 November 1940, 15 November 1940: JKS.
23 Diary entries, 22–23 November 1940, 25 November 1940: JKS.
24 Diary entries, 2 December 1940, 3 December 1940, 5 December 1940, 6 December 1940, 9 December 1940, 11 December 1940: JKS.
25 'North Shore Doctor and a Girl Who Threw Stones', 18. Diary entry, 11 December 1940: JKS.
26 Diary entries, 23 November 1940, 2 December 1940, 3 December 1940, 4 December, 5 December, 6 December 1940: JKS. 'North Shore Doctor and a Girl Who Threw Stones', 18.
27 'North Shore Doctor and a Girl Who Threw Stones', 18.
28 Senior Investigation Officer, PMGD, Memo, 9 December 1940: 'Disconnection of Mrs Kingsley-Strack's Telephone Service': PMGD.
29 'North Shore Doctor and a Girl who Threw Stones', 18.
30 Diary entry, 18 December 1940: JKS.
31 Article submitted to *Truth*, n.d., *c.*18 December 1940 (typed copy): JKS. 'Bitter Lot of Aborigines: Robbed of Children, Shamed, Assaulted', *Truth*, 29 December 1940, 24.
32 Diary entry, 8 April 1941: JKS.

Chapter 19

1 Diary entry, 16 January [1942]: JKS.
2 Postmaster-General's department to J. K. S., 24 January 1941: JKS. Memo, Acting Assistant Superintendent Traffic, 17 December 1940: 'Disconnection of Mrs Kingsley-Strack's Telephone Service': PMGD. Diary entry, 25 January 1941: JKS.
3 J. K. S. to Norman, 24 [February 1941]; J. K. S. to Deputy Postmaster-General, 19 February 1941 (draft); E. J. Ward to J. K. S., 19 February 1941; T. J. Collins, Assistant Postmaster-General, to J. K. S., 31 March 1941; Collins to J. K. S., 24 April 1941: JKS.
4 Letter, J. K. S. to —— [Monaghan?], 23 April 1941 (draft): JKS.
5 J. K. S. to Mr Monaghan, Superintendent, Telephone Branch, PMGD, 5 May [1941] (notes, draft); Monaghan to J. K. S., 7 May 1941, George McLeay (Federal MP) to Senator Cameron, 6 June 1941; Diary entry, 8 [May 1941]: JKS.
6 Jane to Postmaster-General's department, 12 May 1941: PMGD.
7 'Disconnection of Mrs Kingsley-Strack's Telephone Service': PMGD.
8 Diary entry, 6 September 1941: JKS. The handle of the umbrella also survived amongst Ming's belongings: personal possession Melody Haskins.
9 Diary entry, 9 September 1941: JKS.
10 Diary entry, 10 September 1941: JKS.

11 J. K. S. to Cox, 20 February [1942] (draft); Diary entry, 12 September 1941: JKS.
12 Diary entry, 12 September 1941: JKS.
13 Diary entry, 24 September [1941]: JKS.
14 Jane to Postmaster-General's department (Complaints Office) 9 September 1941: PMGD. Though the letter was unsigned, it was in Jane's distinctive handwriting – and the department already had copies of previous letters she'd written.
15 R. W. Hamilton, Deputy Director, Posts and Telegraphs, PMGD, 8 January 1942; Diary entry, 9 January 1942: JKS.
16 Diary entry, 12 January 1942; J. K. S. to Faulkingham, 13 [January 1942] (draft): JKS.
17 Jane to Hamilton, n.d., c.January 1942 (draft): JKS.
18 Chief Investigator's Reports, 9 November 1939, 9 December 1940, 11 December 1940; and PMGD Deputy Director to Director-General Posts and Telegraphs, Melbourne, n.d., stamped 2 June 1941, 'Disconnection of Mrs Kingsley-Strack's Telephone Service': PMGD.
19 Diary entry, 16 January [1942]: JKS.
20 Diary entry, 4 February [1942]: JKS.
21 Articles and commentaries by the doctor are scattered throughout the pages of the leading research journal, the *Medical Journal of Australia*. Between the years 1933 and 1940 I identified five contributions from him, as well as numerous references to his demonstrations. For the privacy of his descendants I withhold the details here as they identify him by name.
22 Jane to Faulkingham, n.d. [two draft letters or notes]: JKS.
23 J. K. S. to Collins, 21 March 1941: PMGD.
24 J. K. S. to Judge [Clancy], 7 February 1942; Jane to Faulkingham, n.d. (draft or note): JKS.
25 'Rheumatism in Children' [unattributed], *Medical Journal of Australia*, II(18), 28 October 1939, 653.
26 Comment, 'Gold Treatment of Rheumatoid Arthritis', *MJA*, II(20), 14 November 1936, 683–4.
27 L. J. A. Parr and Eva Shipton, 'Chrysotherapy in Rheumatoid Arthritis', *MJA*, I(23), 5 June 1937, 864–74.
28 L. Ianuzzi *et al.*, 'Critical Evaluation of 17 Published Studies Carried out since 1940 on Long-acting Agents in Treatment of Rheumatoid Arthritis', *New England Journal of Medicine*, 1983, 309.
29 Letter, J. K. S. to Collins, 21 March 1941: PMGD. C— N— to J. K. S., 1 January 1941, 27 January 1941: JKS.

Chapter 20

1 Diary entry, 3 February [1942]: JKS.
2 Diary entry, 4 February 1942: JKS.
3 J. K. S. to Judge [Clancy], 7 February 1942 (draft): JKS.
4 Diary entry, 12 February [1942]; J. K. S. to Cox, 20 February [1942] (draft): JKS.
5 J. K. S. to Cox, 20 February [1942] (draft): JKS.
6 Diary entry 15 March 1942; Duguid to J. K. S., 24 September 1940: JKS.
7 Duguid to J. K. S., 5 March 1942: JKS.
8 Swann to Elkin, 31 March 1942: EA.

9   APNR minutes, 10 October 1933, 17 April, 19 June, 21 August, 16 October 1934: APNR. [Illegible] to Elkin, 30 January 1940: EA.
10 APNR minutes, 21 April 1942, 20 October 1942: APNR.
11 Duguid to J. K. S., 1 June 1942: JKS.
12 Elkin to J. K. S., 24 November 1941: JKS.
13 FC minutes, 29 July 1941: FC. Street to Premier (Mair), 6 July 1940: PDCF.
14 Baillie to J. K. S., 29 October [1938]; Bennett to J. K. S., 4 January 1939: JKS. Swann to Elkin, 31 March 1942: EA.
15 Sawtell to Ferguson, n.d., *c.*2 April 1941 (copy, forwarded to Elkin by Sawtell, 5 April 1941): EA.
16 Diary entries, 13 March, 15 March, 20 [March], 27 March, 29 March, 10 April 1942: JKS.
17 E. Kent-Hughes to Elkin, 28 February, 12 June 1932, 13 February, 27 April, 15 May, 22 May 1937: AE. Diary entries, 25 April, 26 April 1942; E. Kent-Hughes to J. K. S., 12 May 1942: JKS
18 Diary entry, 28 [March 1943]: JKS.
19 Diary entry, 29 April [1943]; J. K. S. to the editor, *Daily Mirror*, 15 February 1943 (draft): JKS.
20 Diary entries, 28 March, 29 March 1943, undated, *c.*April 1943: JKS.
21 J. K. S. to Cox, 20 February [1942]: JKS.
22 Albert Memmi, *The Colonizer and the Colonized* (London: Souvenir Press, 1974), 123–5, 127–8.
23 Ibid., 40, 38, 43.
24 Clipping, 'Tell-Tale Lipstick on Major's Bed Linen', *Truth*, 27 June 1943: JKS.
25 Clippings, Joyce Burns Glen, 'Painter Pioneers', *Christian Science Monitor* (Boston), 15 October 1953, 6; Wendy Stokes, 'Contemplating Business Venture at "About 70"', not sourced, n.d., *c.*1970s: JKS.
26 C. V. Wedgewood (1944) quoted in John Broomfield, *Other Ways of Knowing: Recharting Our Future with Ageless Wisdom* (Rochester: Inner Traditions, 1997), 8.

Chapter 21

1   Coral Edwards, 'Is the Ward Clean?', Bill Gammage and Andrew Markus, eds, *All that Dirt: Aborigines 1938* (Canberra: History Project Inc., 1982), 8.
2   Jane to AWB, 29 June 1961: AWBCF.
3   Green to Jane, 18 April 1961 (copy); Jane to AWB, 21 April 1961; Jane to AWB, 13 July 1961, Mills to Green, 20 September 1961: AWBCF. Mills to J. K. S., 18 April 1961, J. K. S. to Mills, 18 September [1961]: JKS.
4   Jane to J. K. S. [18 April 1961]: JKS.
5   J. K. S. to Mills, 18 September [1961?]: JKS. Memo, M. Fleming, 4 January 1962 (copy): AWBCF.
6   Jane to J. K. S., 23 December 1961, 7 July 1962, 1963: JKS.
7   Horner, personal communication, 10 September 1993 (notes from interview with Jane and J. K. S., 3 March 1966).
8   Jane to J. K. S., 6 February 1968, May 1973: JKS.
9   Jane to J. K. S., 1977: JKS.
10 Jane to J. K. S., 30 June 1978: JKS.

Bibliography

Aboriginal Historians for the Bicentennial History 1788–1988, working party (Wayne Atkinson, Marcia Langton, Doreen Wanganeen and Michael Williams). 'Aboriginal History and the Bicentennial Volumes', in A. W. Martin, ed. *Australia 1939–1988: A Bicentennial History Bulletin*, no. 3, May 1981. Canberra: Australian National University, 1981.

Amos, Keith. *The New Guard Movement 1931–1935*. Melbourne: Melbourne University Press, 1976.

Attwood, Bain. 'Charles Hammond: Aboriginal Battler', *Gippsland Heritage Journal*, vol. 3, no. 2, 1988.

Attwood, Bain. *The Making of the Aborigines*. Sydney: Allen & Unwin, 1989.

Attwood, Bain and Andrew Markus. *The Struggle for Aboriginal Rights: A Documentary History*. St Leonards, NSW: Allen & Unwin, 1999.

Attwood, Bain, Winifred Burrage, Alan Burrage and Elsie Stokie. *A Life Together, A Life Apart: A History of Relations Between Europeans and Aborigines*. Melbourne: Melbourne University Press, 1994.

Austin, Tony. 'Cecil Cook, Scientific Thought and "Half-Castes" in the Northern Territory 1927–1939', *Aboriginal History*, vol. 14, no. 1, 1990.

Bandler, Faith. 'Birth of the Fellowship', in Faith Bandler and Len Fox, eds. *The Time was Ripe: A History of the Aboriginal-Australian Fellowship (1956–69)*. Chippendale: Alternative Publishing Co-operative, 1983.

Barbalet, Margaret. *Far from a Low Gutter Girl: The Forgotten World of State Wards: South Australia 1887–1940*. Melbourne: Oxford University Press, 1983.

Barwick, Diane. 'Coranderrk and Cumeroongunga: Pioneers and Policy', in T. Scarlett Epslein and David H. Renny, eds. *Opportunities and Response: Case Studies in Economic Develepment*. London: C Huast & Co, 1972.

Broomfield, John. *Other Ways of Knowing: Recharting Our Future with Ageless Wisdom*. Rochester: Inner Traditions, 1997.

Campbell, Eric. *The Rallying Point: My Story of the New Guard*. London: Melbourne University Press, 1965.

Campbell, Rosemary. *Heroes & Lovers: A Question of National Identity*. Sydney: Allen & Unwin, 1989.

Cannon, Michael. *The Human Face of the Great Depression*. Victoria: Today's Australia Publishing, 1997.

Castle, Josie. 'The Australian Women's Guild of Empire', in Elizabeth Windschuttle, ed. *Women, Class and History: Feminist Perspectives on Australia 1788–1978*. Melbourne: Fontana/Collins, 1980.

Christie, M. F., *Aborigines in Colonial Victoria 1835–86*. Sydney: Sydney University Press, 1979.

Clare, Monica. *Karobran: The Story of an Aboriginal Girl*. Sydney: Alternative Publishing Cooperative, 1978.

Clark-Lewis, Elizabeth. *Living in Living out: African American Domestics in Washington, D.C., 1910–1940*. Washington: Smithsonian Institution Press, 1994.

Crawford, Evelyn. *Over My Tracks: A Remarkable Life*, as told to Chris Walsh. Ringwood: Penguin, 1993.

Cummings, Barbara, *Take This Child … from Kahlin Compound to the Retta Dixon Childen's Home* (Camberra: Aboriginal Studies Press, 1990)

Curthoys, Ann. 'Good Christians and Useful Workers: Aborigines, Church and State in NSW 1870–1883', in Sydney Labour History Group, *What Rough Beast? The State and Social Order in Australian History*, Sydney: George Allen & Unwin, 1982.

Damousi, Joy. *Depraved and Disorderly: Female Convicts, Sexuality and Gender in Colonial Australia*. Cambridge: Cambridge University Press, 1997.

Edwards, Coral. 'Is the Ward Clean?', in Bill Gammage and Andrew Markus, eds. *All that Dirt: Aborigines 1938*. Canberra: History Project Inc., 1982.

Ellinghaus, Katherine. 'Regulating Koori Marriages: The 1886 Victorian Aborigines Protection Act', *Journal of Australian Studies*, no. 67, 2001.

Evans, Raymond. '"Soiled Doves": Prostitution and Society in Colonial Queensland – An Overview', *Hecate*, vol. 1, no. 2, 1975.

Evans, Raymond. 'A Gun in the Oven: Masculinism and Gendered Violence', in Kay Saunders and Raymond Evans, eds. *Gender Relations in Australia: Domination and Negotiation*. Sydney: Harcourt Brace Jovanovich, 1992.

Fairchilds, Cissie. *Domestic Enemies: Servants & Their Masters in Old Regime France*. Baltimore: Johns Hopkins University Press, 1984.

Franklin, Margaret-Ann. *Assimilation in Action: The Armidale Story*. Armidale: University of New England Press, 1995.

Gardner, P D. *Our Founding Murdering Father: Angus McMillan and the Kurnai Tribe of Gippsland 1839–1865*. Victoria: Ngarak Press, 1990.

Gardner, P. D. *Gippsland Massacres: The Destruction of the Kurnai Tribes 1800–1860*. Victoria: Ngarak Press, 1993.

Geldard, Tara. 'The Industrial School for Girls at Parramatta: Context, Continuity and Change 1887–1920', BA (Hons) thesis, University of Sydney, 1993.

Gilbert, Stephanie. '"Never Forgotten": Peal Gibbs (Gambarni)', in Anna Cole, Victoria Haskins and Fiona Paisley, eds, *Uncommon Ground: White Women in Aboriginal History* (Canberra: Aboriginal Studies Press, 2005)

Gill, Merri. *Weilmoringle: A Unique Bi-cultural Community*. Dubbo: Development and Advisory Publications of Australia, 1996.

Gillis, John R. 'Servants, Sexual Relations, and the Risks of Illegitimacy in London, 1801–1900', *Feminist Studies*, vol. 5, no. 1, Spring 1979.

Goodall, Heather. 'A History of Aboriginal Communities in NSW, 1909–1939'. PhD thesis, University of Sydney, 1982.

Goodall, Heather. 'Pearl Gibbs: Some Memories', *Aboriginal History*, vol. 7, no. 1, 1983.

Goodall, Heather. '"Saving the Children": Gender and the Colonization of Aboriginal Children in NSW, 1788 to 1990', *Aboriginal Law Bulletin*, vol. 2, no. 44, June 1990.

Goodall, Heather. 'Land in Our Own Country', *Aboriginal History*, vol. 4, no. 1, 1990.

Goodall, Heather. '"Assimilation Begins in the Home": the State and Aboriginal Women's Work as Mothers in New South Wales, 1900 to 1960s', in Ann McGrath and Kay Saunders, eds. *Labour History: Aboriginal Workers*, no. 69, Sydney: Australian Society for the Study of Labour History, 1995.

Goodall, Heather. *Invasion to Embassy: Land in Aboriginal Politics in New South Wales, 1770–1972*. St Leonards, NSW: Allen & Unwin, 1996.

Griffith, Gail. 'The Feminist Club of NSW, 1914–1970: A History of Feminist Politics in Decline', *Hecate*, vol. 14, no. 1, 1988.

Grimshaw, Patricia and Julie Evans. 'Colonial Women on Intercultural Frontiers: Rosa Campbell Praed, Mary Bundock and Katie Langloh-Parker', *Australian Historical Studies*, vol. 27, no. 106, 1996.

Gungil Jindibah Centre. *Learning from the Past: Aboriginal Perspectives on the Effects and Implications of Welfare Policies and Practices on Aboriginal Families in New South Wales*. Lismore: NSW Department of Community Services, 1994.

Hamilton, Jean, Joan and Katherine McKenzie, eds. *Just Lovely*. Coonamble: Joan McKenzie, 1989.

Hankins, Carla. 'The Missing Links: Cultural Genocide through the Abduction of Female Aboriginal Children from their Families and their Training for Domestic Service, 1883–1969'. BA (Hons) thesis, University of NSW, 1982.

Harris, John. *One Blood: 200 Years of Aboriginal Encounter with Christianity: A Story of Hope*. Sutherland: Albatross Books, 1990.

Harwood, Carolyn. 'A History of Aboriginal Women in New South Wales 1930–1950', BA (Hons) thesis, University of Sydney, 1984.

Haskins, Victoria. 'A Better Chance'?: Sexual Abuse and the Apprenticeship of Aboriginal Girls under the NSW Aborigines Protection Board', *Aboriginal History*, vol. 28, 2004.

Heilbrun, Carolyn G. *Writing a Woman's Life*. New York: Ballantine Books, 1998.

Holland, Alison. 'The Child Welfare Department in N.S.W. 1923–1940', BA (Hons) thesis, University of Sydney, 1986.

Horner, Jack. 'Pearl Gibbs: A Biographical Tribute', *Aboriginal History*, vol. 7, no. 1, 1983.

Horner, Jack. *Bill Ferguson: Fighter for Aboriginal Freedom*. Canberra: J. Horner, 1994 [first published 1975].

Huggins, Jackie, Jo Willmot, Isabel Tarrago, Kathy Willetts, Liz Bond, Lillian Holt, Eleanor Bourke, Maryann Bin-Salik, Pat Fowell, Joann Schmider, Valerie Craigie and Linda McBride-Levi, 'Letter to the Editors', *Women's Studies International Forum*, vol. 1, no. 5, 1991.

Huggins, Jackie. *Sister Girl*. St Lucia: University of Queensland Press, 1998.

Huggins, Jackie and Isabel Tarrago. 'Questions of Collaboration: An Interview with Jackie Huggins and Isabel Tarrago', *Hecate*, vol. 16, nos. 1/2, 1990.

Human Rights and Equal Opportunity Commission. *Bringing Them Home: A Guide to the Findings and Recommendations of the National Inquiry into the Separation of Aboriginal and Torres Strait Islander Children from their Families*. Canberra: Human Rights and Equal Opportunity Commission (with AIATSIS), 1997.

Jacobs, Pat. *Mister Neville*. Fremantle: Fremantle Arts Centre Press, 1990.

James, Barbara. *No Man's Land: Women of the Northern Territory*. Sydney: Collins, 1989.

Johnston, Susan Lindsay. 'The New South Wales Government Policy towards Aborigines, 1880 to 1909', MA thesis, University of Sydney.

Kabaila, Peter. *Cootamundra: The Aboriginal Girls' Home*. Canberra: P. R. Kabaila, AIATSIS Research, 1994.

Katzman, David. *Seven Days a Week: Women and Domestic Service in Industrializing America*. New York: Oxford University Press, 1978.

Kingston, Beverley. *My Wife, My Daughter and Poor Mary Ann: Women and Work in Australia*. Melbourne: Nelson, 1977 [first published 1975].

Kociumbas, Jan. *Australian Childhood: A History*. St Leonards, NSW: Allen & Unwin, 1997.

Lake, Marilyn. 'The Politics of Respectability: Identifying the Masculinist Context', *Historical Studies*, vol. 22, no. 86, April 1986.

Lake, Marilyn. 'Frontier Feminism and the Marauding White Man', *Journal of Australian Studies: Australian Frontiers*, no. 49, 1996.

Lines, William J. *Taming the Great South Land: A History of the Conquest of Nature in Australia*. North Sydney: Allen & Unwin, 1991.

Link-Up (NSW) Aboriginal Corporation and Tikka Jan Wilson. *In the Best Interests of the Child? Stolen Children: Aboriginal Pain/White Shame*. Canberra: Aboriginal History Incorporated, 1997.

Marcus, Julie. 'The Beauty, Simplicity and Honour of Truth: Olive Pink in the 1940s', in Julie Marcus, ed. *First in their Field: Women and Australian Anthropology*. Melbourne: Melbourne University Press, 1993.

Maynard, John. 'Fred Maynard and the Awakening of Aboriginal Political Consciousness'. PhD thesis, University of Newcastle, 2003.

Maynard, John. '"Light in the Darkness": Elizabeth Makenzie Hatton', in Anna Cole, Fiona Paisley and Victoria Haskins, eds. *Uncommon Ground: White Women in Aboriginal History*. Canberra: Aboriginal Studies Press, 2005.

McBride, Theresa M. *The Domestic Revolution: The Modernisation of Household Service in England and France 1820–1920*. London: Croom Helm, 1976.

McGregor, Russell, '"Breed out the Colour" or the Importance of Being White', *Australian Historical Studies*, Vol. 33, No. 120 (October 2002), 286–302.

McGuire, Madelaine E. 'The Legend of the Good Fella Missus', *Aboriginal History*, vol. 14, no. 2, 1990.

McMurchy, Megan, Margot Oliver and Jeni Thornley. *For Love or Money: a Pictorial History of Women and Work in Australia*. Ringwood: Penguin, 1985.

Memmi, Albert. *The Colonizer and the Colonized*. London: Souvenir Press, 1974.

Miller, James. *Koori: A Will to Win*. London: Angus & Robertson, 1985.

Moore, Andrew. 'Policing Enemies of the State: The New South Wales Police and the New Guard, 1931–32', in Mark Finnane, ed. *Policing in Australia Historical Perspectives*. Kensington: University of New South Wales Press, 1987.

Moreton-Robinson, Aileen. *Talkin' up to the White Woman: Indigenous Women and Feminism*. St Lucia: University of Queensland Press, 2000.

Morgan, Eileen. *The Calling of the Spirits*. Canberra: Aboriginal Studies Press, 1994.

Munro, Craig. *Wild Man of Letters: The Story of P. R. Stephensen*. Carlton: Melbourne University Press, 1984.

'My Heart is Breaking': A Joint Guide to Records about Aboriginal People in the Public Record Office of Victoria and the Australian Archives, Victorian Regional Office. Canberra: AGPS, 1993.

Nannup, Alice, with Lauren March and Stephen Kinnane. *When the Pelican Laughed*. Fremantle: Fremantle Arts Centre Press, 1992.

Paisley, Fiona. 'Ideas Have Wings: White Women Challenge Aboriginal Policy 1920–1937'. PhD thesis, La Trobe University, 1995.

Paisley, Fiona. 'No Back Streets in the Bush: 1920s and 1930s pro-Aboriginal White Women's Activism and the Trans-Australian Railway', *Australian Feminist Studies*, Vol. 12, No 25 (1997), 119–37.

Paisley, Fiona. *Loving Protection? Australian Feminism and Aboriginal Women's Rights 1919–1939*. Melbourne: Melbourne University Press, 2000.

Pearce, Sharyn. '"The Best Career is Matrimony": First-Wave Journalism and the "Australian Girl"', *Hecate*, vol. 18, no. 2, 1992.

Pepper, Phillip and Tess de Araugo, *What Did Happen to the Aborigines of Victoria, vol. 1: The Kurnai of Gippsland*. Melbourne: Hyland House, 1985.

Pepper, Phillip and Tess De Araugo. *You Are What You Make Yourself To Be: The Story of a Victorian Aboriginal Family 1842–1980*. Melbourne: Hyland House, 1989.

Radi, Heather, 'G. E. Ardill', in Bede Nairn and Geoffrey Serle, eds. *Australian Dictionary of Biography, vol. 7, 1891–1939*. Melbourne: Melbourne University Press, 1979.

Read, Peter. *The Stolen Generations: The Removal of Aboriginal Children in N.S.W. 1883–1969*. Sydney: NSW Ministry of Aboriginal Affairs Occasional Paper no. 1, 1982.

Read, Peter. *A Hundred Years War: The Wiradjuri People and the State*. Rushcutters Bay: Australian National University Press, 1988.

Read, Peter. *A Rape of the Soul So Profound*. Sydney: Allen & Unwin, 1999.

Records Guide, Volume 1: A Guide to Queensland Government Records Relating to Aboriginal and Torres Strait Islander Peoples. Queensland: Queensland State Archives and the Department of Family Services and Aboriginal and Islander Affairs, 1994.

Reiger, Kereen. *The Disenchantment of the Home: Modernizing the Australian Family 1880–1940*. Melbourne: Oxford University Press, 1985.

Reynolds, Henry. *The Law of the Land*. Ringwood: Penguin, 1987.

Riddett, Lyn. '"Watching the White Women Fade": Aboriginal and White Women in the Northern Territory 1870–1940', *Hecate*, vol. 19, no. 1, 1991.

Rintoul, Stuart. *The Wailing: A National Black Oral History*. Port Melbourne: William Heinemann Australia, 1993.

Roberts, Nickie. *Whores in History: Prostitution in Western Society*. London: Grafton HarperCollins, 1993.

Rollins, Judith. *Between Women: Domestics and Their Employers*. Philadelphia: Temple University Press, 1985.

Rutledge, Martha. 'Thomas Ernest Rofe', in Geoffrey Serle, ed. *Australian Dictionary of Biography, vol. 11, 1891–1939*. Carlton: Melbourne University Press, 1988.

Sabbioni, Jennifer. 'I Hate Working for the White People', *Hecate*, vol. 19, no. 2, 1993.

Sabbioni, Jennifer. 'Aboriginal Women's Narratives: Reconstructing Identities', *Australian Historical Studies*, vol. 27, no. 106, April 1996.

Shields, John, ed. *All Our Labours: Oral Histories of Working Life in Twentieth-Century History*. Kensington, NSW: University of New South Wales Press, 1992.

Sicles, Ellen , ed. *The Letters of Elizabeth Kendall Bate*. Surry Hills: E. Sicles, 1967.

Simon, Ella. *Through My Eyes*. Adelaide: Rigby, 1978.

Stone, Janey. 'Brazen Hussies and God's Police: Feminist Historiography and the Depression', *Hecate*, vol. 8, no. 1, 1982.

Summers, Anne. 'The Unwritten History of Adela Pankhurst Walsh', in Elizabeth Windschuttle, ed. *Women, Class and History: Feminist Perspectives on Australia 1788–1978*. Melbourne: Fontana/Collins, 1980.

Summers, Anne. *Damned Whores and God's Police*. Ringwood: Penguin, 1994 [first published 1975].

Tonkinson, Myrna. 'Sisterhood or Aboriginal Servitude? Black Women and White Women on the Australian Frontier', *Aboriginal History*, vol. 12, no. 2, 1988.

Tucker, Margaret. *If Everyone Cared*. Melbourne: Grosvenor Books, 1983 [first published 1977].

Van Krieken, Robert. *Children and the State: Social Control and the Formation of Australian Child Welfare*, North Sydney: Allen & Unwin, 1991.

Walden, Inara. 'Aboriginal Women in Domestic Service in New South Wales, 1850 to 1969', BA (Hons) thesis, University of New South Wales, 1991.

Walden, Inara. '"That was slavery days": Aboriginal Domestic Servants in New South Wales in the Twentieth Century', in Ann McGrath and Kay Saunders, eds. *Labour History 69: Aboriginal Workers*, Sydney: Australian Society for the Study of Labour History, 1995.

Ward, Glenyse. *Wandering Girl*. Broome: Magabala Books, 1987.

Ware, Vron. *Beyond the Pale: White Women, Racism and History*. London: Verso, 1992.

Wetherell, D. and C. Carr-Gregg. *Camilla: C.H. Wedgwood 1901–1955: A Life*. Kensington: New South Wales University Press, 1990.

Wise, Tigger. *The Self-Made Anthropologist: A Life of A. P. Elkin*. Sydney: George Allen & Unwin, 1985.

Woodrow, Marjorie. *One of the Lost Generation*. Narromine: M. Woodrow, 1990.

Index

Page numbers shown in **bold type** are to figures in the text.

273